INFLUENCE OF ISLAM ON INDIAN CULTURE

Tara Chand

First Published 1963
First LG Edition 2018
Reprinted 2024

ISBN 978–93–83723–43–0 (Hb)

Published by
LG PUBLISHERS DISTRIBUTORS
49, Street No. 14, Pratap Nagar,
Mayur Vihar Phase I, Delhi 110091
lgpdist@gmail.com

Printed at
D.K. Fine Art Press, Delhi 110 052

PREFACE

This essay was written in 1922. Circumstances over which I had little control prevented me from revising or completing it. I publish it now as it was written, because I no longer entertain the vain hope that I will be able to devote in the near future adequate time and attention to fulfil my original plan of writing a history of Indian civilization during the middle ages.

The development of Indian civilization is a subject of absorbing interest, and historians are now beginning to pay attention to it. This interest is not merely topical, arising out of the clashes of our present-day life in India. The subject has a wider import and deeper philosophical significance. We are studying to-day the problems of migrations of primitive and pre-historic cultures, and of conflicts of races and of civilizations during the past and in the present. The history of India which furnishes a striking illustration of the impact of many divergent cultures which were gradually transformed by a process of mutual adjustment, surely needs the attention of a student of sociology and history who endeavours to understand the interactions of human mind and the effects of cultural contacts as presented in the customs, religion, literature and art of a people.

Before any generalizations can be made, it is necessary to collect facts. I have sought mainly to collect facts in this essay and facts too connected with only two aspects of civilization—religion and art. I am conscious of the inadequacy of the attempt. It is partly due to the nature of the enquiry—cultural facts are so deeply shrouded in obscurity—and partly to my personal difficulties. But for the encouragement of friends who read the essay in the manuscript and considered its publication worthwhile, it might still lie mouldering in the desk.

My thanks are due to Dr. Banarsi Prasad Saxena for preparing the index and making improvements in the manuscript, and to Mr. Bhagwat Dayal for reading the proofs.

I am indebted to Mr. H. K. Ghosh, the enterprising proprietor of The Indian Press, for undertaking its publication.

TARA CHAND

SECOND EDITION

The book has been reprinted after many years and I have taken this opportunity to correct some mistakes of printing and other inaccuracies.

The work of reading the proofs and making corrections was carried out by Dr. R. K. Parmu for which I owe him thanks.

TARA CHAND

CONTENTS

ILLUSTRATIONS

PLATE NO.

PLATE No.

XXI.—A Picnic (Persian, 1569).

XXII.—Baz Bahadur and Rupmati (Rajput School).

XXIII.—Shikar by night (Bichitar, Rajput School).

XXIV.—Agata-Patika (Rajputana).

XXV.—Ragini Sarangi (Jaipur School).

XXVI.—Dance of Siva (Kangra School).

XXVII.—Birth of Krishna (Kangra School).

XXVIII.—Gai-Charan Lila (Kangra School).

XXIX.—Hori Lila (Kangra School).

XXX.—Rape of Yadava Women (Chaitar, Tehri-Garhwa School).

XXXI.—Hour of Cow-Dust (Chamba School).

XXXII.—Siege of Lanka (Jammu School).

XXXIII.—Siege of Lanka (Jammu School).

XXXIV.—Maharaja Shatrujit on horseback (Bundela School, 1762—1801).

XXXV.—Temple of Visvanath at Khajuraho (Northern style).

XXXVI.—Temple of Nuggehalli, Mysore (Deccan style).

XXXVII.—Temple of Subrahmanya, Tanjore (Dravidian style).

XXXVIII.—Hoysalesvara Temple, Halebid (Sculpture on eastern side).

XXXIX.—Jerusalem—Exterior of the Qubbat As-Sakhrah, (Dome of the Rock).

XL.—Exterior from the East.

XLI.—Cairo, Madrasah of Qayt Bey.

XLII.—The mosque of Sultan Barquq.

XLIII.—Mosque at Tabriz.

Mosque at Ispahan.

INTRODUCTION

INDIAN culture is synthetic in character. It comprehends ideas of different orders. It embraces in its orbit beliefs, customs, rites, institutions, arts, religions and philosophies belonging to strata of society in varying stages of development. It eternally seeks to find a unity for the heterogeneous elements which make up its totality. At worst its attempts end in a mechanical juxtaposition, at best they succeed in evolving an organic system.

The complexity of Indian life is ancient, because from the dawn of history, India has been the meeting place of conflicting civilisations. Through its north-western gates migrating hordes and conquering armies have poured down in unending succession, bringing with them like the floods of the Nile much destruction, but also valuable deposits which enriched the ancient soil, out of which grew ever more fresh and ever more luxuriant cultures.

These foreign impulses have played an important part in India's history. As a matter of fact the process of its cultural development may be envisaged as the blending of three strands producing the characteristic pattern of their cycle.

There have always been two distinct strata of society in India, the one higher and the other lower; the first small in numbers, but in possession of highly developed religions, social ideas and institutions; the second comprising the great mass of the people who occupy a humbler rung on the cultural ladder. The first provides the intellectual and aristocratic and the second the folk element in India's culture.

These two in their interactions have supplied two strands of the pattern, while the third was provided by foreign influences which in peaceful ways or by forcible means entered the country and contributed their share in the perfection of the design. The synthesis of the three and the evolution of new cultures were wrought along its own inherent lines by the peculiar genius of the race, and age after age this process has continued. These ages in Indian history may be fixed and enumerated.

In the first place, Indian history may be broadly divided into three epochs—ancient, medieval and modern; the first beginning from the earliest times to the eighth century of the Christian era, the second consisting of the one thousand years following the eighth century, and the third commencing with the nineteenth century and still running.

The ancient epoch may be subdivided into four ages—the Vedic ending in the seventh century B.C., the Buddhist in the second century B.C., the early Hindu in the middle of the third century A.D., and the later Hindu in the eighth century A.D.

The medieval epoch is divisible into two ages—the early medieval from the eighth to the thirteenth and the later from the thirteenth to the end of the eighteenth century.

In the first age India is discovered as an agitated scene of conflicting tribes and races in which one group attempts to impose its civilisation on the other. The Aryans and the non-Aryans meet in struggle and the war is waged not merely on the plane of politics and economics but also on that of cult and culture. The literature of the Vedic age is a mirror of this vast social conflict, it reflects its various stages (not necessarily successive): the commencement of the Aryan onset when the victors—warriors and priests—exhilarated by their triumph sing joyous paeans in praise of the shinning gods who confer the boons of victory, prosperity and long life; then the process of settlement and spread over Northern India when sobered by reflection and the responsibility of administering newly acquired lands they give utterance to hymns which embody their thinking on problems of social organisation, of cosmic origins, of human destiny and of ultimate reality; and lastly, the assimilation of the victors and the vanquished, when the magic and the ritual attain a position side by side with speculation and philosophy in the sacred arcana of the scriptures, when animistic beliefs and fetish worship lie cheek by jowl with the sublime and subtle concepts of cosmic order and pantheistic godhead.

The Ṛg-Veda (especially its *maṇḍalas* from the second to the tenth) describes the first stage, the religious and social life of these early Aryans in the north-west of India between the banks of the Indus and the Sarasvatī. The first and tenth *maṇḍalas* of the Ṛg-Veda, the Sāma- and Yajur- represent their more advanced state and the Atharva- and the Brāhmaṇas the completion of the Vedic cycle, when the occupation of Northern India to the Gandak (Sadānīrā) was achieved and the original inhabitants were brought into the Vedic social system.

The Vedic age ended sometime between the seventh and sixth centuries B.C. Then began a new age in which the Vedic culture underwent a tremendous development with such force of expansion that it was almost rent into pieces. The impulse came from two sources, in the first place, from an inner urge which represented the assertion of the Kṣatriya class in society; and secondly, from a mysterious and swift interchange of ideas with the Western world. The sixth century was one of the most wonderful epochs of world history, when ideas passed from country to country making their presence felt from far-off China to Egypt, Greece and Rome, radiating from that great centre of culture the city of Babylon which was the clearing house of world commerce and world ideas.

The repercussions of these influences upon the Vedic culture ushered in the new age of science, philosophy and heterodox speculation on the intellectual side and of poetry and art and religious devotion on the emotional, while the basic Vedic religion was both systematised and popularized. During this period of the Upaniṣads and the Bhagavadgītā were compiled, the orthodox schools of philosophy were started, Buddhism, Jainism and other heterodox systems were founded, the first redactions of the epics and of the archetypal Purāṇa were made, devotional elements in Śiva and Viṣṇu worship were introduced, the sciences of metrics, etymology, grammar, astronomy, mathematics and medicine were elaborated, and the arts of war, administration, music, painting, sculpture and architecture were cultivated. The beginning and end of this age coincide approximately with the rise of the Śiśunāga and the downfall of the Maurya dynasties (600 B.C. to 180 B.C.).

About the close of this marvellous era of imperial expansion and cultural glories the north-western horizon again became clouded with the dark appearance of barbarian hordes and alien invaders. Antiochos the Great, Demetrios, Eukratides and Menander hovered on the borders or penetrated into the country and barbarian streams of Yueh--chi and Śakas overflowed the passes and deposited settlements in Sindh, the Punjāb and the plains round Mathurā, and occupied the peninsula of Surāṣtra. How far these events had an effect upon the overthrow of the Mauryas it is difficult to estimate, but they synchronised with the commencement of the new age, in which Hinduism reasserted itself. This was an age of transition. Sanskrit learning was resuscitated by royal patronage, the great epics were re-edited, the popular legendary lore was compiled in the Smṛtis and the earliest Purāṇas, the fluid mass of philosophical speculation was gradually crystallised into systems. Viṣṇu and Śiva worship began to overshadow the worship of the other gods in the religious pantheon. Buddhism expanded into China, Central Asia, and Persia, and although it broke up into the Hīnayāna and Mahāyāna schools and their subordinate branches, it still reigned supreme in the world of art furnishing inspiration for the monuments of Bharhut, Sānchī, Sārnāth and Amarāvatī. Jainism which spread into Gujrat and Tāmil land became divided into the Śvetāṃbara and Digaṃbara schools.

This was the period of the political supremacy of the Brahman dynasties of Śuṇga, Kāṇva and Sātavāhanas, and it lasted from 180 B. C. to 235 A.D.

The curtain fell upon the last age amid a scene of utter anarchy and disorder. The Sātavāhana power broke into pieces and the empire which the Kuṣāñas had built up in Western India dissolved, and the next period was inaugurated in "extreme confusion associated with foreign invasions from the north-west, which is reflected in the muddled statements of the Purāṇas concerning the Ābhīras, Gardabhillas, Śakas, Yavanaṣ,

Bāhlīkas, and other outlandish dynasties named as the successors of the Āndhras." For one hundred years the history of India remained shrouded in darkness which was lifted by the rising sun of the Gupta dynasty in the fourth century. The next four hundred years form a bright epoch in the advancing cycles of Indian culture.

In every department of national life great achievements were made. In religion Hinduism attained its most fully developed form, Śiva and Viṣṇu worship became the dominant cults, Śāktism made its appearance, but Vedic sacrifices began to fall into disuse. Buddhism and Jainism received a definite check and gradually withered away. In Hindu religious literature the last redaction of the Mahābhārata (including the Harivaṃśa) and the Rāmāyaṇa was made, and the Purāṇas were re-edited. In philosophy the six Darśanas were completely systematised, the Vaiṣṇava and Śaiva schools of philosophy (the Pañcarātra Saṃhitā and Śaiva Āgamas), and other sectarian (Tāntrika) and heterodox schools made their appearance. In poetry Kālidāsa, Daṇḍin, Bāṇa, Bhāravi and others adorned the age and in prose the Pañcatantra and other fairy tales which became the storehouse of the world's stories were compiled.

In the sciences Āryabhaṭṭa, Brahmagupta and Varāha-Mihira developed astronomy and mathematics, and Vāgbhaṭṭa compiled the compendium of medicine. In the arts of painting, sculpture and architecture the works of Ajantā, Ellorā, Bāgh, Bādāmī, Sārnāth and other places were accomplished.

With the passing of Harṣa's empire the last period of ancient history closed, and the new epoch which may fitly be called the Middle Age began. The change from the ancient to the medieval times was vast. Politically it put an end to Imperialism based on a loose confederation of practically autonomous principalities acknowledging the overlordship of a suzerain power; it saw the beginnings of feudal particularism, of Rajput tribes waging incessant wars with one another, and paving the way for the Muslim conquest. In religion it marked the almost complete disappearance of Buddhism and Jainism from the land of their birth, the establishment of sectarian Hinduism all over India and its development under the impulses of Islam. In art it witnessed the evolution of Hindu-Muslim schools of architecture and painting, in literature the decline of Sanskrit learning and the rise of Vernacular languages, among them Urdū, and in science the infusion of Arab conceptions into Hindu medicine, mathematics and astronomy. The total amount of change in all departments of social life was so great as to constitute the beginning of a new epoch.

This epoch may be divided into two equal periods of five hundred years each, the first running from the eighth to the thirteenth and the second from the thirteenth to the eighteenth century of the Christian era, the first may be designated the early middle age and the second the later middle age. During the first age Islam began to penetrate into India peacefully in the south and forcibly into Sindh and the north-west, and during the second it became the dominant force practically over the whole of the Indian peninsula.

In order to trace the changes in the culture of the country which Muslim influences produced, it is first necessary to give a description of it as it existed before their advent. It will be convenient to divide culture into two heads—religion and philosophy, and art—and to treat each head separately from the time of the advent of the Muslims into India till the passing of the Moghal empire in the eighteenth century.

THE INFLUENCE OF ISLAM ON INDIAN CULTURE

PRE-MUSLIM HINDU CULTURE

In order to understand the religious conditions prevailing in India at the time of the Islamic impact, it is necessary to introduce some principle of simplification which will indicate the leading tendencies of thought and worship. An exhaustive description of the actual facts of all existing sects and cults, their relationships and conflicts, utterly bewildering in their complexity, will not be useful and need not be attempted.

The Hindus treat their religion from the point of view of emancipation (*mokṣa*) for the attainment of which they recognise three paths—the paths of action (*karman*), of knowledge (*jñāna*), and of devotion (*bhakti*). It will be convenient to arrange all the religions and sects under these three heads. It must, however, be remembered that the three paths are not mutually exclusive and do not necessarily imply antagonism; as a matter of fact practically all the sects recognise their value and enjoin them on their followers. But it is interesting to note that the religious importance of the path of action exclusively was greatest in the earliest times, that of the path of knowledge grew later and that of the path of devotion last. The three have existed side by side but while the influence of the first two has waned that of *Bhakti-Mārga* has increased.

The path of action is the one principally laid down by the *Vedas,* developed and systematised in the *Brāhmaṇas, Kalpa-Sūtras,* and *Karma-Mīmāṁsā* and popularised by *Dharma-Śāstras, Mahābhārata* and the *Purāṇas.* What then is the philosophic basis of this *Karma-Mārga*?

Whatever historical strata Vedic thought may contain, in its mature form it is a well-rounded philosophic-religious system.

In this system one supreme being stands forth as the ultimate reality. It is conceived of as the One[1] (*ekam*), the Person (*puruṣa*), the Creator (*viśvakarman*,[2] *prajāpati*[3]), the Absolute (*tad*[4]), Brāhmaṇa transcendent and immanent,[5] omniscient,[6] upholder of moral law[7] and maintainer of cosmic order.[8] He is the father,[9] the sustainer and supporter of the universe,[10] and the fulfiller of desires. "One All is Lord of what is fixed and moving, that walks, that flies, this multiform creation."[11]

How does He create the world? There are several accounts of it in the Vedic literature. Sometimes the universe is conceived of as the result of mechanical production.[12] It is measured and spread out; it has foundation, support and framework. Sometimes it is the fruit of sacrifice. *Puruṣa* himself becomes the victim and from his parts are made corresponding portions of the universe.[13] More philosophically considered, creation is a process, the evolution of the existent (*sat*) from the non-existent (*asat*).[14] In the beginning not-being and being were both non-existent, there was a dark void in which the One breathed calm and windless, then desire sprang within Him which was the bond of being and non-being and the cause of entire creation. But the account which became popular was that the primeval being created the waters on which floated the golden

1 Ṛg-Veda (Wilson's translation) I, 164, 46; VIII, 58, 2 Bālakhilya.

2 Ibid., X, 81, 82.

3 Ibid., X, 121.

4 Ibid., X, 129.

5 Ibid., I, 164, 45; X, 90, 3 and 4.

6 Ibid., I, 25; Macdonnel: History of Sanskrit Literature, p. 201. Bloomfield: The Religion of Veda, p. 123.

7 Ṛg-Veda II, 28, 5; Bloomfield: The Religion of Veda, p. 124.

8 Ṛg-Veda I, 105, 12; I, 164, 11.

9 Ibid., X, 82, 3.

10 Ibid., X, 82.

11 Frazer: Literary History of India, p. 57.

12 Ṛg-Veda X, 12.

13 Ibid., X, 90.

14 Ibid., X, 129.

egg, he then entered it, and was born from it as *Brahmā* the first of created things. *Brahmā* then created gods, heaven, earth, sky, sun, moon, universe and man.

All these cosmogonies show a frankly pantheistic tendency, for creation either implies transformation of the First Principle into the universe, or the immanence of what was transcendent, or the manifestation of the non-manifest. But within this pantheism lurks the principle of personality, for the universe is the result of desire, creation is the effect of will.

This in fact is the most important conception from the point of view of the path of action. The universe is the theatre of God's will, every being living and non-living is moved by His eternal order and all action and movement is bound in one chain of law. Not only are natural phenomena—day and night, sun and moon, rivers and oceans,—and the gods—*Agni, Soma, Bṛhaspati, Indra Aditi* and *Varuṇa*,—under the sway of law, but the very act of worship—rite and sacrifice—which man offers to the gods obeys the all-comprehending, all-encompassing rule of cosmic law. In fact before the severe majesty of law even the power of the gods pales into insignificance.[15]

Sacrifice is the symbol of this universal order; it is even the source of Prajāpati's power, for when He exhausts it in creation, the gods replenish his pristine vigour with sacrifice. Through sacrifice the gods display their activity in rain and storm and the rising of the sun. Sacrifice is thus the instrument by which the will of God is fulfilled. Man is the creature of God dependent upon His will, seeking to understand and interpret that will, and naturally moulding his actions in imitation of his gods. Sacrifice is, therefore, the means of attaining prosperity here and blessedness hereafter.[16]

The pathway of eternal bliss is that of action, which means sacrifice performed with faith and accompanied with prayer.

15 Bergaigne : Le Religion Védique, Chapitre III.

16 Oltramare : L'histoire des Idées théosophiques dans l'Inde, Chapitre II.

Sacrifices are manifold—they are obligatory and regular (*nitya*), obligatory but occasional (*naimittika*), and optional (*kāmya*). Then there are the great sacrifices which in later times had largely fallen into disuse; and the domestic sacrifices (*gṛhya*) which still play an important part in the life of the individual. The Vedic sacrifices required oblations of animals as well as fruits and milk and cakes of rice; the first, however, disappeared from the ritual, and the followers of *Smṛtis* offered only non-bloody sacrifices.

But sacrifice although symbolic of cosmic law and hence efficacious in bringing about the desired ends is not the whole of human action. Man's life, therefore, is mapped out and man's place in society fixed. Rules are laid down for the governance of each part of the fourfold station of life (*āśrama*) and fourfold classification of society (*varṇa*). The permanence of these duties becomes the essential part of the religion of action (*varṇāśrama dharma*).

Yet another development of this conception takes place in the *Bhagavadgītā* where it is taught that salvation may be won through the path of action, and action is interpreted as performance of duty without attachment to fruits.

This then was the speculative basis of the religion of *Karman*. But in popular practice it meant more or less the offering of sacrifices to the gods and the observance of the domestic rites. In the *Vedas* the gods had been the earliest products of creation. They were semi-anthropomorphised forces of nature, their functions were scarcely differentiated and therefore they easily melted into one another—

> "They call him *Indra, Mitra, Varuṇa, Agni,* and he is the heavenly winged *Garutman.*"[17]

But later they acquired more definite personalities. On the eve of the advent of the Muslims in India the significance and numbers of the ancient deities had greatly changed. Most of them had disappeared from the popular pantheon, the import-

[17] Frazer: Literary History of India, p. 57.

ance of others had enormously varied, and a number of new ones had risen into favour. As beings of a higher order they played an important rôle in the universe and the life of man. Their favour had to be won by prayer and sacrifices and their wrath propitiated by suitable rites and penances. Each of these deities had its group of devotees and particular deities had given rise to sects. It is necessary to gauge the relative popularity and strength of the sects prevalent in India in those times in order to understand the transformations wrought in subsequent times.

The Vedic pantheon was peopled with gods that lived in the heavens or in the atmosphere or upon earth, their number was reckoned as thirty-three, but those to whom the greatest number of hymns were devoted were *Indra, Agni,* and *Soma. Varuṇa* was the most exalted, and *Prajāpati* was the lord of creation, *Viṣṇu* and *Rudra-Śiva* received meagre attention. In older epic mythology *Brahmā* presided over the deities as creator and beneficent ancestor of all, while *Agni, Yama, Varuṇa, Kubera* and *Indra* were most often invoked. Later *Śiva* and *Viṣṇu* attained the predominant position and joined with *Brahmā* formed the great Trinity.

For the seventh and eighth centuries there is a considerable amount of contemporary evidence to show what the state of popular worship was. This evidence consists of the accounts of the Chinese travellers, the Sanskrit dramas, the inscriptions and coins of Indian rulers, and the descriptions of the Arab writers. They disclose that while the non-Vedic religions, Buddhism and Jainism, were on the decline, the old Vedic religion had greatly changed, the worship of *Śiva* was the predominant religion of India, the cult of *Śakti* was rising into importance and *Viṣṇu* and other deities were held in popular esteem in a descending scale.

In the narratives of Fa-Hien[18] one finds that in the fifth century when the traveller came to India, the north-western portion of the country from Kabul and Khotan to Mathurā was

[18] Beal: The Buddhist Records of the Western World, Vol. I, p. xlviii.

still loyal to Buddhism (*Hinayāna*), in the *Madhya Deśa* the assimilation of Buddhism and Hinduism was rapidly proceeding. There were ninety-six heretical sects all of whom allowed the reality of worldly phenomena and the Buddhists professed the *Mahāyāna* doctrine, but the ancient region which had been the cradle of Buddhism was a desert, the *Saṅghārāmas* and *Vihāras* were in ruins and there were hardly any priests in the ancient cities of Śrāvastī, Kapilavastu, Kuśinagar, Vaiśālī, Pāṭaliputra or Gayā. The land was barren, the inhabitants had fled, the roads were infested with wild beasts, and desolation reigned over all. In the east, however, between Campā and Tāmralipti Buddhism still flourished.

When Hiuen-Tsiang visited India two hundred years later he found Hinduism vigorously established by the side of Buddhism. The north-western regions were no longer the seat of a flourishing faith. Everywhere, in Lamghān, in Gandhāra, in Udyāna, in Kashmīr and the Panjāb and right down to Mathurā the *Hīnāyāna* had been displaced by the *Mahāyāna*, and more important still the Deva temples and Brāhmaṇa priests equalled in numbers and importance the Buddhist *Saṅghārāmas* and *Śramaṇas*. In the *Madhya Deśa,* in the east of India, and in the south, wherever he travelled, he found the same state of affairs. Harṣa-Vardhana, the Emperor of Northern India, paid equal reverence to the two faiths and he exhibited his impartiality in the great festival on the plains of Prayāga by installing and worshipping on successive days the image of the *Buddha, Sūrya* and *Maheśvara.*

Hiuen-Tsiang's narrative is full of references to the prevalence of Śaiva worship especially in *Pāśupata* form. In the Swāt Valley the spring of *Śiva* inflicted injury on crops,[19] above Soli to the north-east of Palusha there was an image of *Maheśvara's* spouse Bhīmā, and a temple of ash-smearing *Tirthakas.*[20] In Makrān there were hundreds of *Deva*

[19] Watters : Yuan-Chwang, Vol. I, pp. 229-30.

[20] Ibid., p. 221.

temples and very many professed *Pāśupatas* cult, and in the city there was a large temple to *Maheśvara* which was held in great reverence by the *Pāśupatas*.[21] In *Fa-la-na* (Baluchistan) there were *Deva* temples chiefly belonging to the *Pāśupatas*,[22] in *Maheśvarapura* (east of Sindh) the people were not Buddhists and the majority of temples belonged to the *Pāśupatas*,[23] in *O-tien-po-chi-lo* (a dependency of Sindh) there was a magnificent *Maheśvara* temple and numerous *Pāśupatas*.[24] In Khotan there were *Pāśupatas*, foı a *Pāśupata* engineer was engaged by the Chinese prince to lay the foundations of his capital.[25] In Kashmir the *Kritiyas* had overthrown Buddhism and established heresy (probably Śaivism[26]), in the Panjāb from the Indus to the Sutlej there were numerous heretics, in Jalandhar all the heretics belonged to the *Pāśupatas*[27] (the cinder-sprinkled), in Ahichhatra (*Rāmnagar*) there were sectaries who sacrificed to *Iśvara* and belonged to the company of ash-sprinklers (*Pāśupatas*),[28] in Kapitha (Sankiśa) there were temples where they honoured *Maheśvara* and sacrificed to him,[29] in Kanauj there was a splendid temple to *Maheśvara*,[30] in Benares there were over a hundred *Deva* temples and more than ten thousand adherents of the sects, the majority being devotees of *Śiva* (*Ta-Tseu-Tsai*)—some of these cut off their hair, others made it into a topknot. They covered their bodies with ashes, and by the practice of all sorts of austerities they sought to escape from birth and

21 Wahters : Yuan-Chwang, Vol. II, p. 257.

22 Ibid., p. 262.

23 Beal : Buddhist Records of the Western World, Vol. II, p. 271.

24 Ibid., p. 276.

25 Watters : Yuan-Chwang, Vol. II, p. 296.

26 Beal : Op. cit., Vol. I, pp. 156—58.

27 Ibid., pp. 156—58.

28 Ibid., p. 200.

29 Ibid., p. 202.

30 Watters : Op. cit., Vol. I, p. 352.

death,[31] there was a copper image of *Maheśvara* about 100 feet in height, "its appearance is grave and majestic, and appears as though really living."[32] In Kapilavastu there was a temple of *Iśvaradeva*[33]; beyond Ayodhyā on the Ganges river there were pirates who paid worship to *Durgā* and who annually performed human sacrifice[34]; in Bengal *Śaśāṅka* who was a *Śaiva* persecuted the Buddhists, in the University of Nālandā Hiuen-Tsiang disputed with *Bhūtas* who covered themselves with ashes,[35] and the *Kāpālikas* who wore chaplets of bones round their heads.[36] On the eastern coast there were Hindu sectaries and at Bhramaragiri and Dhanakaṭaka the worship of Durgā prevailed.[37] On Potalaka mountain, east of Malaya, there was a temple of *Śiva*[38]; in Western India Mālwā was famous for its learning, there were hundreds of *Deva* temples and the majority of the sectaries were *Pāśupatas*.[39] Even in Persia, Afghanistan and Central Asia there were *Pāśupatas* besides Buddhists and they performed their rites in their temples.[40]

The literary evidence confirms the account of Hiuen-Tsiang. Śūdraka's Mṛcchakaṭika shows the predominance of Buddhism, but it by no means ignores *Śiva,* for the *Nandī* in invoking benedictions, calls upon *Nīlakaṇṭha* (*Śiva*) whose blue neck is entwined by the arms of *Gaurī* effulgent like lightning.[41] Kālidāsa in the opening lines of Raghuvaṁśa pays homage to

31 Watters: Op. cit., Vol. II, p. 47.

32 Beal: Op. cit., Vol. II, p. 45.

33 Watters: Op. cit., Vol. II, p. 13.

34 Beal: Life of Hiuen-Tsiang, p. 86.

35 Ibid., p. 161. .

36 Ibid., p. 161.

37 Beal: Op. cit., Vol. II, p. 214, note, and p. 224, note.

38 Ibid., p. 233.

39 Watters: Op. cit., Vol. II, p. 242; Beal: Vol. II, p 261.

40 Beal: Op. cit., Vol. II, p. 277.

41 Wilson: The Hindu Drama, Mṛcchakaṭika.

Pārvatī and PARAMEŚVARA.[42] Bāṇa's *Harṣacharita* is replete with metaphors alludinp to *Śiva:* he refers to the yawning gulf of *Mahābhairava's* mouth, to *Śiva's* begging bowl made of *Brahmā's* skull[43]; and among the devotees of various sects to *Mahā-Pāśupatas.*[44] In the *Kādambarī* reverence is paid to *Śiva* as *Mahākāla,* "the pre-eminence yielded in *Kādambarī* to *Śiva* certainly shows that this was then the popular worship."[45] Ujjain was spoken of as a creation of *Mahākāla.* Bhavabhūti in his *Mālatī Mādhava* represents *Mālatī* to have visited the temple of *Saṁkara.*[46] *Śiva* worship prevailed over Western India. There were great *liṅga* shrines at Māndhātā, Ujjain, Nāsik, Ellorā, Nāganātha, east of Ahmadnagar, and at the source of the Bhīmā, and sanguinary rites were still observed at Māndhātā in the twelfth century A.D.[47] In the absence of a fixed chronology for the *Purāṇas* it is difficult to rely upon their evidence, but the important position occupied by *Śiva* both in the *Mahābhārata* and in the *Purāṇas* clearly proves that the cult had obtained such widespread popularity that it had to be given recognition in the Brāhmaṇical system. It is not unlikely that the admission of *Śiva* into the trinity was subsequent to that of *Viṣṇu,* and that the *Vaiṣṇava* redactions of the epic and of the *Purāṇas* are earlier than the Śaiva touches. It is, however, undoubted that the worship of both *Śiva* and *Viṣṇu* existed side by side, and that during the Gupta period *Śiva* was the more popular of the two deities.

The coins of the Kuṣāṇa kings and inscriptions of the various dynasties point to the same conclusion.[48] The Arabs who during the course of the seventh and eighth centuries made many descents upon the coast of Gujarat, the Gulf of Cambay

42 Kālidāsa : Raghuvaṁśa.

43 Cowell and Thomas : Bāṇa's Harṣa Carita, pp. 259, 260

44 J. Vidyāsāgara Bhattāchārya : Harṣa Carita, p. 204.

45 Ridding : Bāṇa's Kādambarī, p. xvii.

46 Bhavabhūti : Mālatī Mādhava, Act III.

47 Pargiter : Introduction to Mārkaṇḍeya Purāṇa.

48 Rapson : Indian Coins, Kuṣaṇas, p. 16.

and the Malabar Coast acquired information regarding Hindu sects which was embodied in their books of religion compiled in the ninth and later centuries. These references shed an interesting light on Indian religious and social customs. The Arabs' attention was naturally attracted to what was peculiar and strange to them, but was usual in the country. Thus, for instance, Sulaimān[49] mentions the ascetics who wandered in hills and forests, who lived on herbs and fruits and who rarely communicated with the rest of the world; and others who wore nothing but panther skins round their loins and performed severe penances; Abu Zaid al Hasan Sirafi saw wandering monks who carried round their neck a cord to which a human cranium was attached out of which they ate their food.[50] Undoubtedly he refers to *Kāpālikas,* a Śaiva sect. Abul Faraj Muhammad ibn Ishāq al Nādim, author of the celebrated *Kitāb-al-Fihrist,* copied the account of Hindu sects from a treatise written in 863 A.D. (probably by Al-Kindi), the information for which was collected by an envoy sent to India at the instance of Yahiyā ibn Khālid, the Barmekide. The *Kitāb* mentions the sect of *Mahākāla,* and describes the idol of *Śiva* in great detail[51] (probably in the temple of Ujjain). Al Shahristānī (1086–1153 A.D.) in his *Kitāb al Milal fi Nihal* speaks of the *Pāśupatas,* (*Bahuvadyah*) whose apostle was a spiritual angel in human form riding on a bull, with a crown of human skulls on his head and a garland of shells round his neck, with a cranium in one hand and a trident in the other, and again of the idols of *Mahākālā* and of Śiva.[52]

Thus it appears that *Śiva* worship prevailed over the greater part of India about the seventh and eighth centuries, but along with it, the worship of other gods was also practised

49 Reinaud: Relations des voyages faits par les Arabes et les Persanes dans l'Inde et à la Chine. (1845). Vol. I, p, 50.

50 Ibid., p. 50.

51 Ferrand: Relations de voyages et texte géographiques Arabes.

52 Rehatsek: Early Moslem Accounts of the Hindu Religion, Journal of Bombay Branch of the Royal Asiatic Society, No. 36, Vol. XIV, p. 29.

though not so extensively; among them that of *Viṣṇu* was the most important. Hiuen-Tsiang, who usually makes mention of *Deva temples* and Hindu sectaries without giving more specific details except in cases where the *Śaivas* are concerned, notices the temple of *Viṣṇu* at Navadevakula[53] (near Kanauj) and of *Nārāyaṇadeva* at Mahāsāra (Masār near Arrah).

The early Muslim accounts are too vague as regards non-*Śaiva* sects to permit of any legitimate inference concerning the prevalence of Vaiṣṇavism. Al-Shahristānī, however, speaks of the *Basuyah* which Haarbrucker reads as *Basuwiya,* i.e., *Vaiṣṇava.* But the description of the cult is not particularly *Vaiṣṇava.*

In the Hindu literature of the period a similar state is revealed. Bāṇa mentions the *Bhāgavatas* and *Pañcarātras* in the *Harṣa Carita,* and the followers of *Kṛṣṇa* in the *Kādambarī.* Mayūra speaks of the claws of *Narasiṁha,* and describes the dread of *Kṛṣṇa.* The epics are dominated by devotion to *Viṣṇu* and some of the *Purāṇas* are dedicated to him but this does not enable one to decide about the diffusion of the creed, for it is difficult to determine whether the Epics and the *Purāṇas* are the expression of the ideas of an intellectual aristocracy, the Court Pundits or of those of the people at large, and is still more difficult to deduce from them any conclusions with regard to the prevalence of the sects in different regions. The evidence as a whole seems to indicate that Northern India of the seventh and eighth centuries was not Vaiṣṇavite but Śaivite although subsequently in the time of Al-Birūnī their relative positions had been reversed. Besides Śiva and Viṣṇu the important cults were those of *Śakti, Sūrya, Candra, Brahmā, Indra, Agni, Skanda, Gaṇeśa, Yama* and *Kubera.*

Hiuen-Tsiang in his itinerary, Bāṇa in the *Harṣa Carita*[54] and *Caṇḍī-Śataka,*[55] *Mayūra* in his *Stanzas,*[56] notice worship

[53] Watters : Yuan-Chwang, Vol. I, pp. 352, 353.

[54] Cowell and Thomas : pp. 232, 259.

[55] Quackenobs : Caṇḍī-Śataka.

[56] Ibid., Mayūra Śataka, p. 231.

of *Śakti* in various forms. In the Mahābhārata there are hymns addressed to *Durgā*,[57] and the *Tantras* which inculcate her cult probably assumed their present form in the sixth century.[58] The cult of the mothers (*mātṛkas*) was closely allied to *Śaktism* and was widely spread.

The *Saura* cult appears to have been widely diffused about this period. Multan had a splendid temple which was seen and described by Hiuen-Tsiang, Ibn Haukal, and Istakhrī. The *Kitāb al Fihrist* mentions *Soma* worshippers who had an image of *Soma* on a chariot drawn by four horses, holding a stone of the colour of fire. Al Shahrastānī gives the same account.[59] Mayūra in his Sūrya Śataka makes *Sūrya*[60] the supreme god and identifies him with *Brahmā, Śiva, Viṣṇu, Yama* and *Kubera*. *Sūrya* is to him not only the god and the primary cause but a kinsman and kind friend, a teacher and a father. Varāhamihira[61] gives directions for the installation and consecration of the images and temples of the sun, and *Harṣavardhana* styles himself a 'great devotee of the sun (*Paramādityabhakta*).'[62]

The worshippers of *Gaṇpati* or *Gaṇeśa, Skanda* or *Kārtikeya, Candra,* and other gods and goddesses hardly need detailed notice.

The followers of the path of action (*karma-mārga*) were found in all the sects and among the devotees of all the gods. Their worship consisted in adressing prayers to the gods before the images at home or in the temple, in performing prescribed rites—domestic and public, in offering sacrifices—rarely human, in some cases bloody, but more often consisting of corn and milk

57 Mahābhārata : Bhīṣma Parvan, Chapter 23, Virāṭa Parvan, Chap. 6 (P. C. Ray's translation).

58 Geden : E.R.E. Tantras.

59 Rehatsek : Early Moslem Accounts.

60 Quackenbos : Mayūra Śataka.

61 Varāhamihira : translated by Kern.

62 V. A. Smith : Gupta Coinage, J.R.A.S. 1889, p. 1.

and fruits. Fasts, pilgrimages, charity, penances and ascetic exercises were part of the good deeds which won the favour of the gods. The path of action was the path of legal duties, and fixed ceremonial; it led to prosperity in this life and to heavenly bliss in the life beyond.

The second path for the attainment of salvation is that of knowledge (*jñāna-mārga*). The *Vedas* and the *Brāhmaṇas* had emphasised the value of action. But when the theory of metempsychosis and the law of *karman* rose, it became apparent to the logical mind of the Hindu thinkers that devotion to action could not lead to deliverance and freedom. It was necessary to discover some other means to break the rigid chain of cause and effect, to bring to an end the otherwise indestructible impulse of primeval action. It became necessary to make a searching enquiry into the very nature of action and to find out the law of its fulfilment and exhaustion. This enquiry was started early by the forest recluses whose bold speculations are embodied in the *Upaniṣads*. It was soon taken up in what Grierson calls the 'Outlands of Āryāvarta,' i.e., among the peoples inhabiting the regions to the south-west and east of the midlands occupied by Vedic Aryans, by Kṣattriyas and other non-Brāhmaṇas. And the profound and earnest discussions of cosmic origin and human destiny, of the nature of the ultimate reality and its relation to the individual, of good and evil and of the psychology of conduct and of the means of deliverance led to the foundation of a number of religio-philosophic, or to use Oltramare's term theosophic systems—*Sāṅkhya, Yoga, Vedānta, Bauddha, Jaina, Śaiva, Vaiṣṇava, Tantra, Lokāyata* and others.

Although each one of these systems proposed a different solution of the problems of life and thought, there are certain features common to all of them which form the basis of the Pre-Islamic Indian culture.

In the first place, all the systems have the same point of departure, i.e., the Vedic conception of law; only they apply it more rigorously than the ancient seers did. This conception of law is combined with the conception of *karman*. Action is a relationship of cause and effect, and it forms an eternal, beginningless, unending chain by which the universe and man are inexorably bound. The conception of *karman* applied to the macrocosm gives the cosmogonies and genetic chains, applied to the microcosm the theory of transmigration or metempsychosis or palingenesis. The essence of *karman* is bondage, and bondage signifies suffering. The goal of human endeavour is to break the chain and end suffering. The preconceptions of time, space and cause which are so to say the media of all thinking are also alike in all the systems. Time and space are not empty voids in which reality happens and lives, but the plastic forms of reality itself, the all-pervading, continuous and universal mediums of reality. Objectively time and space are not homogeneous continuums. They are relative. The time moments differ for different types of beings; for example, the unit of earthly time is one-hundredth part of the unit of higher beings (gods), a millionth of the unit of still higher beings (*Brahmā*) and an infinitesimal part of that of the highest being. Space is gross and subtle and within the subtle are subtler spaces forming thus a series of space within space. Thus the sensible universe does not exhaust the whole of being. Time and space are modes of reality, hence reality is conceived as a becoming, a cyclic process, an eternal evolution and involution, manifestation and reabsorption, and as an inexhaustible articulation of forms and a plenum of worlds upon worlds piled in unending succession.

The ideas of causality involve the notions of agency, material and product and the relation and meaning of them. They have various interpretations, sometimes implying the determination of a product by an agent, sometimes merely denoting a succession of events, and at other times asserting an identity between cause and effect—the manifestation of the unmanifest. Causation is understood in different ways in different schools, and, according to the particular meaning attached to it, is envisaged the relation of the first principle of things to created nature, i.e., God and the universe. Four main interpretations of causation may be distinguished: (1) the theistic, which holds that God created the universe out of nothing, but the universe is real; (2) the realistic, which considers nature co-eternal with God and independent, God being only a demiurge; (3) the pantheistic, which looks upon the universe as the manifestation of God, and makes God and universe synonymous; (4) the idealistic, which maintains that nothing exists besides God.

Besides metaphysical postulates, the methodology of Indian systems is the same. The first assumption is that truth is learnt not merely by ratiocination or faith but by direct experience, and that speculation must begin with these truths of intuition, and philosophy proceed to demonstrate them by reasoning. It follows that philosophical discipline must consist of the hearing (*śravaṇa*) of truths, reflection (*manana*) upon them, repeated meditation (**निदिध्यासव;**); its end being self-illumination.

The presentation of philosophical truth—not the realization of intuitive truth—depends on the prepossessions, temperament and intelligence of the individual, hence considerations of points of view and of personal needs (*pātra*) must arise and be attended to. Looking at things in this way the six different systems of Hindu philosophy constitute one series. *Pūrva Mīmāṁsā* deals with the practical side of religion and explains the Vedic ritual and duties; *Nyāya* lays down the method of reasoning; *Vaiśeṣika* gives a first analysis of metaphysical doctrines and reduces the universe to nine classes of ultimate factors or self-subsisting entities. *Sāṅkhya* carries the analysis a step further and derives the whole of the universe from two ultimate principles—*Puruṣa* and *Prakṛti* or soul and matter; *Yoga* accepts the exposition of *Sāṅkhya* and proceeds to consider the practical method by which the truth of the doctrines can be realised as direct experiences; lastly, Vedānta reduces the two realities of *Sāṅkhya-Yoga* to one absolute reality only, whose appearance is the multiplicity of names and forms, the phenomenal universe of infinite variety.

The religious aspect of the Upaniṣads and the six philosophical systems may be briefly summarised. According to *Sāṅkhya* reality is constituted of two co-eternal substances—soul and matter. Matter in the undifferentiated state consists of three constituents (*sattva, rajas, tamas*) held in equilibrium. Its attribute is change and activity. Souls are infinite in number and conscious but inactive and unchangeable. The presence of the souls excites matter to activity, its equilibrium is disturbed and it enters into the process of development. From undifferentiated matter twenty-five entities are evolved and form the manifested universe including the physiological and psychological vehicles of the soul, body and mind. The soul illumines the processes in the mind, and brings the mechanical and the unconscious into the plane of consciousness, itself remaining passive, at harmony with itself, independent. But the attachment of soul with its vehicles is a bondage and creates suffering and pain. It creates the illusion which involves the souls in the wheel of births and deaths. The ultimate destiny of the soul is, however, liberation and this is attained by the acquisition of discriminating knowledge, by the recognition of the essential distinction of soul from matter. After the attainment of this knowledge and the exhaustion of the results of the works done before soul is freed, mind is dissolved and body perishes. "The soul, therefore, abides eternally released from the delusion and suffering of this world, as a seer who no longer sees anything, a glass in which nothing is any longer reflected, as pure untroubled light by which nothing is illuminated."[63]

Yoga introduces into this system of two co-eternal principles a third eternal principle, that is, God (*Iśvara*). God is conceived as a particular soul, and endowed with all good qualities. He is not a creator or punisher and rewarder, nor a bestower of felicity, but "He in His mercy aids the man who is entirely devoted to Him to remove the hindrances which stand in the

[63] Garga : E.R.E: Sāṅkhya quoted from Oldenberg.

way of the attainment of deliverance." *Yoga* prescribes the exact discipline by means of which the knowledge which emancipates may be attained. This is the famous eightfold discipline of interdictions (*yama*), injunctions (*niyama*), postures (*āsana*), control of breath (*Prāṇāyāma*), retraction of sense activities (*pratyāhāra*), fixation of mind (*dhārṇā*), meditation (*dhyāna*), and concentration (*samādhi*). The first two lay down the decalogue of the necessary virtues among which prominence is given to the suppression of desires, the next three the process of self-hypnosis and the last two the attainment of ecstasy and the unitive state.

The *Vedānta* takes for granted the cosmogony of the *Śāṅkhya* and the eightfold discipline of the *Yoga*, but advances a step further the enquiry into the nature of the soul, matter and God. With regard to the nature of the *ātman* (soul), the *Vaiśeṣika* standpoint is that it is a reality in which consciousness is sustained but of which consciousness is not an absolutely essential characteristic; the *Sāṅkhya* holds that the soul is consciousness or intelligence itself but teaches that souls are infinite in number; the *Vedānta* comes to the conclusion that the soul is not only consciousness itself, but that it is one and the same in all experiencing beings, and that the soul (*ātman*) is identical with God (*brahman*). But soul is overlaid with ignorance and enters into *Saṁsāra* and undergoes suffering, from which release is possible only by the removal of ignorance and the realization of its true nature.

Besides the orthodox schools of philosophy which prescribed the path of knowledge, the India of the seventh and eighth centuries knew of a number of other systems—heterodox and sectarian, which taught liberation by knowledge. Among them the most important were the Bauddha systems.

Buddhism was divided into two schools of *Hīnayānists* and *Mahāyānists* and each of them was further subdivided into two branches. The *Vaibhāṣikas* and *Sautrāntrikas* belonged to the *Hinayāna*, and the *Yogācāras* (or *Vijñānvadins*) and *Mādhyamikas* (or *Śūnyavādins*) to the *Mahāyāna*.

F. 2

Buddhism had started its career as a protest against the formalism of Brāhmaṇism and it fell foul of its essential theories concerning the nature of soul (*ātman*) and God (*brahman*). With regard to both its attitude was one of denial. The soul as a substance did not exist, all that existed was an aggregation of parts (*skandhas*), the coming together of which created a temporary unity. The universe was a plan and it was useless to speculate about its beginning or end. The world as known was a causal order, the first link in the chain was ignorance which gave rise to action, consciousness, mind, body, sense organs, contact, feeling, craving, grasping, becoming, birth, decay, death, grief, sorrow and pain. The *dhamma* of the eightfold path trained away the suffering and put an end to the endless round of births and deaths. This path consisted of right views (*samyak dṛṣṭi*), right thoughts (*samyak saṅkalpa*), right speech (*samyak vāca*), right actions (*samyak karman*), right living (*samyak ājīva*), right exertion (*samyak vyāyāma*), right recollection (*samyak smṛti*), right meditations (*samyak samādhi*). The follower of the eightfold path passed through four stages: first that of the neophyte (*śrotāpanna*) who had broken the first three bonds of human passion (heresy, scepticism and superstitious rites); second, that of the first-returner (*sakṛdāgāmin*) who would be reborn once only in the world of men because he had reduced to a minimum affection, hatred and infatuation; third, that of the never-returner (anāgāmin) who had freed himself from the five bonds (the three of the neophyte, and attachment and antipathy) and who would be born not among men but in a *Brahmaloka,* and, lastly, that of the *Arhat* who had exhausted the *karman* and removed all the bonds, and who would no more be subject to rebirth. The aim of the eightfold path and the fourfold stages was the attainment of *Nirvāṇa.*

> "*Nibbāna* is the highest bliss
> And of all paths the eightfold 'tis
> That unto death-less safety leads."[64]

64 Mrs. Rhys Davids: Buddhism, p. 177.

The *Hīnayāna* and *Mahāyāna* schools differed on questions of metaphysics, on the destiny of the individual, and on ritual. The *Hīnayānists* were realists, acknowledging the real existence of the phenomenal world. The *Mahāyānists* were idealists; the *Yogācāras* denied the real existence of all except consciousness; the *Mādhyamikas* held that the whole of the phenomenal world was unreal and illusory, and in this they were the teachers of *Śaṅkara*. The *Hīnayānists* were concerned with the fate of the individual alone and in Arhathod found his highest possibility of achievement, the *Mahāyānists* aimed at universal salvation and promised the attainment of Buddhahood with all its spiritual powers. Then the first were simple in their ritual, while the second introduced the elaboration of temples and images and the worship of Bodhisattvas, assimilating Buddhism to Hinduism.

Jainism occupied an important position among the religio-philosophical systems then prevalent in India. The Jainas do not believe in one transcendent or absolute existence. They divide reality into soul and not-soul. Under the former category they include two kinds according to the bodies which they inhabit: immobile, e.g., mineral, water, fire, air, and vegetable and mobile, the highest among which are those possessed of five senses. The last are divided into five classes *Siddhas* (liberated), *Arhats* (perfect souls awaiting *Nirvāṇa*), *Ācāryas* (heads of groups of ascetics), *Upādhyāyas* (teaching saints), *Sādhus* (ordinary saints). The soul possesses nine qualities but the chief among them is consciousness (*cetana*). The not-souls (*ajīvas*) are without consciousness. They are classified into five substances (matter, space, time, *dharma* the principle of motion, and *dharma* the principle of inertia). Soul comes into contact with *kārmic* matter (not-oul), becomes impure and obscured of its four great attributes of perfect perception, perfect knowledge, perfect power and perfect happiness. The obscuration of karman keeps the soul tied to the mundane wheel of existence which is the result of a twofold process—(1) the movement of *kārmic* matter towards the soul (*āsrava*), and

(2) the bondage of the soul by *kārmic* matter (*bandha*). This bondage is broken in two steps— (1) by stopping any fresh material ties (*saṁvara*), and (2) by shedding the matter in which soul is entangled (*nirjara*). The end of the process is *nirvāṇa*. The two steps consist of a discipline of vows, penances and austerities by means of which the impurities are gradually (in fourteen stages) washed away and the soul attains the state of pristine purity (*mokṣa*).

The three principal sectarian Hindu philosophical systems are *Vaiṣṇava* (or *Sātvata* or *Pañcarātra* or *Bhāgvata*), *Śaiva* and *Tāntrika*. The history of the various systems included under the three sects goes back to very early times. It is necessary here briefly to give an account of them as they existed in the century following the break-up of Harṣa's empire, without entering into the question of their origin and development.

In the *Pañcaratra* system *Viṣṇu* is the transcendent absolute reality, *Lakṣmī* is the energy, residing in him as Iness in I or moonshine in the moon. *Lakṣmī* has a twofold aspect: as *Kriyāśakti* she represents Viṣṇu's will-to-be, and is independent of space and time, as *Bhūti-śakti* it is the matrix of the universe.

Creation begins when *Viṣṇu* near the end of the night of absorption (*laya*), awakens *Lakṣmī* by his command. The first phase of the manifestation is the appearance of six attributes of God, i.e., Knowledge, Lordship, Power, Strength, Vitality and Splendour. They are the instruments of pure creation. In their totality the attributes make up the body of *Vāsudeva*, the highest personal God. From *Vāsudeva* emanate by self-diremption three *vyūhas* each denoted by a pair of attributes, i.e., *Saṁkarṣāṇa* by Knowledge and Lordship, *Pradyumna* by Power and Strength, *Aniruddha* by Vitality and Splendour.

The second manifestation of pure creation is the *vibhavas*, i.e., the incarnations of God. Two kinds are distinguished among them, the primary when *Viṣṇu* Himself incarnates with a transcendent body, and the secondary when a soul in bondage with a natural body is pervaded by the power of *Viṣṇu*. The

Antaryāmī as the inner ruler of all souls, and *Arca* as the appearance of *Viṣṇu* in images are two other forms of incarnations.

The *vūyhas* bring into play their creative activities by which the non-pure universe comes into existence, in several stages. At first the aggregate of souls (*kutastha puruṣa*) and the primitive form of matter or nature (*Māyā*) are evolved, then the *kutastha* descends into *māyā* and develops the principle of force (*śakti*), regulating knowledge (*niyati*), time (*kāla*), and the three constituents of matter (*sattva, rajas and tamas*). From the three constituents of matter (*mūla prakṛti*) evolves owing to the proximity of soul (*kutasṭha puruṣa*) and the maturing influence of time (*kāla*) the first great product called *Mahat* or cosmic breath, the unconscious. From *Mahat* originates *Ahaṅkāra* (self), from *Ahaṅkāra* mind (*manas*) and the ten senses—the five elements with their five attributes.

In the last stage of creation the elements combine under the influence of *Puruṣa* and form the egg of the universe, out of which come the youths *Sanakādi*, the *Rudras* and the *Prajāpatis*, the universe consisting of fourteen spheres surrounded by seven enclosures, and the five classes of individual souls (*vyaṣṭi*)—the eternally free (*nitya*), the liberated (*mukta*), the pure (*kevala*), the seekers (*mumukṣu*) and the bound (*baddha*).

The individual soul in the world finds itself in bondage. Its original nature is obscured by the acquisition of three taints by association with matter, it loses its original attributes of absoluteness, power knowledge and it becomes limited (*mita*), weak (*akiñcitkara*), and ignorant (*ajñatva*). The taints produce attachment and desire and these lead the soul into *Saṁsāra* and rebirth.

The obscuration can be ended by knowledge (*jñāna*), attained through the grace (*anugraha*) of *Viṣṇu*. The method of the attainment of knowledge consists of the performance of the duties of caste and stage (*varṇāśrama dharma*), the performance of mystical exercises (*mantra and yoga*) under the direction of a teacher, worship (*ārādhanā*), and devotion (*bhakti* or *nyāsa*).

The destiny of the emancipated is to dwell in *Vaikuṇṭhā* enjoying eternal bliss at the feet of *Viṣṇu*.

The period of creation is followed by that of destruction, when the universe is absorbed into *Viṣṇu* from whom it began.

The *Śaiva* system was founded by Lakulīn or Lakulīśa about the second century B.C. Later it was divided into a number of schools forming two groups—(1) *Śaivas, Pāśupatas, Kāpālikas* and *Kālāmukhas*; (2) *Spanda Śāstra, Pratyabhijñā Śāstra* and *Śiva Siddhāntas,* (Kashmir).

The philosophic basis of the *Śaiva* systems of the first group was the recognition of three principles, the lord (*pati*), the individual (*paśu*), and the fetters (*pāśa*). Śiva is the Lord who is endowed with a body made of the five powers of creation, protection, destruction, concealment and benefaction. The individual soul is active, self-conscious, atomic and co-eternal with the Lord. It becomes bound with fourfold fetters by the obscuring power of the Lord. The fetters are taints (*mala*), impression of actions (*karman*), materiality (*māyā*), obstruction (*rodhaśakti*). The fetters may be removed with the help of the beneficent power of the Lord by good deeds (*kriyā*), meditation (*yoga*), and discipline (*caryā*). Good deeds consist in the accomplishment of *mantras,* twilight adorations, worship, mutterings of formulas (*japa*), throwing oblations into the fire, performance of ceremonies and anointing the preceptor and the disciple. Yoga or meditation is constituted by restraint of breath in the circles of the body beginning with the naval (*Mūlādhāra*), attainment of miraculous powers, abstraction, concentration, absorption (*samādhi*). The discipline prescribes penances, the foundation of images or *liṅgams,* the use of the rosary, funeral ceremonies and other practices. The free souls (*muktas*) become identical with *Śiva* himself, retaining their individulity in Him.

The *Pāśupatas* aimed at a mystic union reached by pious mutterings, meditation and the cessation of all action, so that a state of mere feeling (*saṁvid*) was attained. They enjoined a process (*vidhi*) for exciting religious emotions which consisted in besmearing the body with ashes three times a day, and engaging in laughter, song, dance, amorous gestures, uttering loud sounds, executing wild movements and repeating inaudibly certain formulæ.

Their rule of conduct was antinomian, they were required to do a thing condemned by all (*avitatkaraṇa*), as if one were devoid of the sense of discrimination between what should be done and what should be avoided, and to speak nonsensical and absurd things (*avitad bhāṣaṇa*).

The *Kāpālikas* and *Kālāmukhas* carried things to disgusting extremes. They went about wearing garlands of skulls, armed with clubs and lances, carrying wine pots, eating ashes, and performing bloody rites.

The second group which belonged originally to Kashmir spread thence to the Deccan and the extreme south (ninth to twelfth century A.D.). The *Spanda Śāstra* teaches that the soul gains knowledge through intense Yogic contemplation whereby the vision of *Parama Śiva,* the Supreme Lord of the Universe, is realised and the individual soul is absorbed in a mystic trance of peace, quiet and joy. In *Pratyabhijñā* the soul by its own intuition trained under the instruction of a *Guru* (teacher) recognises itself as God and so rests in the mystic bliss of oneness with God. The path of knowledge common to all the sects led by means of the discipline of the *Yoga* to the goal of self-illumination and the realisation of the oneness of the individual soul with the supreme soul.

The third path for the attainment of liberation is that of devotion and faith (*Bhakti-Mārga*). *Bhakti* has been defined as 'the worship of a personal deity in a spirit of love'[65]; as 'personal faith in a personal God, love for him as for a human being, the dedication of everything to his service, and the attainment of *"mokṣa"* by this means, rather than by

65 Barnett : Some Notes on the History of the Religion of Love in India. International Congress for the History of Religions, 1908.

knowledge, or sacrifice, or works,[66] as an affection fixed upon the Lord after acquiring a knowledge of the attributes of the adorable one.[67] *Bhakti* is the emotional aspect of religion, its roots lie in the feeling or affective side of human consciousness, as those of *Jñāna* lie in the cognitive or intellectual, and those of *Karma* in the conative or willing. Psychologically it is impossible that any one of these three aspects should be entirely absent from any religious system, but it is possible that one aspect may be more emphasised than another and in some period of history either will or intellect or feeling may dominate the mind of the people. In this sense, the stream of *Bhakti* which began as a little trickle in the Vedic times went out with the advance of history as a mighty flood sweeping over the whole land. It is necessary to enquire into the origin of this stream and the affluents which entered into it, for it is only by following the course of this stream that the main development of India's religious history can be understood.

The earliest written text of the school of devotion is the Bhagavad Gītā. What then is the character of its devotion?

Kṛṣṇa teaches that it is by unswerving devotion to Him alone that He is reached.[68] God is so pleased that He accepts all that is offered to him with devotion—a leaf, a flower, a fruit, water.[69] "Devotion implies the dedication of all actions to Him,[70] for the devotees live and have their being in God."[71] God extends His ineffable grace to His devotees, for even the sinful worshippers are promised that they will be accounted righteous provided they worship with undivided heart,[72] and that they will never perish.[73] In the sight of God all devotees

66 Sedgwick: Bhakti: Journal of the Bombay Branch of the Royal Asiatic Society, 1910.

67 Grierson: Bhakti Mārga, E.R.E.

68 Bhagavadgītā: VIII, 22 (translation by Bhagvān Dās).

69 Ibid., IX, 26.

70 Ibid., IX, 27.

71 Ibid., IX, 29.

72 Ibid., IX, 30.

73 Ibid., IX, 31.

are equal whether they are born in sin or not, and to whatever caste or sect they may belong.[74] It is by devotion that God may be beheld and known and entered.[75] Devotion is the means of the mystic vision and the unitive state. The devotee is dear to God,[76] surpassingly dear to him,[77] for God is the father,[78] the husband,[79] the mother,[78] and the friend.[79]

Here are all the elements of a religion of devotion, a personal God, divine grace, self-dedication and the love of the devotee, the promise of liberation to all, irrespective of caste and sect, and the mystical union.

The Śvetāśvatara Upaniṣad adds another, that is devotion for the teacher (*guru*) as for God.[80]

The *Nārāyaṇīya*[81] section of the Śāntiaparvan of Mahābhārata is the next important text. It describes the *Ekāntin* religion the ritual of which consisted in meditation and mental recitation (*japa*), the burning of incense, worship with mind, word and deed. The result was the vision of the Adorable by those who possessed faith and devotion, and had won His grace. It declares that the religion of devotion is superior to that of knowledge or of Vedic ritual and enjoins adoration of *Nārāyaṇa* or of one of His manifestations (*vyūhas*).

The ideas of the *Nārāyaṇīya* were more fully stated in the *Pañcarātra Saṁhitā* which, besides knowledge acquired by means of worship (*ārādhanā*) and meditation (*yoga*), recognised devotion (*nyāsa or bhakti*) as a means of emancipation. According to the Saṁhitā, *bhakti* means 'taking refuge in the praying thought: I am a receptacle of sins, naught, helpless,

74 Bhagavadgītā : IX, 32.
75 Ibid., XI, 54.
76 Ibid., XII, 14.
77 Ibid., XII, 20.
78 Ibid., IX, 17.
79 Ibid., IX, 18.
80 Śvetāśvatāra Upaniṣad : VI, 23. (translation by Hume).
81 Grierson : Translation of the Nārāyaṇīya section of the Mahābhārata.

do Thou become my remedy (*upāya*).' The act of taking refuge implies 'austerities, pilgrimages, sacrifices, charities and self-sacrifice than which nothing is higher.'[82]

Bhakti had a parallel development in other systems besides the Pañcarātra, but the most important contribution among them was that of *Buddhism* of the *Mahāyāna* School. Now *Mahāyāna Bhakti* centred round Buddha and the *Bodhisattvas*, but especially about *Amitābha* who is conceived as the eternal God living in *Sukhavatī* (paradise), where the devotees go by His grace and by the help of holy saints. The goal of the devotees of *Aitābha* is not Nirvāṇa (dissolution) but admission into His presence in His heaven. Their devotion is accompanied with acts of worship of *Stūpas* and *Maṇḍalas*, with fasts and pilgrimages, with litanies and formulas for effacing sins, with the reading of Sūtras and the repeating of Buddha's name, and so on.

Buddhism emphasized the democratic side of religion, the spiritual enfranchisement of *Śūdras* and women, and the preaching of religion through the medium of the popular languages, that is, the vernaculars. It also provided examples for the organization of monastic orders.

The survey of Indian religions in the pre-Musalman period of Indian history being completed, it now remains to estimate the relative importance of each of the three paths of religion in the life of the Indian people. The religion of ritual, whether of the higher type laid down in Vedic or Brāhmaṇic or Pauranic literature, or of the lower type as observed in magic performances and animistic worship, was naturally the most widespread of the three. The evidence need not be repeated—sacred and secular literature, observations of foreign travellers, archæological finds and testimony of modern conditions, all confirm it. In the homes of the twice-born—that is, the higher classes—the observance of domestic rites, and among the mass

82 Schrader: Introduction to Ahirbudhnya and Pañcarātra Saṁhitā. Chap. 37.

of the lower classes, the propitiation of malignant deities —like the various forms of dread *Rudra* and *Śakti*,—constituted the greater part of their religion. The path of liberation for the large majority of the people was the religion of good deeds and ceremonial. For the elect it meant the transformation of the will in order to attain harmony with God's wishes—the divine law; for the common people it meant rigid formalism, and for the lowest class of the populace crass superstition.

The religion of knowledge was confined to the learned, the philosophically-minded and the monks. And because it was the path which suited the disposition of those who were chiefly concerned with the writing of books, it naturaly dominates the religious literature of ancient India. The *pandit* and the *sādhu* to whichever denomination he might belong—Buddhism, Jainism, Vaiṣṇavism, Śaivism, Śāktism, etc., had a similar temperament and the realisation of *Mokṣa* or freedom through discriminating knowledge by deep meditation and trance (*samādhi*) made a special appeal to him. Hence the path of knowledge came next in importance to the path of action. Its hold on the intelligentsia was enormous and from them it percolated in a thousand forms to the classes below.

The religion of loving devotion was apparently the least popular of the three. Besides the Bhagavadgītā and the *Nārāyaṇīya* section of the Mahābhārata it is hardly mentioned in the rest of the pre-Muslim sacred literature of Northern Hinduism. In Mahāyāna Buddhist lore as well as in *Śaiva*, Pañcarātra and the Śākta literature *Bhakti* occupies a very subordinate position to *Jñāna*. The worship of *Viṣṇu* or Bhāgavata and devotion to *Amitābha* and *Śiva* have an emotional tinge, but they lack the fierce glow of passion and fervour which has a tendency to run riot in wild eroticism or incoherent ecstatism. These are later growths and it is with their history in either of their aspects—sober and lyrical or Dionysiac and explosive—that the following chapters will deal. It will suffice here to say that the trend of religious development in subsequent times is in the direction of emotionalism, of the transformation of affections suffusing both will and intellect. The rites and ceremonies remain fixed for all time, the philosophies strike no new paths, but devotion finds multitudinous expression and luxuriates in exuberant form.

THE ADVENT OF THE MUSLIMS IN INDIA

THE history of commercial intercourse between India and the Western countries—Arabia, Palestine, and Egypt, goes back to very ancient times. King Solomon obtained his gold from Ophir (the modern Beypur), as well as silver, ivory, apes and peacocks.[1] The Phœnicians traded with India,[2] the Ptolemys founded ports on the Red Sea to encourage Indian commerce,[3] the Saleucidæ followed their example by founding ports in the Persian Gulf.[4] The Greeks[5] imported rice, ginger and cinnamon from the Malabar coast. The Greek and Roman writers were acquainted with Indian geography and wrote about Indian exports and imports, e.g., Hippalus and Pliny in the first century, and Periplus of the Erythrean Sea in the second, Cosma Indicopleustes in the sixth. Ammian Marcellani mentions that the Indians of Ceylon, the Maldives and the Laccadives sent deputations to congratulate Julian. The Peutingerian tables (third century) mention a Roman settlement at Caranganore, and there was a colony of Indian merchants at Alexandria which was massacred by Caracalla in the beginning of the third century.[6] The coins of all the Roman Emperors from Augustus (d. 14 A.D.) to Zeno (d. 491 A.D.) are found in Southern India, attesting to the ample commerce which India had with the west.

The Persians[7] manifested the same commercial activity as the Romans. They founded Obollah at the confluence of the Tigris and Euphrates near Busrah. The Sassanides made Hira,

1 Hunter: History of British India, Vol. I, p. 25.

2 Hunter: History of British India, Vol. I, Chap. I.

3 Ibid.

4 Kennedy: J.R.A.S., 1898, p. 241 ff.

5 Ibid.

6 Thurston: Coins of the Madras Museum, Catalogue No. 2.

7 Reinaud: Géographie d'Aboul Feda, p. 382.

which had been built by the Arabs south-west of ancient Babylon, the capital of a vassal principality, and, according to Arab writers, citizens constantly saw from their houses during the fifth and sixth centuries navigators coming from India and China. Procopius, writing a few years later than Cosma, says that the Persians had become masters of the Indian markets. Under Khusrau Anushīrvān, in the middle of the sixth century, Persian commerce reached its greatest activity; he made an invasion of the Indus Valley, while Darius sent a fleet to Ceylon to avenge the murder of Persians. Tabari mentions the entrance of a flotilla of Indian ships up the Tigris to Obollah during the later days of the Sassanian empire. The use of the term Tājik[8] for a section of Indian Astronomy attests to the influence and amplitude of Persian intercourse with India.

The Arabs[9] naturally took a very active part in the commerce between the Orient and the Occident.[9] A number of entrepots were situated in their territories. Besides Aden they had the town of Shahr, which by its position served as the point of call for mariners who entered or left the Persian Gulf. The Arabs provided the best part of the equipment. Virgil tells us that the Indian and Arab sailors fought under Antony and Cleopatra at Actium. In the Gazetteer of the Bombay Presidency, Khān Bahādur Fazl Ullah Lutfullah Farīdī mentions the settlement of pre-Muslim Arabs at Chaul, Kalyān and Supārā. In the time of Agatharcides[10] there were so many Arabs on the Malabar Coast that the people had adopted tne Arab religion (probably Sabæan). Ptolemy, in his map of India, uses the word *Melizigeris*, the latter part of which is the Arabic *Jazīrah* meaning island. Reinaud says, 'everything points to the belief

[8] Cordier: Melange H. Derenbourg, Notes sur les Musulmanes de Chine.

Bhandâarkar: Search for Sanskrit MSS. Reports.

[9] Reinaud: Relations des voyages faits par les Arabes et les Persanes dans l'Inde et à la Chine, dans le IXe. siècle, Tome I, p. xxxix.

[10] Vincent: Perrplus of the Erythraean Seas, p. 154.

that combined with the Persians they (the Arabs) exercised on those coasts up to the fourteenth century the same ascendancy which the Portuguese did afterwards.'

The rise of Islam in the beginning of the seventh century and the unification of the Arab tribes under a centralised state gave a tremendous impetus to the movement of expansion which was going on since pre-Islamic[11] days. Muslim armies rapidly conquered Syria and Persia and began to hover on the outskirts of India. Muslim merchants immediately entered into the inheritance of Persian maritime trade, and Arab fleets began to scour the Indian seas.

The Arab vessels started either from the coast of the Red Sea or from the southern coast, and, their objective was to disembark either at the mouth of the Indus and in the Gulf of Cambay by sailing along the coast, or on the Malabar coast, in which case they profited by the monsoon to proceed to Koulam and other ports directly. The ships starting from the Persian Gulf followed the same course, and by the help of the monsoon reached Koulam, the Malay Peninsula, the eastern archipelago and China.

The first Muslim fleet appeared in Indian waters in 636 A.D. during the Caliphate of 'Umar, when 'Usmān Sakīfi the Governor of Bahrain and Uman, sent an army across the sea to Tāna.[12] He was rebuked by the Caliph who threatened to meet out dire punishment to his kinsman if the experiment was repeated. About the same time expeditions were sent to Broach and Dabul, but 'Umar's opposition temporarily suspended the activities of the fleet and the policy of armed interference remained in abeyance. During the Caliphate of 'Umar the land approaches to India were explored and a great deal of information was collected, which led ultimately to the conquest of Sindh in the eighth century by Muhammad bin Qāsim. Meanwhile commerce by sea continued, and Muslims made their settlements in

11 Reinaud: Op. cit.

12 Elliot: History of India, Vol. I, pp. 115-16.

three towns along the South Indian coast and in Ceylon. Rowlandson[13] says that the Muslim Arabs first settled on the Malabar coast about the end of the seventh century. Francis Day[14] corroborates this from traditionary accounts, and Sturrock[15] in his account of the Moplahs confirms it. He says: "From the seventh century onwards it is well known that Persian and Arab traders settled in large numbers at the different ports on the western coast of India and married women of the country and these settlements were specially large and important in Malabar where from a very early time it seems to have been the policy to afford every encouragement to traders at the ports." That the Muslims were then living in these countries may be inferred from the account of the immediate causes of Muhammad bin Qāsim's expedition given by Bilādhurī.[16] He relates that the King of Ceylon "sent as a present to Hajjāj certain Muhammadan girls who had been born in his country, the orphan daughters of merchants who had died there." The Bawārij, i.e., the piratical tribes of Kutch, attacked the ships and seized the girls. Hajjāj demanded their release from Dāhir who did not comply with the demand. Upon this Hajjāj sent the expedition led by Qāsim. This expedition was supported by the fleet which assisted in the attack upon Dabul.

The name of Hajjāj is also connected with the settlement of Arabs in the South. Rice[17] quotes from Wilks the account of the origin of the Labbes. According to him, "in the early part of the eighth century, Hijāj Ben Gusaff (Hajjāj bin Yūsuf) Governor of 'Irāq, a monster abhorred for his cruelties even among Musalmans, drove some persons of the house of Hasham to the desperate resolution of abandoning for ever their native

13 Rowlandson: Tuhfat ul Mujāhdīn, Preface.

14 Day: The Land of the Perumāls, p. 365.

15 Sturrock: South Kanara, Madras district Manuals, p. 180.

16 Elliot: Vol. I, p. 118.

17 Rice: Mysore and Coorg, Vol. I, p. 353.

country. Some of them landed on that part of the western coast of India called the Concan; the others eastward of Cape Comorin. The descendants of the former are the Newāyats; of the latter, the Labbes."

In the eighth century the Arab fleets attacked Broach and the ports on the Kathiāwād coast. Their trade and settlements continued to flourish. The first direct recorded evidence of their establishment in India comes from this century. In the Mayyat Kannu, the graveyard of Kollam, there are many ancient tombs, some of which are inscribed. One of the tombs bears an inscription to the effect that 'Alī ibn Udthormān was obliged to leave this world for ever in the year 166 of Hejira, so called after Muhammad the Prophet left Mecca for Medina.'[18]

Henceforth Muslim influence grew rapidly. For over a hundred years the Muslims had been established on the Malabar coast. They were welcomed as traders, and, apparently, facilities were given to them to settle and acquire lands and openly practise their religion. They must have entered upon missionary efforts soon after settling down, for Islam is essentially a missionary religion and every Musalman is a missionary of his faith. Many were undoubtedly held in respectful esteem. They came to India, not like the Christian colonies of Syrians, driven and persecuted from their homelands, but full of the ardour of a new-found religion and of the prestige of conquest and glory. Before the ninth century was far advanced they had spread over the whole of the western coast of India and had created a stir among the Hindu populace, as much by their peculiar beliefs and worship as by the zeal with which they professed and advocated them.

The south of India was then greatly agitated by the conflict of religions, for Neo-Hinduism was struggling with Buddhism and Jainism for the upper hand. Politically, too, it was a period of unsettlement and upheavals.[19] The Cheras

[18] Innes: Malabar and Anjengo District Gazetteer, p. 436.
[19] Iyer: Historical Sketches of Ancient Dekhan.

were losing power and new dynasties were emerging into power. Naturally, the mind of the people was perturbed and they were prone to accept new ideas from whatever quarter they came. Islam appeared upon the scene with a simple formula of faith, well-defined dogmas and rites, and democratic theories of social organisation. It produced a tremendous effect, and, before the first quarter of the ninth century was over, the last of the Cherāman Perumāl Kings of Malabar who reigned at Kodungallur had become a convert to the new religion.[20] According to traditional accounts, his conversion was due to a dream in which he saw the splitting of the moon. He happened just then to meet a party of Muslims who wree returning from Ceylon, their leader Shaikh Sekke Uddīn interpreted the dream, admitted him into the Muslim fold and gave him the name of 'Abdur Rahmān Sāmrī. After his conversion the king left Malabar for Arabia and landed at Shahr where he died four years later. He sent from there Malik ibn Dīnār, Sharf ibn Malik, Malik ibn Habīb and their family to Malabar with a letter of instructions regarding the government of his dominions and the reception of the Muslims. They were treated hospitably and were permitted to build mosques. As a consequence mosques were erected at eleven places on the Malabar coast.

The conversion of the king must have produced a deep impression upon the mind of the people. The memory of the event is still kept fresh in Malabar. For instance, at the installation of the Zamorin, it is the practice to have him shaved and dressed like a Musalman, and crowned by a Mappilla.[21] After the coronation, the Zamorin is treated like an outcaste, he is not allowed to sit and dine with even the members of his own household and no Nāyar would touch him. The Zamorin is supposed to occupy the throne only as a Viceroy awaiting the return of Cherāman Perumāl from Arabia. The Maharajahs of

20 Logan: Malabar, Vol. I, p. 245.

21 Qādir Husain Khān: South Indian Musalmans, Madras Christian College Magazine (1912-13), p. 241.

Travancore on receiving the sword at their coronations have still to declare, "I will keep this sword until the uncle who has gone to Mecca returns."[22] It must, however, be pointed out that the story of the conversion of King Cherāman Perumāl is based on legendary accounts only; and, as in most such stories, many of its details are open to serious doubts. The names of the various personages which appear in it cannot be fixed historically; Cherāman Perumāl is only a title, Sekke Uddīn could not possibly be a contemporary of a ninth century king for the appellation Dīn came into use among Muslims only in the fifth century of the Hejira, and Malik ibn Dīnār was a saint whose appearance in India is more than doubtful. But, as Innes[23] pointed out, "We may perhaps infer from this account that the dynasty reigning at Caranganore came to an end with the abdication of a Perumāl who was converted to Muhammadanism, possibly in the ninth century."

The Musalmans evidently had acquired great importance at this period. They were designated by the name of Mappillas which means either "a great child or a "bridegroom" and was considered a title of honour. It was bestowed on some Christians also, and, in order to distinguish the two communities, the Christians were called Nussaranī Mappillas. Other privileges were showered upon them. A Musalman could be seated by the side of a Nambūtirī Brāhman while a Nāyar could not. The religious leader of the Mappillas, the Thangal, was allowed to ride in a palanquin alongside of the Zamorin.

Under the patronage and encouragement of the Zamorin, the Arab merchants settled in large numbers in his dominions, and not only materially increased his power and wealth by their trade but directly supported him in his campaigns of aggrandizement. The Zamorins who originally hailed from Nediyiruppa in Ernād overran Palanād, the neighbouring territory of Porlattiri Raja, and secured the land thus won at the point of the

[22] Logan: Malabar, Vol. I, p. 231.

[23] Innes: Malabar and Anjengo District Gazetteer.

sword by a fort at Velāpuram. Here, according to tradition, a merchant who had been trading with Arabia settled and established a mart which grew into the flourishing port of Calicut. He became the Koya (Qāzī) of Calicut and his successors fought on the side of the Zamorin against the Rajas of the surrounding Nads. The Raja Valluvakona of Walavanada was defeated and the management of the Mahamakham festival at Tirumavayi and, with it, the predominance in Southern Malabar, passed into the Zamorin's hands.[24] The Muslim family of 'Alī Rajas (Lords of the deep) who were the admirals and ministers of the Kolattiri Rajas were, according to one tradition, the descendants of an Arab Musalman who had been invited from their native land by Cherāman Perumāl and were installed as Chiefs of Kannānūr (Cannanore); according to another tradition, the first chieftain of the family was a Nāyar who was a minister of the Kolattiri and who embraced Islam but was retained in his post on account of his skill and ability.[25]

The Zamorin thought so highly of the Muslims that he definitely encouraged conversion in order to man the Arab ships on which he depended for his aggrandizement. He gave orders that in every family of fishermen (Makkuvans) in his dominion one[26] or more of the male members should be brought up as Muhammadans.

In the following centuries the influence of Islam continued to wax, as the testimony of travellers and geographers demonstrates.

Mas'ūdī[27] who visited India in the beginning of the tenth century (916 A.D.) found over ten thousand Muslims of Siraf, Oman, Basra and Baghdad at Seymore (the modern Chaul), besides numerous others who were children of Arabs born there. They had their own chief whose title was Hazama (probably

24 Logan: Vol. I, p. 278 ff. Innes: p. 44.

25 Innes: Op. Cit.

26 Innes: ,Ibid., p. 190.

27 Elliot: Vol. I, Mas'ūdī.

Hunarmand) and who received his authority from the Hindu king. Abu Dulaf Muhalhil[28] found mosques in the port of Seymore. Ibn Sa'īd[29] in the thirteenth century mentions that Musalmans were living among the inhabitants of the Indian littoral. Ser Marco Polo[30] noticed that the people of Ceylon got Saracen troops from foreign parts whenever they needed them. Abul Fidā[31] (1273–1331) mentions a fine Muhammadan mosque and a square at Koulam. Ibn Batūtah[32] (fourteenth century) in his itinerary from Cambay along the western coast touched at all the ports. He met his co-religionists everywhere and he found them in a flourishing condition. Muslim courtiers paid a visito to him at Kandabār, at Konkah he saw an ancient mosque attributed to Khizr and Ilyās, and met a party of Haidarī Fakīrs with their Shaikh. At Sendāpur there was a mosque which was built in the Baghdad style by the patron of navigators, Hasan, father of Sultan Djemāl Uddīn Mohammad Alhinourī, the ruler of Hinaour (Onore). Onore had a Muslim ruler, a Muslim jurisconsult and Qāzī and a Muslim saint. All along the Malabar coast from Sendabour to Koulam, at all stations on the road, there were houses of Musalmans where their co-religionists could lodge. He notices that the Musalmans were the most highly considered people in that country. At Barcelore, Facanaour (Baccanore) there were Muslim communities with their own Qāzīs and Muftīs. Mangalore had a population of four thousand Musalmans, among them merchants from Fārs and Yemen. Their mosque had a rich treasure and there were a number of students in the mosque. The three Fattans had all mosques and at Fandaraina the Muslims occupied three quarters, and in each of them they had a place of worship. The chief merchant at Calicut was a

28 Ferrand: Relations des voyages, under Yākūt.

29 Ibid., p. 377.

30 Yule: The Book of Ser Marco Polo, Vol. II, p. 314.

31 Ibid., p. 377.

32 Defremery and Sanguinetti: Ibn Batūtah, Vol. III, p. 55 ff.

Musalman, Ibrāhīm Shāh Bander of Bahrain; and there were many Muslim merchants at Koulam; there were a number of mosques here, and the principal one was admirable in its architecture. The Raja venerated the Muslims.

Abdūr-Razzāk[33] (1442), who visited India on the eve of the Portuguese arrival, says about Calicut, "it contains a considerable number of Musalmans, who are constant residents and have built two mosques in which they meet every Friday to offer up prayer." He gives a glowing account of the busy harbour and its merchants from all parts of the world.

These narratives conclusively show that on the western coast of India Muslims had settled early and grown in numbers, wealth and power. It is true that Sulaimān who visited India in the ninth century states that he did not find Muslims or Arabic-speaking individuals there, but his testimony is hardly trustworthy on this point, for he fails to notice the Arab possessions in Sindh, Gujarat or the Gulf of Cambay, and that his compatriots were carrying on rich commerce; and as, according to Reinaud,[34] his main object was a voyage to China without turning to right or left he did not pay much attention to the condition of affairs on the Indian Coast. The traditions enshrined in the Keralolpatti and the legends of the Muslim inhabitants, the evidence of inscriptions and of Muslim historians and travellers and the continuity of Arab commerce with India from early times all lead to one conclusion, that the Muslims appeared on the Indian coast not long after the death of the Prophet and swiftly gained a status of privilege and influence among the Hindu rulers of Malabar.

The Arabs appeared on the eastern coast early. When Darius (519—484 B.C.) dammed up the channels of the Euphrates and Tigris and destroyed the trade of Egypt, the merchants

33 Major: India in the Fifteenth Century; Narrative of the Voyage of 'Abdur Razzāk.

34 Reinaud: Relation des voyages.

of Yemen entered into the inheritance of both.[35] Colonies of Arabs and Jews settled in the early centuries of the Christian era in Ceylon and Southern India. The Greeks and Romans had a considerable trade with the eastern coast. A large number of coins of the Roman Emperors have been discovered in Coimbatore; the Greeks knew Kalkhoi, the modern Kayal; Ptolemy mentions Uraiyur,[36] the ancient capital of the Cholas; and Greek and Roman ships were mostly manned by Arabs. Arab merchants passed along the Coromandel coast on their way to China, where remains of pre-Muslim Arabs are still found at Canton.[37] According to Mr. Cust, "unquestionably the continuous existence of a commerce bewteen Yemen and South India can be asserted from a very remote period."[38]

The Muslims inherited the legacy of the pagan Arabs. The usual route[39] from the ports of Arabia or the Persian Gulf to China passed through the seven seas among which were the Gulf of Palk and the Bay of Bengal, known to the Arabs as *Schelahath* or *Kalahabar* and *Kerdenj*. Sulaimān and Abu Zaid Sīrafī, in the ninth century, and Mas'ūdī, early in the tenth, describe the route and the occurrences in these seas, as if they had been perfectly well known for a long time. Numerous voyagers must have passed along this way and a great deal of commercial intercourse must have been kept up between the Muslim lands and India, for already in the eighth century there was a numerous colony of Muslims established in Canton whose revolt in 758 A.D. created serious commotion.[40]

Their principal settlement on the east coast was Kayalpattanam in Tinnevelly district, near the mouth of the Tamraparni

[35] Kennedy: The Early Commerce of Babylon with India, J.R.A.S., 1898.

[36] Hemingway: Trichinopoly, Madras District Gazetteer.

[37] Edkins: Ancient Navigation in the Indian Ocean, J.R.A.S., 1886.

[38] Ibid., p. 4.

[39] Reinaud: Op. cit.

[40] Cordier: Op. cit.

river, where still the Labbes form the majority of the population, and where Caldwell picked up in large quantities broken pieces of pottery, and, what is more important, a number of Muslim coins bearing dates from the seventh century (71 A.H.) to the thirteenth century A.D.

The Musalmans started their religious propaganda as soon as they had settled down in some numbers. Many of the Islamic communities of the south trace their origin to these times. The Ravuttans of Madura and Trichinopoly believe that they were persuaded to change their religion by Nathad Vali whose tomb exists at Trichinopoly and bears the date of his death 417 A.H. (1039 A.D.).[41] The tradition about Nathad is that he was a Sayyid prince who held territory in Turkey, but abandoned his state and became an ascetic and missionary of Islam. He wandered through Arabia, Persia and Northern India until he reached the city of Trisura, the modern Trichinopoly. Here he settled down and passed the remaining years of his life in prayer and works of charity, converting a large number of Hindus to the religion of Muhammad. His successor was Sayyid Ibrāhīm Shahīd, who was born at Medina (about 1162 A.D.) and who headed a militant mission to the Pāndyān kingdom in his forty-second year. He is said to have defeated the Pāndyā king and ruled for over twelve yeras, but he was at last overthrown and slain. He lies buried at Ervadī. The Dudekulas attribute their conversion to Bābā Fakhr Uddīn the saint of Pennukonda. He became a disciple of Nathad Vali, converted the Raja of Pennukonda and built a mosque there. The date of his death, according to Thurston, was 564 A.H.

In Madura[42] the Musalmans made their entrance in 1050 A.D. under the leadership of Malik-ul-Mulūk, who was accompanied by a great saint, Hazrat 'Alīyār Shāh Sāhib, whose remains were buried near the Hazūr Kacherī at Madura. At the village of Goripaleiyan there is a mosque which acquired

[41] Qādir Husain Khān : Op. cit., p. 294.

[42] Nelson : Madura, p. 86.

six villages for its maintenance from Kun Pāndyā in the eleventh or twelfth century. The grant was subjected to enquiry in the time of Virappā Nāyakan and confirmed in 1573 A.D.[43]

The rulers of the eastern coast pursued an enlightened policy towards the merchants who visited their coasts. The peculiar custom of the western parts, that a vessel driven ashore by stress of weather became the property of the authorities, was not observed, and all vexatious port dues besides the regular custom (kūpasulka) duties were removed, with the natural result that an extensive trade grew up and flourishing trade settlements came into existence under the especial protection of the rulers.[44] The Coromandel Coast became the *Ma'bar* (passage) of the Muslim traders. According to Wassāf,[45] it extended from Koulam to Nilawar (Nellore) nearly three hundred *parsangs* along the sea coast. "In the language of that country the king is called Dewar, which signifies the lord of empire. The curiosities of Chīn and Māchīn and the products of Hind and Sind, laden on large ships (which they call junks) sailing like mountains with the wings of winds on the surface of the water, always arrived there. The wealth of the islands of the Persian Gulf in particular and in part the beauty and adornments of other countries from *'Irāq* and Khorāsān as far as Rūm and Europe, and derived from *Ma'bar* which is so situated as to be the key of Hind."

In the twelfth century the Muhammadans formed a well-established community in these parts, and they seemed to have acquired sufficient importance, for they are noticed along with Vaiśyas as bringing presents to the Ceylonese General who invaded the Pāndyā Kingdom in 1171-72 A.D.[45]

In the thirteenth century the trade, especially in horses, had become so vast that an agency was established at Kayal by Malik-ul-Islām Jamāl Uddīn, ruler of Kis, and later the

43 Nelson : Madura, p. 69.

44 S. K. Aiyangar : South India and Her Muhammadan Invaders.

45 Elliot : Vol. III, p. 32.

farmer-general of Fārs. According to Wassāf, ten thousand horses were annually exported from Fārs to Ma'bar and the Indian ports, and the sum total of their value amounted to 2,200,000 dīnārs. Taqī-Uddīn 'Abdur Rahmān bin Muhammad ul Tībī, brother of Jamāl Uddīn, was the agent, and he had, besides Kayal, the ports of Fitan and Malī Fitan under his control.[46]

According to Rashīd Uddīn,[47] on the death of the Pāndyā ruler in 1293 A.D., Jamāl Uddīn, succeeded him, his brohter becoming his lieutenant. Nelson[48] records a number of traditions relating to the Muhammadan invasion of Madura about this time. Marco Polo[49] describes Taqī Uddīn as the deputy minister and adviser of King Sundar Pāndyā. He was succeeded by his son Sirāj Uddīn and by his grandson Nizām Uddīn in the same position. The Pāndyā ambassador to Kublāī Khān (in 1286 or 1287) was Fakhr Uddīn Ahmad, son of Jamāl Uddīn, who stayed for four years in China and died on board while he was returning. He lies buried in a tomb near that of his uncle's.

There were other Musalman settlements in the Tamil country, for Amīr Khusrau,[50] in his account of the campaign of Malik Kāfūr, mentions the Musalmans of Kandur (Kannanur) who "as they could repeat the Kalīmā" and "though they were worthy of death, yet as they were Musalmans, they were pardoned." Ibn Batūtah,[51] who travelled in these parts after the invasion, states that Ghiyās Uddīn al Damghānī was the ruler of Madura in his time, that Raja Vīr Ballāla had a contingent of 20,000 Musalmans, and that the Muslim ruler of Honawar owed allegiance to his viceroy Hariyappa Odayar.

46 Elliot: Vol. III, p. 32.

47 Elliot: Vol. I, pp. 69, 70.

48 Nelson: Madura District Manual, pp. 78, 79.

49 Yule: Op. cit.

50 Elliot: Op. cit., Vol. III, p. 90.

51 Defremery and Sanguinetty. Op. cit., Vol. III, p. 199.

Thus, before the arrival of Malik Kāfūr's army into the South, Musalmans had established their settlements in the important centres of trade; they had entered into relationship with the people living round them; and from this intercourse of Arabs and Tamils a number of communities of mixed descent had arisen, e.g., the Ravuttans and the Labbes.

The foregoing account shows that the Musalmans made their advent in South India on the western coast as early as the eighth century if not earlier, and in the tenth century on the eastern coast; that they soon spread over the whole coast and in a comparatively short time acquired great influence both in politics and in society. On the one side their leaders became ministers, admirals, ambassadors and farmers of revenue and on the other they made many converts, propagated their religious ideas, established mosques and erected tombs which became centres of the activities of their saints and missionaries. It may, therefore, be premised without overstraining facts that if, in the development of the Hindu religions in the south, any foreign elements are found which make their appearance after the seventh century, and which cannot be accounetd for by the natural development of Hinduism itself, they may with much probability be ascribed to the influence of Islam, provided, of course, they are not alien to its genius.

The question of Christian influence[52] on Hinduism does not arise here, for this influence was exerted, if at all, from the north-west, earlier than the appearance of Islam in the south. It is known that intercourse between Southern India and Alexandria practically ceased in the beginning of the third century, and, before the third century, Alexandria could not be the centre of Christian propaganda, because in the Antonine period the Christian religion was prohibited in Alexandria and the meetings of Christians were held in private. Subsequently, when trade was again resumed between Egypt and India and Christians from Syria and Persia settled in South India, it was

[52] Kennedy : J.R.A.S., 1907, p. 951.

not possible for them to exercise any considerable influence, because the communities were small and insignificant. By the middle of the seventh century, Syria, Persia and Egypt had fallen into the hands of the Muslims; and the Christians had lost their prestige and authority. Hence, although in the eighth century they still existed on the Malabar coast, 'the historic conditions requisite for any real action of Christianity upon Hinduism are wanting.'

In Northern India Muslims began their encroachment during the Caliphate of 'Umar, making their earliest attempts on the ports of the northern coast, and when Persia and Mekrān had been annexed to the empire they invaded Sindh. During the seventh century many raids were made on the borders of Baluchistan and Sindh and the land routes were thoroughly explored. At last in the time of Caliph Walīd, Hajjāj, who was Governor of 'Iraq, organised an expedition which was sent under the leadership of the young and brilliant Muhammad bin Qāsim.[53] He overcame all difficulties, defeated the Hindu rulers of Sindh, overran the whole Indus Valley, and made the provinces of Multan and Sindh appanages of the empire. There, however, the advance of the Muslims was checked, and for the next three centuries they remained confined to this corner of India. Their sphere of influence thus extended during this period over the principalities of Sindh and Multan over which they ruled, and the coastal towns of Sindh, Kathiawar, Gujarat and Konkan where they settled as traders, and till the eleventh century they had no opportunity to reach beyond. In these parts, however, they became fully established, and it is possible that some of their adventurous captains made from there daring forays in Malwa and Kanauj. In any case, Dabul, Somnāth, Broach, Cambay, Sindan, and Chaul became seats of small Muslim communities and nearly each one had its mosque. Most of the Hindu rulers welcomed them in their dominions with open arms and treated them with great hospitality. Sulaimān,

[53] Elliot : Vol. I.

Mas'ūdī, Ibn Haukal and Abu Zaid, all agree in praising Balhāra (the Valbhī ruler of Gujarat) for the friendliness which he exhibited towards the Musalmans. Sulaimān writes, "there does not exist among rulers, a prince who likes the Arabs more than Balhāra, and his subjects follow his example".[54] Mas'ūdī found his co-religionists practising their religion openly everywhere. Speaking of the King of Gujarat, he says, In his kingdom Islam is respected and protected, in all parts rise chapels and splendid mosques where the Muslims say their five daily prayers."[55] Al Istakhrī (951 A.D.) found Muslims in the cities of the Kingdom of Balhāra, and "none but Musalmans rule over them on the part of Balhāra".[56]

Ibn Haukal (968) saw Jāma 'Masjids at Famhal, Sindan Saimūr and Kambāyā; and Idīsrī, in the eleventh century reports, "the town of Anhilwāra is frequented by a large number of Musalman traders who go there on business. They are honourably received by the king and his ministers, and find protection and safety."[57]

Already, before the invasions of Mahmūd of Ghaznā had opened the gates of India wide for the Muslims to enter, they had attained in Western India an influential position, and they used it to disseminate their religion among the people. They were considerably encouraged in the persuit of their aims by the favour of the Hindu rulers themselves. The story that Muhamad 'Ūfī relates throws a great deal of light upon the relations of Hindu princes and Muslim traders.[58] When the Hindus of Cambay attacked the Muslim merchants, Siddh Rāj (1094–1143) held an enquiry into the whole affair, punished the aggressors and gave the Musalmans money to build a new mosque. Some Hindu Rajas seem to have employed Muslim

54 Reinaud: Op. cit., Vol. I, p. 26.
55 Elliot: Vol. I, p. 27.
56 Ibid.
57 Ibid., p. 88.
58 Ibid., Vol. II, p. 164.

mercenaries. The ruler of Somnāth, for instance, had a number of Muslim officers, and the Kasbātīs of Ahmadabad trace their descent from the Khorasānī soldiers of the Vaghela Chiefs.[59]

The Muslim saints followed wherever the Muslim army led or the traders settled. In the ninth century, Abu Hifs Rabī bin Sāhib al Aadi al Basarī, who was a traditionist and an ascetic, came to Sindh where he died in 106 A.H.[60] In the tenth century Mansūr al Hallāj made a voyage to India by sea, and went back overland by way of Northern India and Turkistan.[61] In the eleventh century Bābā Rīhān came to Broach from Baghdad with a company of Derwishes.[62] He is said to have converted the son of the Raja who attacked his father but was killed. About the same time (1067) the religious head of the Shī'ah trading community of Bohras settled in Gujarat from Yemen,[63] and Nūr al Dīn or Nūr Satāgar (1094–1143) converted the Kunbīs, Khārwās and Korīs of Gujarat.[64]

After the invasions of Mahmūd, numerous Muslim men of learning and religion poured into India. It is impossible to compile a list of all of them, but some of the important ones may be mentioned here. Among them was 'Alī bin 'Usmān Al Hujwīrī the author of *Kashful Mahjūb* who was a native of Ghaznā, and who after travelling extensively over Muslim lands came to reside in Lahore where he died in 465 or 469 A.H.[65] Shaikh Ismā'īl Bukhārī early in the eleventh century,[66] and Farīd Uddīn 'Attār the celebrated author of *Mantiq ut Tair* and

[59] Forbes: Rāsa Mālā (1856), Vol. I, p. 276.

[60] Mīr Ghulām 'Alī Āzād: Maāsir ul Kiram, p. 6.

[61] Massignon: Kitāb al Tawā Sīn, Introduction, p. v.

[62] Campbell: Gazetteer of Gujarat, Surat and Bdoach, p. 558 and note.

[63] Forbes: Op. cit., Vol. I, p. 344.

[64] Arnold: Preaching of Islam, Chapter on India.

[65] Nicholson: Kashful Mahjūb, Introduction.

[66] Arnold: Op. cit.

Tadhkiratual Auliā in the twelfth century, visited India.[67] Khwājah Mu'īn Uddīn Chishtī[68] came to Ajmer in 1197 and died there in 1234. In the thirteenth century Shaikh Jalāl Uddīn Tabrīzī[69] a pupil of Shihāb Uddin Suhrāwardi (founder of the sect of the 'illuminati' or eastern philosophers) visited Bengal. Sayyid Jalāl Uddīn Bokhārī[70] settled in Uchh in Bahāwalpur in 1244, and Bābā Farīd[71] at Pākpattan. In the next century 'Abdul Karīm al Jīlī,[72] commentator of *Ibn al 'Arabī* and author of *Insān-i-Kāmil* a famous treatise of Sūfī philosophy, travelled in India (1388), and Sayyid Muhammad Gisūdarāz[73] made conversions in Poona and Belgaum districts. Pīr Sadr Uddīn[74] founder of the Khojah sect, Sayyid Yūsuf Uddīn[75] that of the Momnahs, and Imām Shāh of Pīrāna[76] settled in India in the fifteenth century. Other noted saints who visited India or came to reside there were Sayyid Shāh Mīr[77] son of 'Abdul Qādir Jīlānī, founder of the Qādirī order, Qutb-ud-Dīn Bakhtyār Kākī[78] who is buried at Delhi and whose name is associated with the famous Qutb Mīnār, Bahā Uddīn Zakariā[79]

67 Nicholson : Tadhkiratul Auli'ā of Farīd Uddin 'Attār.

68 Abdul Haq : Akhbār ul Akhiyār, p. 22.

69 Ibid., p. 43.

70 Ibid., p. 60.

71 Macauliff : The Sikh Religion, Vol. VI, p. 356.

72 Nicholson : Studies in Islamic Mysticism, p. 81.

73 Arnold : Op. cit.

74 Bombay Gazetteer, Vol. IX, Part II, p. 40.

75 Ibid., p.27.

76 Ibid., p. 76.

77 Khafī Khān : Muntakhib ul Lubā, Vol. II, Part 2, p. 604.

78 'Abdul Haq : Op. cit., p. 24.

79 Ibid., p. 26.

(d. 1266) and Jalāl Uddīn Surkhposh[80] (d. 1291) who lived in Multan and Uchh, and Muhammad Ghaus (d. 1562)[81] the preceptor of Humayūn, of the Shattarī order. Besides them were antinomian Derwishes like Shāh Madār[82] (eleventh century) and Sakhī Sarwar[83] (twelfth or thirteenth century).

There were men of high rank in Muslim religious biography[83]—undoubtedly along with them a host of others of less renown—who lived and laboured in India, and by their personal contact and influence spread the ideas of Islamic philosophy and mysticism through the length and breadth of India, with results which will be estimated in the following chapter.

80 'Abdul Huq: Op. cit., p. 60.

81 Abdul Qadir Badaoni: Muntakhib ut Tawarikh, Vol. III, p. 4. (Bibliotheca Indica).

82 Arnold: The Saints and Martyrs of India, E.R.E.

83 Ibid.

MYSTICISM IN ISLAM

THE land where Islam arose is one of the least hospitable regions of the earth. Vast tracts in Arabia are mere empty plains of drifting sands. Only on the coast is it possible for human beings to live with moderate comfort and to create institutions of civilization. And here in ancient times kingdoms grew and cultures flourished and they partook of the ancient commerce of the world and were its intermediaries. But in the sixth century the legends of antiquity had become effaced from the mind of the peoples and the Arabs had sunk into a life of barbarism. Mecca, one of the principal places in the country, was a materialistic commercial town "where lust of gain and usuary reigned supreme, where women, wine and gambling filled up the leisure time, where might was right and widows, orphans and the feeble were treated as superfluous ballast."[1] Religion consisted of ceremonialism without meaning, of the worship of stars, stone and deities, in which no one believed. The notions of right and wrong were rudimentary, no moral guilt attached to murder, little sanctity to marriage. Women had no rights; property, loyalty and honour were held in scant respect, and sensuality was rampant.[2]

In this physical and moral desert there were here and there oases which gave shelter to high aspiration and noble thought. Communities of Jews and Christians were settled in scattered places, itinerant monks and wise men from the East travelled about with caravans. In some way they supplied some kind of nourishment to the otherwise starved souls, and from their contact arose the early reformers known as the Hanīfs who

[1] Hurgronje : Momammedanism, p. 28.

[2] Ibid.

strove to mend men's ways and to turn their hearts to the worship of God.

The stir in moral life was an echo of the stir in social life. Already, before the sixth century, Arab tribes, driven by economic causes—growth of population and others—were moving in the directions of Mesopotamia and Syria, and their movements and contacts with the settled civilizations were reacting on the peoples left behind.[3]

In the midst of such conditions the Prophet of Islam was born. He belonged to a family whose means were small and he was left an orphan at an early age. He grew up to manhood untutored and uncared for, amid circumstances of great poverty and hardship. The stress of personal misery, and the sense of humiliation caused by the inglorious condition of his people deeply affected his sensitive soul. The teachings of the Hanīfs, the ascetic practices and lonely self-communings on Mount Hira led to a religious crisis in his highly strung and mystically inclined nature, and occasioned the ecstatic religious experiences which changed his entire outlook upon life.

Out of the living fear of the approaching day of judgment, the crushing conviction of sin, out of the hopeless emptiness of Meccan ritual and the utter wretchedness of social life, his soul-illuminating experience redeemed him. The revelation tore asunder the veil of illusion and ignorance and gave him that knowledge than which no other possesses greater certitude and higher coercive power for action.

Muhammad became the recipient of God's commands, His messenger on earth and His apostle to the people of Arabia. In him, as in other deep religious mystics, religious fervour was combined with intense practical sense, and he became not only the prophet of a new religion but also the leader and creator of a new nation.[4]

[3] Cambridge Medieval History: Chapter on Islam.
[4] Hurgronje: Op. cit.

The religion which he preached was exceedingly simple. It possessed the minimum of doctrine and ritual, for, according to the *Qorān*, God wanted to make the burden of men light and easy. His central doctrine was the unity of God, and his most important ritual the daily prayers. Fasts, alms, pilgrimage and belief in Muhammad as the Prophet of God were the main pillars of the faith. On the social side its most impressive feature was the assertion of the equality and brotherhood of Muslims and hence the absence of a priestly class. The doctrine of the unity of God implied complete rejection of the worship of deities or the adoration of idols. The characteristics of the Muslim religious consciousness were vivid realisation of the ever present nearness and all-encompassing power of God, lively dread of the awful consequences of disobedience to His will, and a feeling of profound submission and entire dependence on His mercy and grace; altogether, a consciousness of calm and stern resignation.

Within a short period after the death of the Prophet his simple faith had begun to branch out into sects and systems under the pressure of life and logic. Politics was the cause of the first divisions. The sects of the *Khārijīa, Shī'ah, Murjīa* and *Qādirīya* were the earliest to make their appearance. The *Shī'ahs* who soon spread into Persia had a most luxuriant growth of fantastic systems of great interest. The extreme *Shī'ahs* known as the Ghulāt[5] had doctrines curiously resembling those found in Hinduism. For example, they believed in excess (*ghuluv*) and defect (*taqsīr*), by the former of which they meant that man might be raised to the position of God and by the latter that God might be reduced to the status of man. As a consequence of these doctrines they raised their leader and preceptor to the position of divinity. Then they believed that God could pass into human form (*hulūl*) and also in the doctrine of metempsychosis (*tanāsukh*), of an anthropomorphic God

[5] E. G. Browne: Literary History of Persia, Vol. I p 310; Vol. II, p. 195.

(*tashbīh*), of change in divine purpose (*bid'a*), and of the return of the *Imām* (*rajā'*). These extreme sects were known by various names, *Khurrumiyah* in Isfahān, *Qudsiyyah* in Ray, *Mazdakiyah* and *Sindbādiyah* in Āzarbaijān, *Mahammirah* (redrobed ones) and *Mubayyazah* (white-robed ones) in Transoxiana. But of peculiar interest among them were the *'Alī-Ilāhiyās*[6] who seemed to have come into existence early in Islamic history. They were settled in Persia and India and came under the notice of the author of *Dabistāni-Mazāhib*.

The *'Alī-Ilāhīyās* were an extreme *Shī'ah* sect who belived in the divinity of *'Alī*. They did not go to mosques, did not recognize ritual uncleanliness, did not permit polygamy or divorce, and allowed men and women to dance together in weddings. They believed in five emanations from God which took part in the creation of the universe. They held a communion (*khidmat*) which consisted in sharing and eating in common sugar-candy or a sacrificed sheep or, on solemn occasions, a bull. According to them man was swayed by two forces, reason (*'aql*) and lust (*nafs*). Their order had a hereditary head (*pīr*), who was assisted by a conductor of ritual ceremonies (*khādim* or *delīl*) and by a representative (*khalīfa*) who distributed portions of the meal of communion. The poet Al Sayyid al Himyārī[7] (723–789 A.D.) was claimed by them as belonging to their sect.

There were others among *Shī'ahs* who refused to believe in the open meaning of the *Qorān* and who interpreted it allegorically. To them prayer meant supplication to the *Imām*, charity (*zakāt*) donation to the *Imām*, and pilgrimage (*haj*) visit to the *Imām*.[8]

The *Shī'ahs*, whether of extreme or moderate parties, held one cardinal tenet, that of the *Imāmate*; for *Shiism* centres

6 Patton: Shī'ahs, E.R.E. Encyclopædia of Islam: 'Alī Ilāhiya.

Colebrooke: On the Origin and Peculiar Tenets of Certain Muhammadan Sects. Asiatic Researches, Vol. III, p. 338 ff.

7 Brockelmann: Geschichte der Arabischen Litteratur, p. 75.

8 Friendlander: Heterodies of Shiites, J.A.O.S., Nos. xxviii, and xxix.

religious authority in an inspired person whose presence is the only true guarantee of right guidance. The *Imām* originally had two functions, the one of leading in prayer and the second of ruling the Muslim community; but the death of 'Alī and his sons Hasan and Husain extinguished the hope of political dominion. "The *Shī'ahs* made the best of necessity and gave themselves now to an ambition for religious leadership. The representatives of the house of 'Alī became the indispensable heads of Islam, the *Imāms* of the believers."[9] His claim was twofold, the right by virtue of inheritance, and "the further claim that the celestial light substance which was lodged in Muhammad was likewise received into the souls of the *Imāms* in succession."[10] The *Imāms* were infallible and sinless, and, because of the light within them, incorruptible and immortal. "The extreme sect of the *Shī'ahs* exaggerated the enduement of the *Imāms* and claimed that some or all of them were of divine nature or incarnate manifestations of God. On this belief they offered to them divine honours."[11] According to Nicholson, "the notion of Theios anthropos (of the Hellenists) passed over into Islam through the *Shiites* and became embodied in the *Imām,* regarded as the living representative of God and as a semi-divine personality on whom the world depends for its existence.[12]

From such early *Shiite* sects grew the later Seveners[13] and Twelvers.[14] The founder of the first was 'Abd allah ibn Maymūn, a refined Persian sceptic whose aim was the overthrow of Arab supremacy. The number seven had a mystic significance in his system. He taught that there were seven prophets who

9 Patton: Op. cit.

10 Ibid.

11 Ibid.

12 Nicholson: Studies in Islamic Mysticism, Preface, vi.

13 E. G. Browne: Op. cit., Vol. I, p. 130 ff.; Vol. II, p. 194 ff.

14 Ibid.

Blochet: Le messianisme dans l'hétérodoxie musulmane.

had seven helpers, and that between each prophet and his successor there were seven *Imāms,* he himself being the last and greatest of all. In his metaphysics God was an absolute being who had no attributes and no name. He was the Pre-existent One, and from His thought emanated the second being or God who created and governed the world. In these two beings, one without attribute and the other with attributes, there is close analogy to the *Brahman* and *Iśvara of* the Hindu systems.

The Prophet was the hypostasis of the Divinity, an emanation some degrees removed from the Creator; in fact all living beings formed a chain of such emanations from the Pre-existent, their only difference being their distance from Him. Hence all would ultimately return to Him after an indefinite number of hypostases. The initiate in the order passed through various stages with the help of his teacher till he attained the station of the Prophet.

The Karmathians were a branch of the *Ismā'īlians* (Seveners) who separated from the parent sect in 890 A.D.

The Twelvers (*Asnā 'Asharīya*) believe in twelve *Imāms,* descendants of 'Alī, the last of whom was Muhammad ibn Hasan who disappeared in 873 A.D. and whose return is expected. The Safvids who conquered Persia in 1502 A.D. belonged to this sect.

Besides these were the Assassins whose stronghold was Almūt in Iran and Masyaf in Syria and who were stamped out by Hulākū; also the *Fātimides,* the *Druzes* and the *Nusairis.*

Of still greater importance were the developments in other sects, which were mainly divided on theological grounds. The questions which agitated the minds of Muslim theologians related principally to the nature of God, His relation to creation, His relation to man, the nature of soul and the nature of the knowledge of God. The most influential among the early sects were the *Mu'tazalites,* the rationalists of Islam.[15]

15 Goldziher: Forlesungen über den Islam, translated by Felix Arin. Chapter III.

They were the successors of the *Qādirites* who believed in the freedom of will, and the first to employ philosophy in religious discussions. The *Mu'tazalites* were originally a group of ascetics who lived in retirement and who gave an impetus to the movement which gathered round itself the rationalists of Islam. They also had a close connection with the *Shiites* who had an intellectual affinity with them.[16]

The founder of the school was Wāsil bin 'Atā, a pupil of the famous teacher Abul Hasan Basrī who seceded from his master and earned the name by which his followers became famous. The other noted leaders were Amïr ibn Ubaid (d. 144 A.H.), Abul Hudhail (d. 226 A.H.), An-Nazzām (d. 231 A.H.), Bishr ibn Mu'tamir (contemporary of Al-Rashīd), Abu' Ubaida Ma'mar (d. 210 A.H.), Thumamma ibn Ashras (d. 213 A.H.), Al Jāhiz (d. 255 A.H.), Al Khaiyāt (d. 230 A.H.), Al Zubair (d. 303 A.H.).

The general tendency of the *Mu'tazalites* was to turn from the objective and eternal standards of truth to a subjective, critical, even sceptical attitude of mind. Naturally they made reason (*'aql*) the chief source of religious knowledge. The point of view which dominated their theological reasoning was to purify the monotheistic idea of all obscurities and deformations which it had acquired in popular belief, both in ethics and in metaphysics. Like Śankara they combated vigorously for the monistic conception of God. In this they had to fight against the anthropomorphists who pointed to the passages of the *Qorān* and the *Hadīs* which have anthropomorphic tendencies. These passages were explained by them according to their own methods of interpretation (*tāwīl*). Then they had to fight those who held that God possessed the attributes of knowledge, power and so forth. The attribution of eternal qualities to God was to admit plurality, to admit the existence of other eternals besides the one eternal God. Like the Hindu monists, Abul Hudhail held that God was knowing, powerful,

16 Amīr 'Alī: Muhammadan Law, Vol. II, Introduction.

loving, but his knowledge, power and love constituted His very essence (*dhāt*), that God's qualities could only be described in negatives, and that they existed only as hypostases of the divine essence. In the hands of Ma'mar ibn 'Abbād this unity of God became merely an abstract possibility of which nothing could be predicated, hence God became unknowable. The disciples of Nazzām took the next step forward and recognized besides the absolute God who was unpredicable, the contingent God who was creator and ruler.

With regard to creation Abul Hudhail taught that creation meant change, and annihilation repose, and that they alternated eternally. Others held that creation was the actualisation of pre-existing potentialities or the manifestation of what was hidden. An-Nazzām established the idea of law, and of the gradual evolution of the world from the pre-existent unmanifest state in accordance with an internal necessity. Thus, in relation to the universe, God was an efficient cause only; the universe followed its own immutable law.

The outstanding characteristic of *Mu'tazalā* metaphysics was unity and that of their ethics, justice. The idea of justice for them was all-comprehensive, so that even God could not conceivably transcend it; even His power was limited by the exigencies of justice. It followed from this that as God had created man for his good, it was necessary for Him to send His prophets to guide man and instruct him in His ways, so that divine grace was obligatory (*lutf wājib*); human welfare demanded that it should be necessary. Another important consequence of the principle was that good and evil were determined not by the arbitrary will of God, but according to an absolute standard—the law of the categorical imperative which bound God Himself.

Man's will was free and hence the responsibility of choosing good or evil rested on him, and, according as he chose one or the other, he merited punishment or reward. The *Mu'tazalite* view of life was tinged with asceticism. Mas'ūdī in praising their ideas quotes 'Āmir ibn 'Ubaid's words. He said, "Desire blinds man, and death separates him from his hopes. The world is a station where the voyager camps but for a moment and then goes away. Its pleasures are woes, its snares are fatal, its serenity agitation and its kingdom revolution. The quiet of man is disturbed by perpetual alarms, both peace and unrest are unreal, for death is man's end, who is the plaything of adversity, the offspring of destiny. Let one fly to save himself and there death is in ambuscade, let there be one false step and there is a fall. Man exhausts himself, but his efforts benefit only his inheritors and the tomb gathers the fruits of his exertions."[17]

Lastly, in regard to revelation they held that the *Qorān* was not the eternal, uncreate, infallible word of God. Thus they were upholders of a progressive revelation which is in consonance with the growing needs of humanity.

The vigorous application of logic to theology led to the formulation of an abstract, impersonal, absolute God, which hardly fulfilled the two universal needs of man—dependence on a power greater than his own, and devotion to a person or ideal which evokes the deepest emotions of love. As a reaction against *Mu'tazalism* these two tendencies already in existence made vigorous headway, while two other tendencies—both results of rationalism—made their appearance: that is, philosophic speculation and agnosticism or downright atheism. Of the first set of these tendencies the traditionalists and the jurists were the chief representatives; the six celebrated collectors of the sayings of the Prophet, and the four great *Imāms* who compiled the codes of laws. The ascendancy of the liberals (*Mu'tazalites*) did not mean the triumph of liberty, for their hand had fallen heavily upon their rivals and one of the most respected of the jurists, Ibn Hanbal, had to suffer the consequences of his honesty and independence. It was only in the reign of Mutwakkil (847–61 A.D.) that the adherents of the old regime were able to raise their head.

17 Carra de Vaux: Avicenne, p. 20.

Abul Hassan Al Ash'arī[18] was the leader of this movement. He was born in 873 A.D. (260 A.H.) and was descended from Abu Mūsā, a respected companion of the Prophet. He spent a large part of his life in Baghdad. He began as an adherent of the *Mu'tazalites* and for forty years remained with them. In the end he quarrelled with his teacher Jubbai on the question of necessary grace, and after a short but sharp internal struggle became a convert to traditionalist ideas. He publicly abjured *Mu'tazala* and henceforth spent his whole energy in combating heterodox views by public lectures and books. He died some time between 931 and 941 A.D.

Ash'arī occupied a position midway between the extreme absolutists, the Mu'tazalites, and the extreme anthropomorphists, the *Mushabbihites* and Khārijites. He utilised the dialectics of the *Mu'tazala* but combined it with ancient traditions and thus established a new school of theology. His view of God's nature was different both from the impersonal abstraction of the rationalists and from the gross realism of the materialists. According to him, God possessed all good qualities, but they did not bear any resemblance with human qualities. Similarly, with regard to matter, he conceded existence to it and did not hold that existence was conferred upon it by God, and with regard to human destiny and conduct he believed in the acquisition of grace by man's own effort, and in the intercession of the Prophet with God's permission.

Ash'arī's ideas were developed a century later by Bāqillānī who died in 1012 A.D. and by the latter's successor a hundred years after, Al Ghazālī[19] (1057–1112) who set the seal upon Muslim theology. He is regarded by the Muslims as their

18 Mehren: Exposé de la réforme de l'islamisme commencée au IIIème siècle de l'Hégire par Abou-l-Hasan 'Alī El Ash'arī. Third International Oriental Congress, St. Petersburg.

19 Carra de Vaux, Ghazālī.

Macdonald: Ghazālī, J.A.O., Vol. 20.

Claude Field: The Alchemy of Happiness.

greatest authority in theology, the Proof of Islam (*Hujjat-al Islām*); Renan considered him "the most original mind among Arabian philosophers," and Tholuck's opinion of him was, "this man, if ever any have deserved the name, was truly a 'divine.'"

Ghazālī was born at Tūs. He early lost his father and was brought up by a *Sūfī* friend. He studied theology and canon law, but soon broke away from authority and tradition and then devoted himself to dialectics, logic, science, philosophy and Sufism. The fame of his learning spread widely, and in 1085 he was appointed by Nizām-ul-Mulk to the Nizāmia academy at Baghdad. Ten years later he was struck with a mental malady and was obliged to leave Baghdad. He became a sceptic and lost all faith in religion. Out of his doubts he was lifted by his mystic experiences, and then abandoning reason he came to rely upon mysticism. He rejected the teaching of the traditionists because it appeared to him childish, but he found no satisfaction in scholasticism (*kalām*), nor in science or philosophy. The only true way of knowledge was through ecstasy and direct intuition. Therefore he devoted himself to mystical exercises in retirement from the world and at last acquired the peace of mind which he desired. In 1106, he was appointed to the academy of Nīshāpur, but he soon left it, and went back to Tūs where he established a school and a monastery (*khānqāh*). Here he wrote his book in refutation of philosophy (*Tihāfatul Filāsafa*), and here in 1112 he died.

Ghazālī made important contributions to Islamic theology. In the theory of knowledge he discarded, as above stated, the ultimate authority of reason, and made direct realisation (the *Samādhi* of Hindus) the proof of religion. Like the Hindu philosophers, he argued that through ordinary means of knowledge man can know only the relative, and, as God is absolute, he cannot gain any positive knowledge of His qualities or nature. He must therefore depend upon revelation—prophetic or personal—to obtain that knowledge. He further taught that it was possible to know God because God's nature was not different in essence from that of man, and that the human soul partook of the divine and would after death return to its divine source.

On the plane of the relative he accepted the teaching of science concerning the universe, although he maintained that behind the order of nature lay the Absolute Being whose will dominated all. The universe existed in three modes—the world of sense or change (*'ālam-ul-mulk*), the world of power (*ālam-ul-jabrūt*), and the world of eternal repose (*ālam-ul-malakūt*). The three worlds were not discrete in time and space but were modes of existence like the ideas of Plato.

Ghazālī completed the circle in which philosophic speculation ever moves. The *Mu'tazala* had started the circle by making reason the arbiter in religion, but the pitiless course of their own logic led to its final dethronement at the hands of Ash'arī and Ghazālī. Outside the ranks of the dialecticians the movement of speculation ran into several channels. Scholastic rationalism branched off into atheism, or rather scepticism, into pure philosophy, and into a complete denial of intellectualism, that is, mysticism.

The sceptics and atheists were usually found among the poets, the scientists and others who had all come under the influence of Persian and Indian thought. The names of the early sceptics have been enumerated by Jāhiz (869 A.D.) and their doctrines noted by Tabarī. Ibn Hazm (d. 1064 A.D.) and Ghazālī have attempted to classify them. They generally deny the existence of a personal God, and an immortal soul, show contempt for the prophets and for religious ordinances, and believe in the eternity of the universe, or in the eternity of two or three principles.[20]

The Caliph Yazīd (d. 744 A.D.) was rockoned among them, the poets (Abu Tammām (d. 846 A.D.) and Mutnabbī (d. 965 A.D.) were suspected of sceptic leanings, but of course the

20 Margoliouth: Atheists of Islam, E.R.E.

greatest of them all were Abul 'Alā Ma'arrī (d. 1057) and 'Umar Khayyām.

Regarding Abul 'Alā, the translator of his Dīwān, Henry Baerlein, says, he "was not merely saddened by the politics and the religion of the period; his meditations had been most profound; they had been influenced by Buddha."[21] Abul 'Alā was a believer in transmigration, a rigid vegetarian who disapproved of the use of milk, honey and leather, and had a tender regard for animal life, an abstemious ascetic in his clothing and food, a recluse, an upholder of celibacy. Yet he was one of the greatest of Arab poets, a deeply learned scholar who gathered round him hundreds of students from all lands, and a kindly helper to those who stood in need of his aid. Abul 'Alā was a foe of external piety and formal religion, for he sang:

> Abandon worship in the mosque and shrink
> From idle prayer, from sacrificial sheep,
> For Destiny will bring the bowl of sleep
> Or bowl of tribulation—you shall drink.[22]

and again,

> So, there are many ways and many traps
> And many guides, and which of them is lord?
> For verily Mahomet has the sword.
> And he may have the truth—perhaps! perhaps![23]

and with regard to prophets and paradise,

> "There is no God save Allah!"—that is true,
> Nor is there any prophet save the mind
> Of man who wanders through the dark to find
> The paradise that is in me and you.[24]

21 Baerlein: Abul 'Alā, the Syrian. p. 19.

22 Baerlein: Dīwān of Abul'Alā, Poem No. 1.

23 Ibid., Poem No. 35.

24 Ibid., Poem No. 81.

His view of the world is that it is illusory,

> Perchance the world is nothing, is a place
> Of dream, and what the dreamland people say
> We sedulously note, and we and they
> May be the shadows of a shining race.[25]

And he is a confirmed pessimist, who revels in pain and finds in it man's opportunity to live nobly.

> We suffer—that we know, and that is all
> Our knowledge. If we recklessly should strain
> To sweep aside the solid rocks of pain,
> Then would the domes of love and courage fall.[26]

'Umar Khayyām is so well known that it is hardly necessary to do more than just mention him.

The philosophers of Islam[27]—Al-Kindī, Fārābī (d. 950 A.D.), the Brothers of Purity (Ikhwān-us-Safā), Ibn Maskāwaih and Ibn Sīnā (d. 1036 A.D.) in the east, and Ibn Bājā (d. 1138 A.D.), Ibn Tufail (d. 1185) and Ibn Rushd (d. 1198) in the west, do not need extended notice. Their metaphysical systems were largely based on Greek philosophy and exerted influence in India only in so far as they became part of *Sufi* thought. It is, however, interesting to note that Al-Nadīm obtained information about Indian religious sects for his *Fihrist* from a treatise compiled by Al-Kindī, who in his turn depended on the account of an envoy sent by Yahiyā ibn Khālid, the Barmekide, to India. Fārābī was an encyclopædic writer, for besides logic and metaphysics he wrote on ethics, politics and music. He attempted to combine the systems of Plato and Aristotle, and his logic became the basis of Ibn Sīnā's philosophy. Ibn Sīnā shares with Ghazālī and Ibn Rushd the premier position among the Muslim thinkers. His canon is almost the last word on Muslim

25 Baerlein: Dīwān of Abul 'Alā, Poem No. 96.

26 Ibid., Poem No. 71.

27 Boer: History of Muslim Philosophy.
Iqbāl: Development of Metaphysics in Persia.

medicine, and in philosophy he is unsurpassed for the penetrating keenness of his mind and the subtlety of his thought.

The philosophers introduced neo-Platonic ideas of emanation into Muslim thought and sowed the seeds whose intellectual harvest was gathered by the *Sufis*. If Ghazālī starting from dogma landed into mysticism, Ibn Sīnā whose point of departure was Greek philosophy reached the same destination. He held that reason was of value in science only, but beyond reason was intuition which gave a simpler, more direct, and more adequate knowledge of the absolute truth. His metaphysics served as grist to the Sufistic mill, for he conceived of the ultimate reality as eternal beauty, whose nature being self-expression, it saw itself reflected in the universe-mirror. This self-expression is love, for love is appreciation of the beauty which is perfection. Love is thus the moving energy of the world, it makes beings strive after their original perfection from which in creation they have travelled away, and it is by love that the human soul realises its unity with the ultimate reality.

Every avenue of thought thus led to *Sufism*, whether it was *Mu'tazalah* dialectics, orthodox scholasticism or pure philosophy. Apparently the causes of such a convergence were not merely logical necessity, there were deeper social causes—among others the exhaustion of the energy which had led to the establishment of a world-wide empire, and the rise of the nationalistic spirit which brought about the downfall of the Abbaside Caliphate. Their result in the domain of thought is clear: from the twelfth century onwards the sway of Sufism becomes increasingly dominant over the Muslim mind; literature, philosophy and religion become all subject to its sovereign power.

It is time then to turn back and trace the beginning and gradual development of *Sufi* tendencies in Islam.

Sufism is a complex phenomenon; it is like a stream which gathers volume by the joining of tributaries from many lands. Its original source is the *Qorān* and the life of Muhammad. Christianity and neo-Platonism swelled it by a large contribution. Hinduism and Buddhism supplied a number of ideas, and the religions of ancient Persia *Zoroastrianism, Manism,* etc., brought to it their share.

Muhammad was a mystic, and the mystical note sounds clearly in the utterances of the *Qorān.*[28] The Mecca *Sūras* mainly and the Medina *Sūras* occasionally are charged with deep religious devotion and ascetic feeling. They teach absolute dependence and renunciation. God is spoken of as the light of the heavens and earth.[29] God says concerning the believers, "He loves them and they love Him"[30] and therefore He bears the beautiful name of lover (*wudūd*).[31] Again, the *Qorān* says, "Those who walk meekly on the earth, and when the ignorant speak to them answer 'Peace' shall be rewarded with the highest place in Paradise."[32] Then from the earliest times there were among the Muslim devotees who were continually engaged in reading the *Qorān,* and the penitents (*Bakk'āūn*)[33] who kept fasts and made orisons. In spite of Muhammad's insistence upon moderation, asceticism and abstinence were regarded as specially commendable by those called *Zāhid* (abstainers) and *'Ubbād* (servants), whose motto was 'flee from the world' (*al-firar min-al-duniya*). These ascetics developed the ordinary rites by works of supererogation, their prayers were more numerous and more highly spiritualised, their fasts more continuous and severer. Naturally their ethics and mode of living were held up as an example of saintly life, and their services utilised in roles of preachers, arbiters, ambassadors and leaders.[34]

When the Muslims came into contact with the Christians these tendencies were accentuated—in liturgical matters, medi-

28 Qorān, xxiv, 35 (Rodwell's translation, p. 446).

29 Ibid., I. 15 (Ibid., p. 92).

30 Ibid., v. 59 (Ibid., p. 492).

31 Ibid., lxxxv. 14 (Ibid., p. 43).

32 Ibid., xxv, 64 (Ibid., p. 163).

33 Goldziher: Op. cit., Chap. IV.

34 Margoliouth: Early Development of Muhammadanism, Lecture V.

tation and repetition of God's name and prayer (*dhikr*); and in ethical, complete detachment from the affairs of personal interest, utter dependence upon God (*tawakkul*), rejection of material goods (*fuqr*), idifference towards suffering or sickness, praise or blame. Abu 'Abdallah al Hārith al-Muhāsibi (d. 857-58), who is the earliest *Sufi* author whose work is preserved, shows evident traces of the use of the Christian Gospels, one of his works beginning with the Parable of the Sower and another being an expansion of the Sermon on the Mount.[35]

The neo-Platonists strengthened the feeling of contempt for the world and supported the leanings towards divine life by their doctrines of emanation and of dynamic pantheism. The neo-Platonic ideas passed into Islam when, in the beginning of the ninth century, Greek works were translated into Arabic.[36]

The third foreign source of Muslim mysticis was Indian. It has been pointed out in an earlier chapter that India and the Persian Gulf had close commercial intercourse; with trade, undoubtedly, ideas were exchanged. It stands to reason that if things of material use like Indian steel and sword[37] and Indian gold and precious stones,[38] and if things of artistic value like the pointed arch and the bulbous dome,[39] reached Persia and Iraq, Indian philosophical ideas should have travelled there too. Many Indians held posts in the financial department at Basra under the early Umayyads[40]; the Caliph Muāwiya is reported to

[35] Margoliouth: Notice of the Writings of Abu 'Abdallah al Hārith Bin Asad al-Muhāsibī. Transactions of the Third International Congress for the History of Religions, 1908.

[36] Nicholson: A Historical Enquiry Concerning the Origin and Development of Sufism, J.R.A.S., 1906.

[37] Brockelmann: Uyūn al Akhbār,' p. 119, l. 3.

[38] Margoliouth: Table talk of a Mesopotamian Judge, p. 189.

[39] Rivoira: Muslim Architecture, pp. 152, 153.

Choisy: Histoire de l'architecture, Vol. II, pp. 92, 102.

[40] Jean Perier: Vie d'al Hadjdjadj ibn Yūsuf, p. 249.

have planted a colony of them in Syria specially Antioch,[41] and Hajjāj to have established them in Kāshgar.[42] "The black-eyed and olive-complexioned Hindus" were brushing their shoulders[43] against those of the Muslims in the cities of the Caliphate. The eastern dominions of the empire, that is, Khorāsān, Afghanistan, Sīstān and Baluchistan were Buddhist or Hindu before they were converted. Balkh had a large monastery (*Vihāra*) whose superintendent was known as the Paramukh. His descendants became the famous Barmakide Vizirs of the Abbaside Caliphs.[44]

Then the Arabs familiarised themselves from early times with Indian literature and sciences. They translated Buddhist works in the second century of the Hijra, for instance, *Kitābal-Bud,* and *'Bilāwhar wa Budāsif'*[45]; treatises on astronomy and medicine called *'Sindhind'* (*Siddhānta*) and *'Shushrud'* (*Susruta*) and *Sirak* (*Charaka*)[46]; story books like *Kalilah Damnah* (*Panchatantra*) and *Kitāb Sindbād*[47]; ethical books of *Shanaq* (*Chāṇakya*) and *Bīdpā* (*Hitopadesa*)[48]; and treatises on logic[49] and military science.[50]

They were exceedingly keen on informing themselves of the customs, manners, sciences and religions of the people with whom they came into contact. Al-Kindī wrote a book on Indian religions, Sulaimān and Mas'ūdī collected information in their travels which they used in their writings. Al-Nadīm,[51]

[41] Jean Perier: Op. cit.

[42] Ibid., p. 249.

[43] Ibid., p. 252.

[44] Nicholson: A Literary History of the Arabs, p. 259.

[45] Duke: Influence of Buddhism upon Islam, a Summary of Goldziher's Paper, J.R.A.S., 1904.

[46] Fluegel: Fihrist.

[47] Ibid.

[48] Ibid.

[49] Ibid.

[50] Ibid.

[51] Ibid.

Al-Ash'arī,[52] Al-Birūnī,[53] Shahrastānī[54] and many others devoted chapters in their books to describe and discuss Indian religious and philosophic systems.

The legend of Buddha entered into Muslim literature as the type of the saintly man, and Muslim hagiologists assimilated the stories of Ibn Adham to the Buddhist legend.[55] Indian ascetics travelling in pairs and staying not more than two nights at one place were directly known to the Muslim adepts, who took from them their fourfold vows—of cleanliness, purity, truth and poverty—and the use of the rosary.[56]

What wonder then that the conception of *Nirvāṇa*, the discipline of the eightfold path, the practice of *Yoga* and the acquaintance of miraculous powers were appropriated in Islam under the name of *Fanā*, *Tarīqā* or *Sulūk*, *Marāqabah* and *Karāmat* or *M'ujizā*.[57]

Two periods may be distinguished in the history of *Sufism*. The first from the earliest times to the beginning of the ninth century, and the second from the ninth century onwards; during the first period, *Sufism* was merely tendencious and possessed no system; during the second, it developed metaphysical systems and the organization of monastic orders.

The leaders of saintly life in the first period were ascetics, quietists and recluses. Kūfa and Basra were their two main centres. The name *Sufi* was first applied to Abu Hāshim of Kūfa[58] who died in 778 A.D. But the *Sufi* writers include

[52] Mehren : Op. cit., p. 192.

[53] Sachau : Al-Birūnī's India.

[54] Rehatsek : Op. cit.

[55] Goldziher : Op. cit., Chap. IV.

[56] Ibid.

[57] Ibid.

Duka : Op. cit.

[58] E. G. Browne : Literary History of Persia, Vol. I. p. 298.

among the early mystics[59] Imām Ja'far Sādiq (d. 765 A.D.), Hasan al Basrī (d. 728 A.D.), Uwais al Qaranī (fl. 1st cent. A.D.). Dāūd al-Taī (d. 781 A.D.), Shaqïq Balkhī (d. 810 A.D.), Ibrahim ibn Adham (d. 777 A.D.), Rābi'a al 'Adawiya (d. 753 A.D.), Habīb' Ajmī (d. 899 A.D.), Abu Hanīfa N'umān (d. 768 A.D.), al'-Kharrāz (pupil of Hasan), Fuḍayl ibn 'Ayaz (d. 803 A.D.).

The chief characteristic of their belief was the submission of human will to God. They were seekers more of piety and other-worldliness than of divine knowledge, they had an exaggerated consciousness of sin and an overwhelming dread of divine retribution, yet they had early developed emotional and ecstatic features and they negated the externalia of religion.

Among Rābi'a al 'Adawiya's sayings there are many which show emotional tendencies. For instance, "Consume with fire, O God, a (presumptuous) heart which loveth Thee."[60] "I reserve my heart for Thy converse, (O Lord!) and leave my body to keep company with those who desire my society. My body is thus the companion of the visitor, but my dearly beloved is the companion of my heart."[61] She is reported to have said that the love of God had so taken possession of her soul that there was no room left even for the love of the prophet, much less of hatred for the devil.[62] The fear of death and of the day of judgment was expressed in many ways. Rābi'a says, "O my soul! how long wilt thou sleep to rise no more, till the call shall summon thee on the day of resurrection."[63]

59 Nicholson : A Historical Enqurry.

E. G. Browne : Literary History, Vol. I.

60 De Slane : Ibn Khallikan, Vol. I, p. 515.

61 Ibid., p. 516.

62 E. G. Browne : Literary History, Vol. I, p. 299.

63 Nicholson : Kashful Mahjūb, p. 91.

Uwais Qaranī speaking to Hārun ibn Hayyān said, "my father died, Adam and Eve died, Noah and Abraham died, Moses, son of Amran died, David, Caliph of God, died, Muhammad, the prophet of God, died, Abu Bakr, his Caliph, died, my brother 'Umar died, and my friend died....and this is my last advice to thee, keep always before thee the Book of God and the path of the righteous, and do not for a moment allow thyself to become heedless of death."[64]

The second period of *Sufism* began in the ninth century; the calm monotheistic quietism of the first, having absorbed *Shī'ah* theories and foreign notions, blossomed out in surprisingly short time into full-fledged pantheistic mysticism. The Sufis of the period fall into several groups, men of similar temperaments clustering together round some pious leader. These groups eventually evolved several orders and different systems, according to the differences of emphasis on particular doctrines, details of organization, and philosophical schemes. In this manner arose the early schools[65] which Hujwīrī has described fully. Among them were the followers of Muhāsibī who has been mentioned above as a writer of Christian tendencies; opposed to them were the *Qassārīs* or *Malāmatīs* who pushed detachment from the world to extremes and voluntarily sought the contempt of men. The followers of Junaid of Baghdad were prudent and sober; they condemned formalism and preached a religion of sincerity. The *Sahlīs* laid emphasis on self-mortification. Abu Saíd Kharrāz was the first to explain the states of annihilation (*fanā*) and subsistence (*baqā*). Lastly, there were the extreme *Sufis* who held the doctrines of incarnation (*hulūl*), commixture (*imtizāj*) and transmigration of spirits (*naskh-i-arwāh*).

But the man who produced the greatest stir in the Islamic world by the boldness of his doctrines was Husain bin Mansūr

64 Nicholson : Tadhkirat-ul-Auliyā, pp. 20, 21.

65 Nicholson : Kashful Mahjūb.

al Hallāj.[66] His theories were later worked up in the systems of Ibn al Arabī and 'Abdul Karīm Jīli and in the poetry of Ibn al Fārīdh and Abu Sa'īd Ibn Abul Khair and their influence spread to far-off countries including India. Ghazālī, Hujwirī and 'Attār attempted to reconcile him to orthodoxy. The story of Mansūr's life is well known. He started his career as an ordinary *Sufi* under the guidance of such well-known *Shaikhs* (preceptors) as Tushtarī and Junaid. But afterwards he threw away the *Sufi* garments and put on worldly clothes. He began to preach as an apostle of God and offended the *Jurists*—for apostleship was a breach of traditions—and the government, because, it savoured of Shīah legitimism. He travelled about in many lands, among them India, and thrice visited Mecca. At last his activities became so obnoxious that he was arrested. He was kept in prison for a long time, was tortured and at last executed in 922 A.D. As Kabīr, Dādū, Nānak and other Indian saints used the language of Muslim *Sufism,* it is necessary to briefly explain Mansūr's mystical system, for his terms became the current coinage of *Sufism.*

Before creation, God was in His unity, holding ineffable discourse with Himself and contemplating the splendour of His own essence, and this radical simplicity of His admiration is Love, "which in His essence is the essence of essences," beyond all modelisations in attributes. In His perfect isolation (*infirād*) God was illuminated by Love, and from this illumination came the multiplicity of His attributes and names. Then in order to see His supreme joy He projected out of the pre-eternal (*azal*) an image of Himself, that is, of His attributes and names. This was Adam. Thus the absolute God in His divinity (*lāhūt*) became in Adam God in Humanity (*nāsūt*). Mansūr conceived of the relation of God with man as the infusion of the divine into the human soul; in Hindu terms, the illumination of *buddhi* by

66 Massignon : Kitāb Tāwal Sīn.

Massignon : La passion d'Al-Halladj et l'ordre des Halladjiyyah Mélanges H. Derenbourg. 1909. *cs,ici cohtBA 'p*

Puruśa. The divine spirit produces the illumination where, "I become that which I love, and that which I love becomes mine. We are two spirits, infused in one body, to see me is to see Him, to see Him is to see us."[67] Apparently Mansūr was not a thorough-going monist in spite of his declaration, "I am God", (*anal Haq*), for according to him there was still some difference of level or potential between the Absolute and His image.

Qushairī (d. 1072) introduced into *Sūfi* thought the neo-Platonic idea of creation by intermediary agencies, and Ibn Sīnā the conception of ultimate reality as eternal beauty, seeing its reflection in the universe-mirror. Thus the idea that God was both transcendent and immanent grew, and from the pantheistic view it followed that all 'otherness' was mere illusion, and the feeling of separateness was due to ignorance, which could only be dissipated by knowledge. This school[68] had three basic ideas—in the first place, the ultimate reality was knowledge through a supersensual state of consciousness; secondly the ultimate reality was impersonal; and thirdly, the ultimate reality was one.

There were many other schools of mystic speculation, but two are of special importance: those who regarded the ultimate reality as light (*nūr*), and those who regarded it as thought. The chief exponent of the first was Shaikh Shahāb-Uddīn Suhrāwardī (d. 1209), and of the second Ibn al'Arabī (d. 1241) and his commentator 'Abdul Karīm Jīlī (d. 1406). Shahāb-Uddin[69] began his studies at Maragha and then migrated to Aleppo. The independence of his thought made him suspect in the eyes of the authorities. He was denounced by the *Qāzis* and executed by the order of Saladin. He wrote a number of works on what is called *Hikmat al Ishrāq* (illuminative philosophy). The chain of ideas links him with Plotinus, Mānī, and Zoroaster. In his philosophy the ultimate principle of all existence is Light

67 Massignon : Op. cit. *r wlTT*

68 Iqbāl : Op. cit.

69 Carra de Voun : La philosophie illuminative d'apres Suhrawardy Maqtūl, J. A., 1902.

(*Nūr-i-Qāhir*), whose essential nature consists in perpetual illumination. This light is self-existent, self-manifesting, indefinable. Not-light is its negation and is necessary for its manifestation. Not-light like the Indian *Māyā* is non-existent. Light is the source of existence. It has two kinds of illuminations. First, the abstract, which is without form or limitation and is not an attribute of any other substance. Its essence is consciousness or knowledge. It is the principle of universal intellect and of its distant reflection, the individual intellect. Secondly, the accidental, which has form and which is capable of becoming an attribute. It is a reflection of the abstract light and is contingent upon it.

To not-light, which is the principle of absolute matter, two kinds of material beings belong—(1) the obscure substance or atom which is beyond space, and (2) the forms which are necessarily in space. These two give rise to all material bodies.

From the abstract Light to material bodies the whole universe is a continuous series of circles of substance all depending on the Original Light. Those near the source receive more light than those that are distant, and all strive to move towards the original fountain of Light with the intense passion and eternal attraction of Love. Thus the universe lives in and moves by Love.

The human soul is the highest dwelling place of the abstract illumination, which enters the body of man which is composed of not-light, through the medium of the animal soul which is midway between not-light and light. The human soul longs for greater and greater illumination in order to gain complete freedom from the world of form or not-light; this is realised through knowledge and action.

The human soul has five external and five internal senses which belong to the power of light; and it has faculties or functions like growth, assimilation, digestion, which belong to the power of not-light. They together form the unity of the organism, they are associated with abstract illumination as the enlightened but passive *Puruśa* is associated with the blind but active *manas.* There are three constituents of the human soul (*manas='aql*)—(1) reason or intelligence (*sattva*), (2) courage and ambition (*rajas*), and (3) lust, hunger and passion (*tamas*). The harmonisation of the three results in juitice which is the highest virtue.

The individual soul is ever progressive. It strives unceasingly for total illumination and final absorption. Death does not end its strivings. When the material machinery which it adopts in one life is exhausted it takes up another body and rises higher and higher in different spheres of Being until it reaches its destination, which is the state of absolute annihilation (fanā).

When all the souls which are journeying towards their common source have reached their goal the universe is dissolved and then another cycle of creation follows, similar to the first one; and so cycles of absorption and evolution continue.

The spiritual goal of man is enlightenment. He has to tread the path of saintship in order to attain it. On the path are stations, five of which may be distinguished. First is the stage of '*I*', feeling of personality and selfishness; second of '*Thou art not*', complete absorption in self; third of '*I am not*', a reaction of the second; fourth of '*Thou art*', complete resignation to God; and the fifth of '*I am not, and thou art not*', cosmic consciousness, annihilation of distinctions of subject and object.

Ibn al 'Arabī (d. 1241)[70] is one of the greatest authorities on *Sufi* philosophy. He regarded both nature and man as the mirrors which displayed God Himself. "God manifests Himself in every atom of creation; He is revealed in every intelligible object and concealed from every intelligence except the intelligence of those who say that the universe is His form and *ipseity* (*sūrah wa huwīyah*), inasmuch as He stands in the same relation to phenomenal objects as the spirit to the body.[71]

70 Nicholson : Tarjumān-al-Ashwāq.

71 Ibid.

Regarding the relation of God and man he says, "man is the form of God, and God is the spirit of man."[72] By means of man God beholds the objects which He has created. "Man is the substance of every attribute wherewith he endows God; when he contemplates God he contemplates himself, and God contemplates Himself when He contemplates man."[73]

Attainment of the knowledge of God was the only end of man, for complete union with Him was not possible as long as the body lasted. The knowledge is gained by faith and contemplation, in which human reason divests itself of its discursive or reflective faculty. The end of knowledge is transcendental consciousness, where the phenomenal vanishes in the presence of the eternal.

The practical inference from this pantheism was that God could be worshipped in innumerable ways, and that all religions contained truth. For if all things are a manifestation of the Divine substance, God may be worshipped in a star or a calf or any other object, and consequently there should be complete tolerance towards all creeds. He says, "every one praises what he believes, his God is His own creature, and in praising it he praises himself. Consequently he blames the beliefs of others, which he would not do if he were just, but his dislike is based on ignorance. If he knew Junaid's saying, 'the water takes its colour from the vessel containing it,' he would not interfere with the beliefs of others, but would perceive God in every form and every belief."[74]

About a century and a half later than Ibn al 'Arabī lived 'Abdul Karīm Al Jīlī[75] (d. 1406–17), who wrote a commentary on his predecessor's work, *Futūhāt-al-Makkiyah* and an independent treatise on *Sufism* called 'the Perfect Man' (*Insān al Kāmil*). Jīlī does not rank in intellectual power or philoso-

72 Nicholson : Tarjumān-al-Ash[illegible]q.

73 Ibid.

74 Ibid.

75 Nicholson : Studies in Islamic Mysticism.
Iqbāl : Op. cit.

phical insight as an equal of 'Arabī. His treatise is full of digressions on all kinds of occult subjects and his philosophy can only be pieced together with such patient labour as has been bestowed upon it by Nicholson and Iqbāl. From their accounts the following abstract of his system is drawn.

There is one Being which exists in two modes, the absolute or unmanifest and the qualified or manifest. The absolute is unknowable *per se*, for it is beyond all relation, beyond being and not-being, a sum of contradictions. This absolute (*wujūd-i-mutlaq*) which is devoid of all qualities and relations exists enveloped in cecity (*'ama*). The first step in its manifestation is when it emerges from the darkness without becoming externally manifest; it is still free from name and attributes and is a unity comprehending diversity. The external aspect of this bare potentiality is abstract oneness (*ahadiya*), when Being is conscious of itself as a unity. The second step is taken when the abstract unity (*ahadïya*) manifests itself in two aspects of He-ness (*huwīya*) and I-ness (*'annīya*). In the first or inward state the Being is conscious of itself as negativing the many (attributes), in the second or outward state as the truth of the many. The third step is that of Unity in Plurality (*wāhidïya*), when Being identifies itself as one with itself as many. The last step brings the absolute out of darkness into light, out of the unconscious into the conscious out of *nirguṇa*, into *saguṇa*, into the sphere of Divinity with distinctive attributes embracing the whole series of existence. At last the absolute has become the subject and object of all thought, the noumenal has become the phenomenal.

The Divinity (*ilāhīya*) is the highest manifestation of the absolute. It is a name for the sum of the individualisations of Being, for the sum of all the attributes. It is revealed in two aspects of mercy and lordship; in the first it is in the relation of creator (*al-haqq*) to the created things (*al-khalq*); and in the second it is as the preserver and maintainer in their respective order of the created things.

The Divinity is known through its names and attributes. The names appertain to its essence (*dhāt*), beauty (*jamāl*), grandeur (*jalāl*) and perfection (*kamāl*). The principal attributes are life, knowledge, will power, speech, hearing and sight.

The universe is the embodiment of the Divine idea, the objectification of the absolute. The universe is ice, God, water, God is the substance (*hayūla*) of the cosmos. The sensible world is idea, thought or dream, but not unreal, it is reality as presented to itself through and in the cosmic consciousness of the perfect man which holds all the attributes of reality together. The thing-in-itself is the collection of attributes, it is built of idea and has no other existence. In *Jīlī's* cosmological myth, the idea of ideas (*haqīqat al haqā'iq*) existed as a white chrysolite (*yāqūt-al-baidha*) in which dwelt God before He created the creatures. He looked at it with the eye of perfection and it became water, and then with the eye of grandeur (*jalāl*) and it surged into waves, and from its grosser elements seven earths were created and from its suble elements seven heavens and from the water seven seas with their presiding angels and inhabitants.

Man in perfection is the image (*nuskha*) of God. He is a mirror to God reflecting His names and attributes. He is the archetype of nature, the link between God and the universe. He is the microcosm in which the absolute becomes conscious of itself in all its diverse parts. He is the unifying principle between reality and appearance, the axis (*qutb*) round which the spheres of existence revolve. He is the first created spirit (*rūh*) in which God first manifests Himself in His essence. He is the archetypal spirit of Muhammad (*Haqīqat al-Muhammadiyah*), and one of his names is the Word of God (*amr-i-Allah*). Regarding this spirit (*rūh*), Jīlī says, "I am the child whose father is his son and the wine whose vine is its jar......I met the mothers who bore me, and I asked them in marriage, and they let me marry them."[76] These phrases bear curious resemblance to the Vedic cosmologies where the *Aditis* are spoken of as mothers as well as wives of their sons.[77]

[76] Nicholson : Studies in Islamic Mysticism, pp. 112, 113.

[77] Macdonnel : History of Sanskrit Literature.

The first theatre of the manifestation of the spirit was Adam, then there were angels of light and darkness, and then five kinds of souls,—animal, passionate, active or good, penitent and tranquil. All souls are potentially perfect, some are actually so. Among the latter, one stands above all, namely, Muhammad. In every age there are perfect men who are an outward manifestation of the essence of Muhammad, the Logos of God.

The absolute descends by many stages into man; in man the mystical ascent takes place by which man returns to the Divine. The process of ascent or spiritual perfection has four stages. In the first stage man completely surrenders himself to the will of God. In the second, he meditates on the names of God and is illuminated by the splendour of the name, the individual will is destroyed. In the third stage takes place the illumination of the attributes; man participates in the divine attributes and acquires miraculous powers. He hears the ringing of bells (*silsilat-al jaras*), experiences the dissolution of the bodily frame, and beholds "lightening and thunder and clouds raining lights and seas surging with fire."[78] In the fourth stage he crosses the domain of name and attribute and enters into that of Essence and becomes perfect (*Insān-i-Kāmil*), God-man.

Jīlī was an idealistic monist. For him all beliefs were thoughts about one reality, and all modes of worship expressive of some aspect of that reality. The differences were due to the variety of names and attributes and all together contributed to the perfection of the whole. Jīlī was acquainted with Hindu religion, for among the ten principal sects he noted the *Brāhimā*[79] (*Brạhmaṇ*). About them he says that they worship God in His absolute aspect, without reference to prophet or apostle. The scriptures of the *Brāhmiṇā*, according to him, were revealed to them not by God but by *Abraham* (*Brahmā*); they contained five books, the fifth on account of its profundity was unknown to most of the Brahmans, but those who read it invariably became Moslems. Apparently Jīlīs fifth book is the

78 Nicholson : Studies in Islamic Mysticism, p. 129.

79 Ibid., pp. 132, 133 note.

Vedānta whose monistic philosophy in the eyes of Jīlī made it indistinguishable from Islam.

Theoretical *Sufism* had reached the highest point of its growth; the writers of subsequent times wrote text-books for students and popular treatises without adding much of original value. Of these Jāmī's *Lawāih* in Persian is the best summary of *Sufi* philosophy and deservingly attained the widest repute. Arabic and Persian poets who became increasingly imbued with *Sufism* made it more than the philosophers the religion of the high and the low. Among the former Abu Sa'īd ibn Abul Khair (d. 1048) and 'Umar ibn al Farīdh, and among the latter Hakīm Sanā'ī (d. 1150 A.D.), Farid-ud-Dīn 'Attār (d. 1229-30), Jalāl-ud-Dīn Rūmī (d. 1273), Shabistarī (d. 1317 or 1320) give the best exposition of *Sufi* doctrines.

Besides the philosophical and the poetical, and of equal importance with them, is the practical[80] aspect of *Sufism*. The practical aim of the *Sufi* is absorption in God. According to the orthodox (*Bā Shara'*) school there are three stages in the attainment of this goal. The first is the stage of good actions, the surrender of will to the commands of God, the obedience of law (*sharī'at*). As a preliminary step to the first stage the seeker (*tālib* or *sālik*) has to repent of his sins (*taubah*) and to acquire faith (*imān*). Then he has to carry out scrupulously all the injunctions regarding cleanliness (*tahārat*), prayer (*salāt*), fasting (*saum*), almsgiving or charity (*zakāt*), and pilgrimage (*Haj*). By ascetic practices, fasting, silence and solitude the evil propensities of the self (*nafs*), that is, ignorance, pride, envy, uncharitableness, anger and others are mortified, for it is absolutely essential that the lower self should die in order that the higher should live in God. The inward or spiritual aspect of obedience to law is designated the path (*tarīqat*). The second stage is that of gnosis (*m'arifat*), the attainment of spiritual knowledge. In this stage logical reasoning is discarded because its inadequacy to gain the knowledge of God is realised. Intellect

80 J. P. Brown: The Derwishes.
Malcolm: History of Persia.

(*'aql*) and demonstration (*istidlāl*) are abandoned, and the restless soul seeks relief only in the mercy of God, for it is only by His grace (*faidh*) and favour (*'ināyat*) that gnosis takes place. Then the Sufi finds out that otherness is an illusion and therefore attachment to created things and fruits of good actions utterly vain. With Abul Hasan Khirqānï he holds, "I do not say that paradise and hell are non-existent, but I say that they are nothing to me, because God created them both, and there is no room for any created object in the place where I am."[81] To the gnostic the following of law is relatively insignificant. Inward light transforms his intellect and will, and he no longer stands in need of outward action; for instance, the object of mysticism in traversing wilderness and deserts is not the sanctuary (*k'aba*) itself, for to a lover of God it is unlawful to look upon His sacntuary. No; their object is mortification in a longing that leaves them no rest, and eager dissolution in a love that has no end."[82] Junaid pointed out how outward pilgrimage without spiritual progress was futile.[83]

But gnosis is not enough. It must lead to the next and the highest stage: complete union with the Divinity (*haqïqat*), the transformation of the whole of man, will, intellect and emotions and the attainment of the unitive state. In this state the mystic passes away from the self (*fanā*) and lives in essential unity with God (*baqā*). The illusion of subject and object vanishes, the sense of individuality dies and law and religion lose their meaning; but this is only the negative aspect of the cosmic consciousness which has a rich, positive content. The sanctified mystic comprehends both the inward and the outward aspects of Reality, the one and the many, the truth and law, in the unitive state he becomes one with God, he exclaims with Mansūr "I am God" (*ɔnal Haq*). "I am He whom I love, and He whom I love is I."[84]

81 Nicholson : The Mystics of Islam, Chap. III.

82 Nicholson : Kashf-ul-Mahjūb, p. 327.

83 Ibid., p. 328.

84 Nicholson : The Mystics of Islam, Chap. VI.

The stages by which a novice rises to union with God have many stations (*maqāmāt*) and their corresponding states (*hāl*). The seven stations[85] usually recognised are— (1) repentance (*taubah*), (2) abstinence (*wara'a*), (3) renunciation (*zuhd*), (4) poverty (*fuqr*), (5) patience (*sabr*), (6) trust (*tawakkul*), (7) satisfaction (*radha*). The states[86] are meditation (*murāqaba*), nearness to God (*qurb*), love (*muhabbat*), fear (*khauf*), hope (*rija*), longing (*shauq*), intimacy (*uns*), tranquillity (*itmīnān*), contemplation (*mushāhada*), certainty (*yaqīn*). The stations are self-acquired, but the states are given by God.

In the copious literature of Sufism all the stages, stations and states have been described with superabundant zest and consummate resourcefulness. The legends of saints overflow with stories illustrating ascetic, contemplative and unitive states, and the language of poetry and symbolism has been exhausted in giving expression to all the emotions—of fear, hope, longing and love—which the mystic experiences. For a student of mysticism and of varieties of religious experiences no richer mine of information exists than the lives of Muslim saints and the poetry of Muslim mysticism. Sobriety and intoxication, quiet piety and frenzied love bordering on insanity, profound thinking and fantastic occultism, writhing anguish, abject humility, joyous elation and exuberant hope; there is not a note in the whole gamut of human feeling and thought which has not been touched and made to yield its rich and hidden music. All kinds of physico-psychical phenomena, the hearing of sounds and voices and the seeing of visions and colours, the melting of sound into sight and of colours into music, the ravishing scents of flowers and musk and the soft touch of morning zephyrs, the trance produced by song and dance and death caused by the reciting of a line of poetry—all of them are there, offering an endless feast to the psychological gourmand hungry for esoteric facts.

85 Nicholson : The Mystics of Islam, Chap. I.

86 Ibid.

The Muslim mystic who sets out upon the path of union (*wasl*), of absorption (*fanā*) always needs a spiritual guide, for "if a man has no teacher, his *imām* is Satan."[87] The guide or the preceptor (*pīr* or Shaikh) is the pivot round which the whole machinery of *Sufi* monachism moves. His authority is divine, for the *Sufi* preceptor has inherited the whole significance of Shīa'h Imām.[88] In the order to which *Sufi* belongs he is sovereign. The order provides the companionship of saints which is necessary for spiritual welfare, the *Shaikh* regulates the conduct of the companions and watches over their spiritual progress. He is a saint who has completed the journey and reached the goal. He has become one with God and therefore his position and status are divine. Ma'rūf Karkhī[89] asked his disciples to swear to God by him, and Dhul Nūn[90] asserted that a true disciple should be more obedient to his master than to God Himself, Jalāl-ud-Dīn Rūmī spoke of his master Shams-i-Tabrīz, as 'that monarch supreme who had come out from behind the door clothed in the garment of mortality.'[91] In this way the *Sufi* professing to adore a universal abstraction makes individual men the object of his real worship.[92] The disciple is advised to keep his *Murshid* constantly in mind, to become mentally absorbed in him through constant meditation and contemplation of him, to see him in all men and in all things, and to annihilate his self in the *Murshid*. From this state of self-absorption in the *Murshid*, the master leads him on through several stages at last to absorption in the Deity.[93]

87 Nicholson : A Historical Enquiry, etc., etc.

88 Patton : Shīa'hs, E. R. E.

Nicholson : Studies in Isalmic Mysticism, Preface.

89 Nicholson : A Historical Enquiry, etc., etc.

90 Ibid.

91 Nicholson : Dīwān-i-Shams-i-Tabrīz, Introduction, xxii.

92 Nicholson : A Historical Enquiry, etc., etc.

93 J. P. Brown : The Derwishes.

Muhammad taught surrender to God (*islām*), *Sufism* surrender to the teacher who is the representative of God upon earth.

The discipline of the seeker is *dhikr*, which ordinarily means remembering God and repeating His name, but which includes all the devotional practices which induce ecstasy and trance. There are two kinds of it, *dhikr i jalī* or reciting aloud and *dhikr i khafī* or reciting mentally. Malcolm[94] and Brown[95] have described the processes. They are very similar to the meditation and the breathing exercises (*prāṇāyāma*) of the Indian Yoga. Shiblī pointedly brings out this feature of *Sufism* in his definition. "*Tasawwuf*" (Sufism) is control of the faculties and observance of the breaths.[96] In the *Naqshbandī* order, the *Murīd* (disciple) closes his eyes, shuts his mouth, presses his tongue against the roof of his mouth, holds his breath and recites in his heart. The "*lā*" goes upward, the "*illaha*" to the right, the whole phrase "*lā illaha*" is formed upon the cone of the heart and through it passed to all the members of the whole frame. The breath is drawn from the navel to the breast, from the breast to the brain, from the brain up to the heavens and then again repeated stage by stage backwards and forwards.

Another method of bringing about trance is by song and dance (*sama'*). There has been much dispute among theologians as to the lawfulness of music and dancing regarded as religious exercises. Ghazālī speaks of them as novelties which had not been received in Islam from the first followers of the Prophet, but which were therefore not forbidden. He himself approves of them for by their means the *Sufis* "stir up in them selves greater love towards God, and by means of music, often obtain spiritual visions and ecstasies, their heart becoming in this condition as clean as silver in the flame of a furnace, and attaining a degree of purity which could never be attained by any amount of mere outward austerities. The *Sufi* then

94 Malcolm : Op. cit., p. 146.

95 J. P. Brown : Op. cit., p. 127.

96 Hadland Davis : The Persian Mystics, p. 28.

becomes so keenly aware of his relationship to the spiritual world that he loses all consciousness of this world, and often falls down senseless."[97] Hujwīrī quotes traditions and the opinion of early *Sufis* to show that audition is lawful, and fulfils a necessary function, and although footplay (*pāy bāzī*) was bad in law and reason, the ecstatic condition "when the heart throbs with exhilaration and rapture becomes intense and the agitation of ecstasy is manifested and conventional forms are gone, that agitation is neither dancing nor footplay nor bodily indulgence but a dissolution of the soul."[98] Jalāl-ud-Dīn Rūmī laid great emphasis upon music and dance, so much so that his order, the *Maulavīs,* has become known as the 'dancing Derwishes.'[99] Both the Chishtī and Suhrawardī orders included them as essential features of their *dhikr*. Of Shaikh Badr-ud-Dīn (a saint settled in India in the thirteenth century) it is related that "in his old age when he was unable to move, the sound of a hymn would excite him to ecstasy and he would dance like a youth. When asked how it was that the Shaikh could dance notwithstanding his decrepitude, he replied, 'where is the Shaikh, It is Love that dances.' "[100]

Sufism indeed was a religion of intense devotion, love was its passion; poetry, song and dance its worship; and passing away in God its ideal.

97 Field : Ghazālī : The Alchemy of Happiness, p. 67.
98 Nicholson : Kashful Mahjūb, p. 416.
99 J. P. Brown : Op. cit.
100 Blochmann and Jarrett : Ā'in-iAkbarī, Vol. III, p. 368.

HINDU REFORMERS OF THE SOUTH : I

THE history of the Hindu religion sketched in a previous chapter shows a continuity in development from the earliest times to the beginning of the eighth century. This development took place principally in Northern India where all the great movements originated and from where they spread to the south. All through this period the north was the leader in culture, for there all the scriptures were written, and most of the heterodox faiths, Buddhism and Jainism, philosophical schools and sects arose. But after the eighth century came a change; the north lost its leadership and the initiative passed to the south. From the eighth century to the fifteenth the south is the home of religious reform; it is there that *Vaiśṇava* and *Śaivite* saints start the schools of *Bhakti*, and Śankara, Rāmānuja, Nimbāditya, Basava, Vallabhāchārya and Mādhava expound their philosophical systems. From the south the impulse was transmitted to the north through Rāmānanda, a pupil of Ramānuja.

This sudden shifting of the scene of activity from the north to the south was the result of the political and social changes that came over India at this time. In the north the empire of Harśa broke up; political unity disappeared and a number of principalities were established which were engaged in unending internecine wars with one another; Buddhism became decadent and by gradual steps merged into *Śiva* and *Śakti* cults and was displaced by Paurāṇic Hinduism. The establishment of Rajput kingdoms did not infuse new life into the old systems and when they were overthrown by the Muslim invasions the Hindu society was thoroughly enfeebled.

In the south, on the other hand, Hinduism was a conquering faith. It had entered into conflict with Buddhism and Jainism and emerged victorious, and triumph had given it fresh inspiration. Again, the Hindu kingdoms in the south enjoyed a long lease of prosperity and power under the rule of the Cholas and the Vijayanagar kings; and above all it was there in the south that Islam first came into contact with Hinduism and leavened the growing mass of Hindu thought.

From the earliest times in spite of geographical difficulties—the barriers of rivers and mountains, the northern people had communications with the inhabitants of the Deccan and the extreme south. Currents of culture had passed continuously and affected their beliefs and customs. The deities of hills and forests in Tamil lands were assimilated to Aryan gods and goddesses. Small colonies of Brahmin pioneers had settled down in the Dravida kingdoms bringing with them the Vedic religion and Sanskrit learning, and modifying the life of the Southern peoples.[1] Buddhist and Jain missionaries had arrived soon after the promulgation of these religions in the north, and converted thousands to their faiths. Thus in the early centuries of the Christian era there was a mixture of religions in the south. Animism, devil worship, Śaivism, Viśṇuism, Buddhism, Jainism and other persuasions—all existed side by side in happy confusion, in perfect neighbourliness.[2]

In the fifth century the establishment of the Gupta Empire gave a strong impetus to the process of cultural conquest. Fresh waves of the missionaries of rejuvenated Hinduism overran the country; Brahmin emigrants settled in Kerala lands, poured new life into faiths and prepared them to enter upon a deadly conflict with heterodox systems. In the seventh century Hiuen-Tsang still found Buddhism and Jainism strongly entrenched, but *Śaivism* rising swiftly as a formidable antagonist. Of the Śaiva uprise het Pallavas were the great protagonists. While Harśa was holding tolerant sway over the north encouraging equally Hinduism and Buddhism; and Pulakesin II celebrated his *Aśvamedha* sacrifice which indicated the revival of Brahmanism, Narsingh Varmā Pallava, their southern contemporary,

[1] A. Govindāchārya : The Coming of the Brahmans to the South of India, J.R.A.S., 1912.

Innes : Malabar and Anjengo, Madras, District Gazetteer.

[2] S. K. Iyengar : South Indian History.

was vigorously advancing the cause of *Paurāṇic* Hinduism by building the great pagodas of Mahāmallapuram. During the seventh and eighth centuries the Chālukyas and Pallavas, the two dominant powers south of the Nerbudda, were engaged in two common aims—to revive Hinduism and to destroy one another. Before the end of the eighth century they had succeeded in both aims. They had given a mortal blow to Buddhist ascendancy and thus secured the triumph of Hinduism; and they had so worn themselves out as to allow the Cholas from the south and the Rāśtrakutas from the north to usurp their dominions.[3]

The eighth century was thus a period of revolutionary activity in religion and politics, of ceaseless conflict of ideas and of peoples, of dramatic rise and overthrow of dynasties, of philosophical debate in schools and sectarian dispute in temples. Such an atmosphere gave a tremendous impulse to thought and feeling, Men's minds were for the time being freed from the tyranny of old traditional ways and thrown open to receive suggestions from unfamiliar quarters.

It was during this period of strenuous activity that the foundations of later religious development in the south were laid. The *Śaiva* and *Vaiśṇava* saints combined to wean the people from their allegiance to Buddhism and Jainism to *Śiva* and *Viśṇu* worship. They sought to attain their aim by making an appeal to the heart, and so in affecting verse they sang of devotion and of the happiness of dwelling in the presence of God and of seeking of His grace. Their poems were all in the language of the people, and in this as in other matters they were indebted deeply to the religions which they attempted to supplant. For they took over from Buddhism its devotionalism, its sense of the transitoriness of the world, its conceptions of human worthlessness, its suppression of desires and asceticism as also its ritual, the worship of idols and *stūpas* or *lingams,* temples, pilgrimages, fasts and monastic rules and its idea of the

[3] K. V. Subrāhmaṇya Aiyer: Hisorical Sketches of the Deccan, Books II and III.

spiritual equality of all castes; from Jainism they took its ethical tone and its respect for animal life.

The assimilation of these ideas into *Paurāṇic* theology and the pervasion of the whole with warm human feeling was the achievement of the saintly hymn-makers of Tamil land, the celebrated *Adiyārs* (the *Śaiva* saints) and the *Ālvārs* (*Vaiśṇava* saints), who flourished between the seventh and the twelfth centuries.

These devotees of *Śiva* and *Viśṇu* developed the cult of Bhakti, and their works are looked upon as those of the highest authority by the followers of the two creeds. The *Śaiva* literature[4] was arranged into eleven groups, called Tiru-murai by Nambiāndār-Nambi of Tanjore in the time of Rājarāja Kulśekhara Chola (985—1013 A.D.). Of these eleven groups, the first three are the works of Tirujñāna Sambandamūrti Swāmī, the next three of Tiru-nāwukkarasu (Appar) and the seventh of Sundarar. These seven together form the *Devāram*. They contain hymns offering praise and prayer to God, and are used on ceremonial and religious occasions like the Vedas. The eighth book which corresponds to the Upaniśads is the *Tiruvāchakam* of Māṇikka Vāsahar, the ninth is the *Tiru-Isaippa*, a compilation of minor poets, the tenth contains songs of Tirumūlar, and the eleventh consists of miscellaneous writings of Nakkīrar, Nambi-āndār and others. These eleven books with the *Periya Purāṇa* (a *Śaiva* hagiology) constitute the sacred lore of the Śaivas.

The *Vaiśṇavas*[5] have a parallel collection of their hymns. This collection was compiled and arranged by Nāthmuni (tenth century) probably under the editorship of Nammālvār. This is known as *Nālāyira-Prabandham,* and is considered as sacred as the *Vedas.* The number of the Alvārs is reckoned as twelve. Four of them, Poygaiar, Pudattar (Bhūtattar), Peyar,

[4] & [5] Barnett: British Museum Catalogue of the Tamil Books.

Srīnivāsa Aiyangar: Tamil Studies.

Sundaram Pillai: Some Milestones in the History of Tamil Literature.

Tirumalisai were Pallavas and were the most ancient; three were Cholas—Tiruppanar, Tondarad ippodi, and Tirumangai; one was a Chera, Kulaśekhara; and the remaining four came from the Pāndya country—Periyār, Āndāl, Nammālvār, Madhurakavi.

Their history is of importance in the evolution of Hindu religions and it is necessary to give an account of the careers and achievements of the most important among them.

Tirujñāna Sambandhar[6] was born of Brahmin parents at Shiyāli in the Tanjore district in the seventh century. According to legend he began to compose hymns while he was only three years of age. When he grew up he wandered as a pilgrim to all the *Śaivite* shrines in Southern India singing *Śiva's* praises. His fame as a saint reached the court of Kūn Pāndya (Nedumaran) who ruled at Madura. The king professed the Jaina faith, but the queen Mangaiyarkkarasi and the chief minister Kulachchirai Nayanār were both staunch *Śaivites* and they invited Tirujñāna to exert his influence to change the mind of the king. He met the Jaina teachers in the royal presence and defeated them in discussion. The king was converted, but the Jainas refused to abandon their religion and so a large number of them were executed. He was an inveterate enemy of the Buddhists as is borne out by the uniform imprecations pronounced upon them in every one of his hymns. He appears to have entered into disputes with the Vaiśṇava saint Tirumangai Alvār also and in every way he was so stout a champion of *Śaivism* that the revival of the faith is mainly ascribed to him; he holds the foremost place among the great *Śaiva* preceptors and is actually regarded as an incarnation of *Śiva.*

The following hymns give an idea of his conception of God and of man's relation to Him:

For the Father is *Ārūr*
Sprinkle ye the blooms of love;
In your heart will dawn the light,
Every bondage will remove.

[6] Kingsbury and Phillips: Hymns of the Tamil *Śaivite* Saints.

Him the holy in *Ārūr*
Ne'er forget to laud and praise;
Bonds of birth will severed be,
Left behind all wordly ways.
In *Ārūr*, our loved one's gem,
Scatter golden blossoms fair.
Sorrow ye shall wipe away,
Yours be bliss beyond compare.[7]

Tirunāvukkarasu[8] (Appar) was an elder contemporary of Tirujñāna Sambandhar. He belonged to the Vellāla caste. He was left as an orphan at an early age and was brought up by his sister as a devotee of *Śiva*. But he forsook his faith and became a Jaina. Later he returned to the *Śaiva* fold and became a powerful influence in its growth. In his verses a deeper note of devotion is struck, his consciousness of sin is intense and his sense of dependence on *Śiva's* grace and of the ultimate breaking of the bonds of sin by His grace is certain. How close and intimate is God's relationship to man is brought out in this hymn:

Thou to me art parents, Lord,
Thou all kinsmen that I need,
Thou to me art loved one fair,
Thou art treasure rich indeed.
Family, friends, home art Thou,
Life and joy I draw from Thee,
False world's good by Thee, I leave,
Gold, pearl, wealth art Thou to me.[9]

In his exalted moods he rises high above all external forms of religion leaning unaided upon the mercy of God alone. He then knows that no ceremonial will help him, and that bathing

7 Kingsbury and Phillips : Op. cit., p. 25.

8 Ibid.

Pūrṇaliṅgam Pillai : Ten Tamil Saints.

9 Kingsbury and Phillips : Op. cit., p. 49.

in the Ganges, pilgrimages to Comorin, chanting of the Vedas, study of the *Śastras*, asceticism, penance and fasts, will not eventually avail.[10]

> "Release is theirs, and theirs, alone, who call
> In every place upon the Lord of all."[11]

Appar's *Śiva* is not a crude anthropomorphic conception but the being which dwells in all. "He is ever hard to find, but He lives in the thought of the good. He is the innermost secret of scripture, inscrutable, unknowable. He is honey and milk and the shining light. He is the King of the *Devas,*

> Immanent in *Viśṇu,* in *Brahmā* in flame and in wind,
> Yea, in the mighty sounding sea and in the mountains."[12]

Sunderamūrti,[13] the third of the joint authors of the *Devāram,* was a Brahmin. He was bron in the South Arcot District and lived in the eighth or ninth century. He was not rigid in his adherence to caste principles, for although he married twice, neither of his wives was a Brahmin. He was probably the last of the *Adiyārs,* for he has sung the praises of his sixty-two predecessors. The dread of death and faith in ultimate deliverance inform many of his hymns.

> The young saint refuge sought from Death;
> To save him, Thou grim Death didst slay,
> Such deeds might accomplisheth.
> And I who have beheld them pray,
> "O Father, should dread *Yama* press
> On me, forbid Him. 'Tis my slave';
> Do Thou in green *Pungūr* confess.
> I've reached Thy foot, and Thou canst save."[14]

10 Kingsbury and Phillips: Op. cit., p. 57.

11 Ibid., p. 57.

12 Ibid., p. 65.

13 Ibid.

14 Ibid., p. 79.

Māṇikka Vāsahar[15] (Māṇikya Vāchakar), the greatest among *Śaiva* saints, was born at Tiru Vathavur on the Vaigai river near Madura, of parents who belonged to the Amittiya section of the Brahmins. Māṇikka was a precocious lad and at the age of sixteen had acquired the whole of Sanskrit learning. His fame reached the ears of the Pāndya King who called him to the Court and appointed him Chief Minister. But although he lived surrounded with pomp and luxury the infinite woe of the world oppressed him. The story of his conversion is overlaid with miracles. It is related that the king sent him on commission to purchase horses which had arrived from the 'Aryan land' (Arabia). He started with great eclat, his march was a procession. On the way, he met a saintly Brahmin whose personality so impressed him that he accepted him as his *guru* (teacher). He spent the king's treasure in feeding the ascetics and returned without executing the commission. This brought upon him the wrath of the king, but at last he escaped through the *guru's* grace, for he was no other than *Śiva* himself. The *Guru* then laid upon him an injunction to convert the Tamil country to *Śiva's* faith. He became a wanderer visiting holy shrines singing *Śiva's* hymns, till at last he came to Chidambaram where he rested. He attended an assemblage of Buddhist priests which was gathered together by the King of Ceylon and attended by the Chera King. In discussion the Buddhists were worsted and the King of Ceylon became a *Śaivite*. This was the last triumph of Māṇikka's life, for some time after this he died. It is difficult to fix correctly his date, but in all probability his career lay in the ninth century.

There is deeper passion and fervour in his verses than in those of his predecessors, and without a doubt they must have powerfully affected the heart of his hearers. Dr. Pope says, "the effect of these songs—full of a living faith and devotion—was great and instantaneous. South India needed a personal God, an assurance of immortality, and a call to prayer. These

15 Pope : Māṇikka Vāsahar.

are found in Māṇikka Vāsahar's compositions."[16] Here are a few specimens of his songs:

"*Indra* or *Viśṇu* or *Brahma*,
Their divine bliss crave not I;
I seek the love of Thy saints,
Though my house perish thereby.
To the worst hell will I go,
So but Thy grace be with me.
Best of all, how could my heart
Think of a God beside Thee?"[17]

"I have no fear of births, but quake at thought that I must die.
E'en heav'n to me were naught; for earth's whole empire what care I?
O *Śiva* wreathed with honeyed blossoms, when shall come the morn,
When Thou wilt grant Thy grace to me? I cry with anguish torn."[18]

"Myself I cannot understand, nor what is day or night;
He who both word and thought transcends has reft my senses quite,
He who for bull has *Viśṇu*, and in *Perundurai* dwells,
O light supreme, in Brahman guise has cast on me strange spells."[19]

"I had no virtue, penance, knowledge, self-control
A doll to turn
At others' will I danced, whistled, fell. But me He filled in every limb,
With love's mad longing, and that I might climb there whence is no return,
He shewed His beauty, made me His. Ah me, when shall I go to Him."[20]

16 Pope: Op. cit., p. xxxvi.

17 Kingsbury and Phillips: Op. cit., p. 89.

18 Ibid., p. 91.

19 Ibid., p. 121.

20 Ibid., p. 127.

Of other *Śaiva* saints Tirumūlar, Nakkīrar, Nambiāndār Nambī, Śekkirār there is not much to write. They followed the same line of thinking and added to the volume of feeling created by their forerunners.[21]

The separation of the *Vaiṣṇava* cult from *Śaivism* and its development as a distinct sect was due to the *Ālvārs*.[22] They drew their ideas largely from the Sanskrit epics and the *Purāṇas.* Their hymns were collected together in the tenth century, and they were themselves canonised two or three centuries later, when their images were set up in temples and prayers were addressed to them to mediate for securing salvation. The *Ālvārs* were ardent worshippers of *Viṣṇu* and most of them were zealous opponents of Buddhism, Jainism and *Śaivism.* Some of them came from lower castes; some were Brahmins; one, Āndāl, was a woman; and Kulaśekhar was a king.[23] Tirumanpai wrote the larpest number of hymns, and Nammālvār was the foremost among the saints. Nammā's poems (*Tiruvāy-moli, Tiruvāśiriyam, Tiruviruttam* and *Tiruvantādi*) are considered as the four Vedas.

The hymns of *Vaiṣṇava* saints show the same type of thought and feeling as those of the *Śaivas.* They, however, substituted *Viṣṇu* in place of *Śiva* and sang his praises above all other gods; they also differed in regard to the belief in incarnation, for while *Viṣṇu* came down several times upon the earth to save mankind, *Śiva* did not do so, at any rate in the *Vaiṣṇavite* manner. A few extracts to illustrate their teachings are given below. The spirit of love of God and reliance upon His grace breathe through them.

"Mighty Lord of the Celestials! Thou hast made my heart Thy tabernacle. So intimate and close is Thy union with

21 Pūrṇalingam Pillai : Ten Tamil Saints.

22 Bhandārkar : Vaiṣnavism and Śaivism.

T. Rājagopālachariar : The Vaiṣṇava Reformers of India.

Other Literature as cited above.

23 Bhandārkar : Op. cit.

me that I beseech Thee never more to leave me,—me so lovingly clinging to Thee."[24] (Nammā)

"As dote I on the Lord of *Katkatai,*
Whose streets with scarlet lily are perfum'd,
My heart for His wonderful graces melts
How then can I, my restless love suppress ?"[25] (*Nammā*)
"The errors of I-ness, my-ness,
With roots pluck out, and join the Lord."[26]
"If men are drunk with the love of God, they ought
To dance like madmen in the streets; if they cannot
They are not love-smitten."[27]

The relation of devotee to God is like that of wife to her husband.

"Thou hast not yet been gracious enough to extend Thy sympathy towards Thy consort (*Ālvār*). Before she gives up her ghost in despair owing to Thy indifference show so much at least of Thy mercy as to send word to Thy consort through Thy messenger and vehicle *Garuḍa* the storehouse of kindness, not to pine away, but to take courage a little, till Thou, Lord and Master returnest as expected, which will assuredly take place soon."[28] (*Nammālvār*)

"O Lord, mayest Thou graciously hear the humble supplications of thy devotees......O Thou Lord of *Srīranga*! the Reliever of the great elephant (*Gajendra*).....Condescend to wake up from Thy conscious sleep to extend Thy gracious look on Thy servants."[29] (*Tondaradippodi*)

"I shall wed, if at all, none other than the Supreme Lord."[30] (*Āndāl*)

24 Govindāchārya : The Divine Wisdom of the Dravidian Saints, p. 103.
25 Ibid., p. 109.
26 Ibid., p. 2.
27 Ibid., p. 52.
28 Nityānusanādhanam Series, Book 3, p.54.
29 Ibid., Book 2.
30 Ibid., Book 2, (Andal).

The hymn singers of Tamil land were the creators of that powerful religious feeling which swept Buddhism and Jainism out of their country. The great scholastics who appeared simultaneously with them forged the intellectual instruments with which the resuscitated Hinduism fought and conquered. Among them the earliest and the most remarkable was Śankara.[31]

Śivaguru, a Nambūtiri Brahmin, and his wife Āryamba resided at Kaladi, a village situated on the north bank of the Alvar river on the Malabar coast. They were the parents of Śankara who was born at some time in the last quarter of the eighth century. The death of the father while he was young made the mother his sole guardian. She appears to have bestowed great affection and care upon him and his education. Śankara was a precocious child, he soon learnt all that his teachers could impart to him, he had an insatiable desire for learning and he was early smitten with the sorrow of the world. He left home and became a *Sanyāsin*, and took Govind Yogi, who was a pupil of *Gauḍapāda*, and who resided on the banks of the Narmada, as his teacher (*Guru*). He passed rapidly through all the stages of an ascetic's life and his *Guru* conferred upon him the degree of *Param Hamsa*. He then betook to travelling all over the country, discussing with religious teachers of all denominations and sects. His biographer Ānandaigri names nearly fifty different sectaries with whom Śankara had intellectual combats, and by defeating whom he celebrated his *Digvijaya* (world-conquest). Śankara visited Malabar several times after his retirement from the world. One of these occasions was when his mother died. The story is that the Brahmins raised objections to his performing the

31 *For Śankara's Life*, Krishnaswāmī Aiyar : Śankara and His Times.
Bhāsyāchārya : Age of Śankara.
Ānandagiri : Śankarra Vijaya.

For Śankara's teachings :—
P. Deussen : Philosophy of the Upaniśads.
,, Outline of the Vedānta.
G. Thibaut : The Vedānta Sūtras, S.B,E,, Vols. 34, 35.

funeral rites because he was a *Sanyāsin*, but he overbore the objections. His name is connected with great reforms in Malabar; and, according to legends, the Kollam era of that country which began in 825 A.D. marks the new epoch which these reforms inaugurated. Among these reforms none was more important than the banishment of Buddhism, and the abolition of rites connected with it and with other sects. He was also the organiser of monastic orders (*maṭha*), he opened the ranks of *Sanyāsins* to recruitment from all castes, but he excluded women from monastic life. If the story of the *Chanḍāla* who met him on the banks of the Ganges and asked him why he made a difference between his teaching and practice is true, then he appears to have been inclined towards social reform also. He wrote in the *Manuśa Panchaka*[32]: "He who has learned to look on phenomena in this light (monistic) is my true Guru, be he a Chanḍāla or a twice-born. This is my conviction." A consideration of his legendary life seems to indicate that Śankara was not a blind follower of the ancient ways, he attempted to introduce change, though cautiously, and he appears to have received opposition and opprobrium from orthodox Brahmins. He died young in the beginning of the ninth century.

Śankara's career is the great watershed in the history of Sanskrit learning. Behind him lies the world of ancient ideas, half reconciled systems, profound but scattered thoughts, rival philosophies struggling for ascendancy, the changing pantheon and theologies in a fluid condition, a living culture almost anarchic in its exuberance; before him the medieval world of set ideas, fixed systems, scholastic ingenuity, accretion not growth, explanation not invention, commentaries not philosophies, a stereotyped uniformity. The living stream of culture abandons the ancient bed of Sanskrit and flows through new channels—Tamil, Telugu and Canarese in the south, Hindi, Bengali, Marathi and Urdu in the north—but the abandonment

32 Krishnaswāmī Aiyar: Op. cit.

is never quite complete, an increasingly thinning rill continues to linger in the old beds.

Śankara's philosophy[33] which, in so far as thought systems may be considered to be causes of events, dealt a fatal blow to Buddhism, attempted to rally the Hindu sects together. The one aim of Śankara's endeavours was to remove the fatal weakness of Hinduism, the fissiparous tendency of its religious sects, which all claimed their authority from the same source, namely, the *Śrutis.* He employed the whole power of his keen analytic mind and his matchless dialectical skill in overthrowing all systems which disagreed with one another, and in establishing one logical system. It is a tremendous recognition of his genius that all later thinkers have taken Śankara as the starting point (*prasthāna*) of their thinking and more or less confined their labours to establishing, amending, or disproving his doctrines and interpretations. In doing so they have all become tinged with his ways of thinking and his methods of exposition.

Śankara had to establish that the sacred scriptures of the Hindus had one consistent teaching to impart; and that the differences of schools were due to misunderstanding and lack of true insight. Monism, according to him, was the outstanding feature of Hindu theology, a monism uncompromising, absolute, idealistic. God was one and there was no other besides Him. God was the only reality, all else was illusion. His nature was absolutely homogeneous. He was a pure being and pure intelligence. He was without attributes or qualities. He was not a thinking or knowing being, but thought or knowledge itself. The world was merely a phenomenon, an appearance, not a true reality. It evolved out of the principle of illusion (*māyā*). *Māyā* by self-modification gave rise to individuals distinguished by name and form, and the individuals made up the whole universe. In fact, however, the multiplicity of individuals is only apparent; in reality they are one. The plurality of sentient beings is equally illusory. The human ego is identical with God, his individuality is *Māyā,* his reality is *Brahman.* It

[33] See under 31.

is due to ignorance that he does not perceive the identity, and so lives a miserable existence in the phenomenal world which is only a creation of illusion.

As long as this ignorance lasts the weight of the phenomenal presses upon man. The phenomenal appears real and during the period of ignorance has to be taken into account. This phenomenal world has a god, *Īśvara,* who is endowed with good attributes. He is the creator who evolves and dissolves the world in cycles. The human soul looks up to Him for reward and punishment, for grace and forgiveness. It realises its good through knowledge of *Īśvara.*

Thus there are two worlds, one real, the other unreal; and there are two kinds of knowledge, one, the higher, for the removal of ignorance and the realisation of the absolute *Brahman,* the other, the lower, to win *Īśvara's* favour. But the lower knowledge and its end *Īśvara* are both phenomenal and true freedom is only attained by rising above it to the real. As, besidse the soul, the mind and intellect, the ordinary instruments of cognition are the products of *Māyā,* the higher knowledge cannot be gained as long as the activities of the mind are not completely controlled and stopped. In the moment when the mind is still and the path of impression is cut off and the state of deep trance (*Samādhi*) is induced, the soul realises its unity with the absolute and rids itself of the illusion of the phenomenal.

Śankara established a logical monistic system, but the cost at which it was done was great. On the one hand, God's unity was raised to such a giddy height of abstractness as to daze the ordinary mortal. On the other, by compromising this idealism by the acceptance of a world of lower good and lower truth, he almost handed over this poor mortal bound hand and foot to the mercies of the priest and his elaborate ceremonial. What he tried to drive out of the front door thus re-entered through the back door, and while he started to condemn, he remained to bless those very practices and doctrines which were fit only for the feeble and the ignorant.

Śankara's system, however, had a unique success. It dominated by the grandeur of its conception, the amplitude of its knowledge and the subtlety of its philosophy the thought of generations of men. Time has not yet dulled the freshness of its impress upon the Indian mind.

Śankara was the great protagonist of the path of knowledge, and among the learned and the philosophically minded his exposition of *Vedānta* had an extraordinary influence. Also vast bodies of *Smārtas* in the south and the west as well as in the north became his followers. But the religion of love and devotion, which the *Alvārs* and the *Adiyārs* were making popular, soon found its own philosophic exponents who entered the field of controversy and disputed the theories of Śankara. These were the *Vaiṣṇava Āchāryās*, and the *Śaiva Siddhānta* teachers.

The first among the *Vaiṣṇava Achāryas* was Nāthmuni who lived at Srīrangam in the tenth century. His grandson and successor was Yamuna-muni who was also known as Alvandar (victor). He was the teacher of Rāmānuja, and he directed him to write a commentary on Bādrāyaṇa's *Brahma Sūtras*, to refute the theory of illusion or Māyā, and to establish the religion of Bhakti.

Ṛāmānuja[34] was born in 1016 at Tirupati or Perumbur in the neighbourhood of Madras. His father Keśava was a Dravida Brahman of Harīta family and his mother's name was Kāntimati. He became at first the pupil of Yādava Prakāśa

[34] *For life of Rāmānuja* :—

Bhandārkar : Vaiṣnavism and Śaivism.
Rangāchārya : Life and Teachings of Rāmanuja.
K. S. Aiyangar : Rāmānuja.
Rajagopālāchāriar : Rāmānuja.

For his philosophy :—

G. Thibaut : Vedānta Sūtras, S.B.E., Vol. 48.
Sukhtankar : The Teachings of Vedānta According to Rāmānuja.
Bhandārkar : Op. cit.

Bhandārkar, Research for Sanskrit MSS. in Bombay Presidency for 1883-84.

who was a follower of Śankara at Conjeeveram, but he disagreed from his teacher on the interpretation of sacred passages and was dismissed from the class. He was then invited by Yamunāmuni, who taught at Srīrangam, to become his disciple. Soon after, the teacher died, and Rāmānuja was appointed his successor. He continued to study and teach, till at length he considered himself fit to carry out the directions of his *Guru* to write the promised commentaries, and then he composed his *Vedānta Sangraha,* the *Bhāśyas* of *Bādrāyaṇa's Vedānta Sūtras* and the *Bhagavadgītā.*

He had before becoming an author taken to *Sanyāsa,* and now he started on his travels accompanied by his disciples. He visited many northern countries as far as Kashmir and then returned to Srīrangam. Here he was threatened with persecution by the Chola King Kulottunga I (1095) who wanted him to renounce *Vaiśṇavism* for *Śaivism.* Rāmānuja took refuge in the dominions of the Hoysala Yādava princes, and converted Vithaldeva, brother of Ballāladeva. After the death of Kulottunga I in 1118, Rāmānuja returned to Srīrangam where he died in 1137.

The aim of Rāmānuja's teaching was the refutation of Śankara's absolute monism and *Māyāvāda* and the establishment of *Bhakti* within the philosophy of *Vedānta,* and, incidentally, also to obtain recognition for the non-Vedic *Panchrātra* in the Vedic literature.

According to him, *Brahman* is the one supreme reality possessed of unsurpassable greatness both in his nature and in his qualities. He is the Lord of all (*Īśvara*), and, as the universal soul, the Highest Person (*Puruśottama*). He is devoid of imperfections and endowed with numberless auspicious qualities of unequalled excellence. He has unconditional and unlimited power to realise His wishes and purposes. He creates, destroys and preserves. He does not create out of nothing, for creation out of absolute non-existence is inconceivable. His creation means change from one state to another, from existence in the causal condition (*kārana*) to existence in the effect condition (*kārya*). At first *Īśvara* was one without a second, but from within Him appeared matter and souls (*Prakriti* and *Jīva*), which form His body. They are both real, they do not bind *Īśvara* but are subservient to His will, and are dependent upon Him for existence. At the end of each *kalpa* (cycle of creation) the world is dissolved, the grosser substance in to subtler, till at last the ultra-subtle matter called darkness (*Tamas*) alone remains. This is the body of *Brahman*, but it is so subtle that it does not deserve a separate designation and is, as it were, non-existent. In this causal condition *Brahman* is one without a second, for the body (*Tamas*) is undistinguished by name and form and is non-existent. Then *Brahman* wills to become many and transforms itself into the effect condition, into the gross world of names and forms, into creation. Effect is no more than the evolution of the cause.

For purposes of meditation and worship *Īśvara* appears in five different manifestations: (1) as *Parā* or the highest in which form as Nārāyaṇa he lives in *Vaikuṇṭha* attended by gods, goddesses, eternal spirits and delivered souls; (2) as *Vyūhas* or hypostases of *Parā* in the four forms of *Vāsudeva, Saṁkarśana, Pradyumna* and *Aniruddha;* (3) as *Vibhava* or the incarnations of *Nārāyaṇa*; (4) as *Antaryāmin* in which mode he dwells within the heart and is seen in the Yogic trance; and, (5) as idols or images (*archa*) set up for worship.

The individual souls are the modes of *Brahman*. They are divided into five classes: (1) the *Nitya,* who never enter the cycle of births and deaths; (2) the *Mukta,* who have broken their fetters and attend on God as His servants; (3) the *Kevalas,* who have purified their hearts and who are free from birth and death; (4) the *Mumukśu,* who desire liberation and are endeavouring to attain it; (5) the *Bāddha* who are still bound.

The soul is conscious, self-illuminated, joyous, eternal, atomic, imperceptible to senses, unchangeable, the substratum of knowledge, unthinkable agent, subject to God's control, dependent for its existence upon Him, and an attribute or mode of God.

The soul attains God by *Bhakti*. It first purifies itself by sacrifice and the performance of duties (*karma*), and acquires concentration and meditation (*Jñāna*) which lead to actual visualisation (*Bhakti*). The three upper classes alone could practise *Bhakti*; for others there was the path of self-surrender or avoidance of opposition and resolution to yield (*Prapatti*), with complete trust in the preceptor (*Achārya abhimāna*).

The end of the path was release, a glorious freedom in which the soul enjoys eternal blessedness in the presence of God, partakes of His joys and, excepting creation, shares in his powers, transcending all prohibitions and commands and ranging freely through the universe.

Rāmānuja, although he still maintained the ancient privileges of the higher castes, opened a way for the *Śūdras* and the outcastes. He arranged that the outcastes should be able to attend certain temples on a fixed day in the year and he gave instruction to the *Satanis* who were a group of *Śūdras* whom he attached to his *Sampradāya*. His teaching with regard to *Prapatti* led to the formation of two schools. The northern branch (*Vadagalai*) holds that God's grace is co-operative, that is, the process of deliverance must begin with an act of a person seeking it. The southern branch (*Tengalai*), on the other hand, considers God's grace obligatory, for God must take entire possession of the soul of the devotee and lead him to Himself, his function being to surrender himself completely. The Northerners describe *Prapatti* as one of the ways of liberation, the Southerners as the only way. They also differ regarding their treatment of persons belonging to inferior castes, and in other details.

Nimbārka,[35] a younger contemporary of Rāmānuja, carried the doctrine of devotion further. Philosophically his system was based on the theory known as *bhedābhed* (difference without difference), that is, that God, the individual soul and the inanimate world are identical yet distinct. In religion he gave

35 Bhandārkar: Vaiṣṇavism and Śaivism.

predominance to the principle of self-surrender (*prapatti*), and to the worship of *Krisna* and *Rādhā*. Nimbārka although originally a Tailanga Brahman born in the Bellary district, spent most of his life in the North, in Brindaban near Mathura, whence the cult of *Rādhā* and *Krisna* spread in the North and in Bengal.

Ānandatīrtha or Madhva[36] (1199–1278) rejected both the unqualified Monism of Śankara and the qualified Monism of Rāmānuja, and established a system of frank dualism, based mainly upon the *Bhāgavata Purāṇa*. His object was to emphasize the independence and majesty of God which was compromised by his predecessors, who made Him the material cause fo the universe. Madhva's concepiton of God was that of the sovereign who ruled the world, and whose grace conferred deliverance on man.

A number of other *Vaiṣṇava* teachers developed these doctrines and spread the cult of devotion among the people. Among them were Viṣṇu Swāmī, Pillai Lokāchārya (born in 1213), Vedānta Desika (born in 1268), and many others in subsequent centuries.

Among the *Śaiva Āchāryas*[37] the earliest was Nambiāndār Nambī, a contemporary of Nāthmuni. He collected the *Śaivite* hymns into the *Devāram* (the divine garland) and the *Tiru-Murāi* (the sacred books). But the first of the *Śaiva* theologians was Meykandar Deva who was a *Śūdra* and lived in the thirteenth century on the bank of the Pennar river to the north of Madras. He translated the Sanskrit Raurava Āgama *Sūtras* into Tamil and called it *Śiva-jñāna-bodha* (Introduction to the Knowledge of Śiva). His disciple Arulnandī Deva wrote a commentary on the master's work and a polemic criticizing

[36] Bhandārkar : Vaiṣṇavism and Śaivism.

[37] Pope : Op. cit., Introduction.
Barnett : Museon, 1909.
Barnett : Śaiva Siddhānta, Siddhānta Dīpikā Vol. XI. Nos. 2, 3.
Barnett : J.R.A.S., 1910.
Frazer : Dravidians (South India) E. R. E.
Frazer : Śaivism, E. R. E.

other schools. A Śūdra disciple of Arulnandī was the author of another work on *Śaiva Siddhānta,* and the *Śūdra's* disciple was Brāhmana Umāpati (1313) who was the greatest theologian of the sect.

The Tamil *Śaiva Siddhāntas* were affiliated to Kashmir *Śaiva* Schools which had arisen in the ninth and subsequent centuries. The central doctrine of both was the trinity of *Pati* (lord), *Pāśu* (individual soul), and Pāśa (bond).

The systems into which this doctrine was expounded bear analogies with *Vaiṣṇava Pancharātra* systems. But, whatever the metaphysics of *Śaiva Siddhānta,* the practical religion was that of love and devotion. Its chief elements were: (1) faith in *Śiva* and his grace; (2) unquestioned belief in the teacher; (3) loving devotion and worship; (4) discipline of *Yoga* demanding concentration and accompanied with song, dance and ecstatic rapture; (5) toleration of all creeds; (6) protest against the externalia of religion, ritual and idol worship; and (7) religious equality of all irrespective of caste or sect or worldly position.

The distance which the Indian mind has travelled from the sober moderate, contemplative devotionalism of the north and the fervent ardour and explosive passion of the religion of *Bhakti,* of the south, is great. The mystic note is struck clearly in both. But mysticism is universal and eternal. It appears in all cultures and in all periods of man's history. It is an activity of the human mind obscure and ill-understood, arising out of dark regions carefully protected from the intrusion of intellect, a phenomenon of the subconscious self, a function of the subliminal consciousness. The mystic feeling dwells where abide libido, and impulse of sex and fear and desire.[38] It has thus a world-wide significance and a history coeval with that of man.

[38] Evelyn Underhill: The Essentials of Mysticism.
Bertrand Russel: Mysticism and Logic.
Pratt: Psychology of Religious Life.
Starbuck: Psychology of Religion.
Cohen: Religion and Sex.
William James: Varieties of Religious Experiences.

It is obviously futile to attempt to discuss the origins and migrations of mysticism in history, for mystical experience is implicit in all religions. But mysticism is a protean phenomenon. Its expression takes infinite forms. In different lands it has different intellectual formulas and theories; it employs different phrases and idioms, and in doing so it borrows language and imagery; it accentuates certain aspects of faith and tends to ignore others. It is possible to observe the modifications of form and expression and to render an account of the debts which one culture owes another.

The growth of the emotional religion, the *Bhakti* school, both in the ancient epoch in the north and in the early medieval times in the south, has been traced above. The development of the speculative side of religion and of its social aspects through the efforts of poet-saints and theological thinkers has also been described. It now remains to enquire into the causes of its growth, the reasons of the striking differences between the ancient beliefs and practices and the early medieval ones.

Much of the difference may be accounted for by the social upheavals, religious conflicts and political movements of the times, in short by the fact that thought moves as life moves. Much may be due to natural developments in the intellectual field, the logical springing forth of schemes from seeds in earlier systems. It may, for instance, be urged that the passionate *Bhakti* of the later age is the necessary outcome of the devotion in the *Bhagavadgītā, Svetaśvatara Upaniṣad* and *Mahāyāna Buddhism,* that the increasing emphasis on the unity of God is the extension of the ancient monotheism of the Upaniṣads, that the rejection of externalia or caste is a reversion to the purer forms of ancient Buddhism and Jainism.

All this may be granted, yet the progressive simplification of the faith and the deepening of its emotion as time passes does not seem to be completely explained by the causes just mentioned. These circumstances seem to point to the working of a steady force with fixed tendencies in reference to which the movement of Hindu thought pressed onwards, and whose influence, which began to operate early, continued to grow with time. The need for such a cause has been felt for a long time and most writers on the history of Hindu religion have sought to discover it. Grierson[39] felt it strongly, as appears from his remarks in reply to Keith and Kennedy's criticism of his paper *Modern Hinduism and its Debt to the Nestorians.*

Pope,[40] in the introduction to the translation of *Mānikkā Vāsahar,* notes two features of this *Bhakti* which appear to him new. He says, "here can be no doubt but that the idea of special devotion is expressly taught in the Gītā, but the devotion of the *Śaivite* to the *Guru*—who is a man, a holy, humane, divinely endowed teacher—differs very widely from this, or any previous Hindu conception of loving service." Again, "*Bhakti,* or loving piety, is the main idea of the *Śaiva* system, and the fervent self-negative love and worship of *Śivan* is represented as including all religion, and transcending every kind of religious observance, and since all are capable of this, men of all castes can be received as devotees and saints in the *Śaiva* system.... In fact, it (love) seems to be something pertaining to the semitic religions especially."

Burnell,[41] Weber,[42] Logan,[43] Caldwell,[44] Hopkins[45] and Bhandārkar[46] along with Pope and Grierson ascribed these changes to the influence of Christian communities in the south. Barnett,[47] Macnicoll,[48] Estlin Carpenter,[49] hold more or less ex-

39 Grierson: Modern Hinduism and its Debt to the Nestorians, J.R.A.S., 1907.

40 Pope: Op. cit., p. lxvii.

41 Burnell: Indian Antiquary, Vol. III, p. 308; Vol. IV, p. 183.

42 Weber: Indian Antiquary, Vol. III, pp. 21, 47.

43 Logan: Malabar.

44 Caldwell: A Comparative Grammar of the Dravidian Languages

45 Hopkins: India Old and New.

46 Bhandārkar: Vaiṣnavism and Śaivism.

47 Barnett: Heart of India, Bhagwad Gīta, etc.

48 Macnicoll: Indian Theism, Appendix C.

49 Estlin Carpenter: Theism in Medieval India; Noe on Christianity in India.

plicitly that the development was due to internal causes only, because the historical conditions necessary for Christian contact in the south were wanting. Fawcett,[50] however, in his Notes on *Some of the People of Malabar* suggested that Islam was probably the needed factor. He wrote, "something may be said of the legendary story surrounding the great Śankarāchārya, the apostle of the Nambutris. He was born at Kaladi near the Eluvayi river when the country was in peril. Her king had been converted to Islam, and that religion was gaining ground. Brahmanism must be revived, so *Śiva* was re-incarnated in the child of a widow." The circumstances of his practical excommunication with all his family by the Brahmans, and his seeking a Nāyar's aid in performing the rites of the dead on the demise of his mother, point to the same conclusion. And Barth[51] in the *Religions of India* argued in a similar strain. He says, "The Arabs of the Khilāfat had arrived on these shores in the character of travellers and had established commercial relations and intercourse with these parts long before the Afghans, Turks, or Mongols, their co-religionists, came as conquerors. Now, it is precisely in these parts that from the ninth to the twelfth century, those great religious movements took their rise which are connected with the names of Śankara, Rāmānuja, Ānandatīrtha and Bāsava, out of which the majority of the historical sects came and to which Hindustan presents nothing analogous till a much later period."

It is necessary to repeat that most of the elements in the southern schools of devotion and philosophy, taken singly, were derived from ancient systems; but the elements in their totality and in their peculiar emphases betray a singular approximation to the Muslim faith and therefore make the arguments for Islamic influence probable. It is true that among the schools discussed so far the evidence is all circumstantial and the argument for borrowing cannot be substantiated by direct proof, philological

50 Fawcett : Anthropology, Bulletin, Vol. III. No. I. Edited by Thurson.
51 Barth : Religions of India.

or otherwise; but it must be remembered that the Hindus were a proud race as Alberunī remarked. They were great artists in the assimilation of foreign ideas and they did not allow their prestige to be lowered by crude imitations which could be easily detected. The history of the whole of Indian culture in the ancient period is a testimony to the correctness of these statements.

The influence of Islam was in the first stages indirect and selective. It was not the result—so far as can be ascertained—of a study of the Muslim literature, but of the teaching from the mouth of religious ascetics or of observation of their rites and customs. In a previous chapter the occasion of contact and the opportunities of influence have been discussed. There were plenty of Muslims settled on the coasts where the great Tamil teachers arose, they wielded sufficient power to attract notice and held a sufficiently respected status in the land to enter into intercourse with the people. The history of the development of Islamic thought shows how in the Muslim countries ideas had been evolved which were analogous to the Hindu ideas and which could therefore be presented without shocking them. The material of contact although peculiar, was not thus entirely heterogeneous. It is necessary to examine it in order to find out what contribution it could have made to the development of Hindu thought.

HINDU REFORMERS OF THE SOUTH: II

THE parallels between the Indian systems developed in the south by Śankara and his successors and the schools of Muslim theology and mysticism are startling in their similitudes. Both systems of thought appear to have undergone an evolution which ran on similar lines. The Indian mind starting with *Śruti* and the Muslim with the *Qurān,* both enjoining a religion of action, passed through the stage of rationalisation to devotional and emotional religion. Sabara and Kumāril, the predecessors of Śankara, were *Mīmānsakas* who tried to re-establish the religion of action and sacrifice. Their appearance marked the turning point in ancient Indian religious thought. Śankara found a philosophic basis for this new movement and set definitely the direction in which the Hindu mind was to work in subsequent ages.

The difference between the aspect of religious history in the pre-Śankaran or ancient, and post-Śankaran or medieval periods is great. In the ancient period there is not one religion but many religions—Brahmanism, Buddhism, and Jainism. Brahmanism itself is in a curiously fluid condition, syncretism is taking pace in its pantheon on at least three lines—*Śiva, Viṣṇu* and *Śakti.* Along the first line the *Rudra* of the Vedas gathers under his expanding wings the gods of hills and forests, of the Himalayas, the Vindhya and the Tamil land, the red lord of terror and the bright lord of healing combine, the dread human and animal sacrifices and Vedic rites combine, the magic of ruder tribes and the speculations of the civilised combine, and these produce the *Śiva* of the *Mahābhārata,* the *Pāśupata* and similar philosophical systems, and the *Śaiva* cults. Similarly, along another line the Vedic *Viṣṇu,* the *Vāsudeva* of the *Sātvaṭas,* the *Kriṣṇa* of the *Yādavas,* the *Gopāl Kriṣṇa* of the *Abhīras* are joined in one conception of an *Ekāntin* God, the cults of various tribes are merged inot Bhāgvata and Pancharātra worship and their speculation in the Bhagavad Gītā and Vaiṣṇava Samhitas. Śākta philosophy, worship and cult follow exactly the model of the *Śiva* sect. In Buddhism and Jainism the influence of neighbouring sects and the assimilation of alien elements produce complexities which have been described elsewhere. All these processes which go on throughout the ancient period leave on the mind an impression of great complexity and bewilderment, although as time passes the confusion begins to simplify.

According to some sociologists, all religions in their beginning must have been monotheistical; each tribe had one god whom it worshipped. As tribes joined together, either because of war or of struggles for means of living, their gods were brought together and polytheism arose; and as the joint tribes became uniform and gained in solidarity so again the many gods coalesced into one dominant god. If this theory is correct, it throws a great deal of light upon the process of the emergence of the three deities *Śiva, Viṣṇu* and *Śakti* in India. After the Guptas had vanquished the barbarous Huṇas in the fifth century, no large accession of foreign tribes took place in India for the next five or six hundred years. The Muslims, who settled on the western borders or on the coast from the eighth century onwards, came in small communities and did not produce any large disturbance in the settled populations. The fluid mass of thought and religion had therefore time to settle. The peoples of India in the ancient times were divided into numerous tribes politically independent or semi-independent, and culturally diverse as the literature of the Vedic and Buddhist[1] periods clearly attests. The incursion of the Scythians, Yueh-Chis, Huṇas and others added to the diversity already existing. The assimilation of the tribes and their cultures was the task of the various periods of ancient history. During the Gupta period the last of the syntheses took place, and gave to Brahmanism a unity of which

[1] Rhys Davids: Buddhist India.

the literary expression is the *Mahābhārata* and the religious symbol the Trimurtī.

Śankara was born when this modification had been accomplished and Hinduism was already triumphing over its rivals, Buddhism and Jainism. He was thus a child of the times, but he was also the precursor of a new age. Monotheistic worship had been vindicated, by the labours of his predecessors, but it had to be established on the firm foundations of philosophy, so that not merely the will but also the intellect might become convinced and its permanence be assured.

The establishment of this monotheistical tendency received a powerful impetus from the appearance of so uncompromisingly monotheistic a religion as Islam. Śankara was born at a time when Muslims were beginning their activities in India, and, if tradition is correct, when they had gained a notable success in the extension of their faith by converting the king of the land. He was born and brought up at a place near which many ships from Arabia and the Persian Gulf touched. If his extreme monism, his stripping of the *One* of all *semblance* of duality, his attempt to establish this monism on the auhtority of revealed scriptures, his desire to purge the cult of many abuses, had even a faint echo of the new noises that were abroad, it would not be a matter for great surprise or utter incredulity. But Śankara's life is wrapped in legend and direct testimony of any kind is completely lacking to establish a connexion between him and Islam.

His successors, Rāmānuja. Viṣṇuswāmī, Madhva and Nimbārka, and the hymn-makers, in their speculations and religious tone, show closer parallelism. In the give and take of culture between Muslims and Indians it is difficult to assess accurately the share of each. It is true that the Muslims received many ideas from India and perhaps India received through Islam a reflection of its own contribution. It is true that Christian and neo-Platonist thought deeply coloured Islam and therefore some writers have found in Hinduism traces of those systems. But the fact remains that a number of elements were absorbed into Hinduism through its direct contact with Islam and these elements were presented to India impressed with the Islamic mould.

In Rāmānuja's time Muslims were to be found in the ports of the Coromandel coast. Muslim saints like Nathad Valī were preaching Islam to the people and converting numbers of them, and Hindu kings like Kuṇ-Pāndya were giving grants of land for the erection of mosques. The existence of the Christians at Malaipuram is more than doubtful; and, in any case, the small uninfluential community professing a corrupt form of that religion could hardly influence the thoughts of its neighbours. As Barth has pointed out, it was not in general the monotheism of the Christian religion which most struck the Hindus.[2]

Ramānuja's philosophy recognised a god with good attributes and inculcates His worship with faith and devotion. He exhibits a desire to open the doors of religion to the classes which had so far been shut out of it. Love finds a place not only in the relations of man and God, but also of man and man, although in the latter case the advance is timid. Viṣṇuswāmī, Nimbārka and Madhva's metaphysical discussions regarding the nature of God and man almost recall the debates of Nazzām, Ah'arī and Ghazālī. But these resemblances may be easily fanciful or due to the nautre of the enquiries themselves, and no reliance can be placed upon them for deducing any inference regarding cultural borrowings.

Certain other characteristics of South Indian thought from the ninth century onwards, however, strongly point to Islamic influence. These are the increasing emphasis on monotheism, emotional worship, self-surrender (*prapatti*) and adoration of the teacher (*Guru bhakti*) and in addition to them laxity in the rigours of the caste system, and indifference towards mere ritual.

It is hardly necessary to expatiate at length on the first point. The conception was ancient, but was not dominant.

2 Barth : Religions of India.

Practical religion consisted in either the performance of good actions and sacrifices, or in following a system of mental and spiritual training (*Yoga*) without dependence on a god with whom intimate personal relationship could be established. This is mainly the teaching of the *Dharma Śāstras, Mahābhārata* and *Sānkhya-Yoga* philosophy. The Upaniṣads and the unorthodox Bhāgavatism were exceptional. They appealed to a small esoteric coterie, the last to tribes outside the pale of Vedic Brahmanism, till they were admitted inside the fold and their systems were recognized.[3] Philosophical religion dwelt in the region of abstraction and only practical needs forced it to take account of the conception of God. Buddhism and Jainism were largely atheistical; only in later times did Mahāyāna develop a theistic cult, but the worship of *Amitābha* was only one of the numerous sects.

In medieval times monotheism becomes the prevailing religion of India. The One God may be called by different names, *Śiva, Viṣṇu* or any other, and there may be different theories about His existence, creation and relation with man. But He is One above all. Then He is a personal god. Again the conceptions of personality may differ. He may be king and master, father or mother, friend and teacher, spouse and lover. In every case the human relation with Him is emotional, usually tender. The emotion in the earlier times is calm, and restrained, in later times exuberant, passionate, violent.

The hymns of the *Alvārs* deprecate externalia in religion, fasts and pilgrimages, and, occasionally, image worship, and inequality in worship. Rāmānuja admitted the *Śūdras* (under restrictions) to temples and provided the faith of self-surrender (*prapatti*) and of adoration of the *Guru* (*āchāryābhimāna-yoga*) for their spiritual welfare. These features of the reform movements could hardly be due to Buddhism and Jainism for both were in their later days rigidly bound up with ceremonialism and image worship, which was indeed one of the many

3 Ram Prasada Chanda : Indo-Aryan Races.

causes of their downfall. They could scarcely be derived from the prevailing types of the Hindu religion, for the worship of *Viṣṇu, Śiva* or *Śakti* was ritualistic as well as that of the other Vedic sects. Some of them might be affiliated to older and purer froms of Buddhism and Upaniṣadism, but *Prapatti* and *Guru-bhakti* not quite.

The idea of *Prapatti* attains importance in the school of Rāmānuja, where *Bhakti* is permitted to the three higher classes alone, but not to the *Śūdras*.[4] The last are *Prapannas,* who take refuge in God, feeling themselves poor and helpless. They fling themselves on the will of God, renouncing everything worldly, seeking the advice of a preceptor and acquiring from him the impulse to action. Later the *Vaiṣṇavas* were divided into two branches on the question of *Prapatti.* And Nimb-ārka gave great predominance to this method of winning the grace of God.

Prapatti is closely connected with the adoration of the teacher (*āchāryābhimāna-yoga*) which consists in surrendering oneself completely to a teacher and being guided by him in everything.

Bhandārkar is of opinion that both these elements may be traced to the influence of Christianity.[5] It is more likely, however, that they came from Islam. Both were very prominent features of that religion. The word *Islam* means surrender, and the Muslim is verily a *Prapanna.* It has been shown that submission to the will of God is an essential part of the Muslim religious consciousness. Historically also there is no insuperable difficulty in supposing that Rāmānuja adopted it from Islam.

Absorption in God through devotion to a teacher is again an important Muslim conception. It was started by the *Shī'as* and from them taken by the *Sufis.* But it may be urged that the reverence to a teacher is an ancient Indian idea. Without going further back one may find it in the *Gṛhya Sūtra* and the

[4] Bhandārkar: Vaiṣṇavism and Śaivism.
[5] Ibid., p. 57.

Dharma Śāstras.[6] They lay down rules governing the relation of *Guru* and *Brahmachārī* (student). The student is asked to regard his *Guru* as more than his father, to pay him perfect obedience during the period of studentship and to hold him in reverence throughout life. The teacher is even compared to God.[7] But this ancient homage that the disciple paid to the preceptor is not the same thing as devotion to a spiritual director who is human yet divine, who is a link in the hierarchical chain of preceptors (*pīr, shaikh, murshid* or *qutb*), each the successor receiving inspiration from his predecessor and being the keeper of the traditions of the sect to which the novice once admitted belongs for ever.

This *Sufi* conception of the deified teacher was incorporated in medieval Hinduism. Ānandagirī's conception of Śankara as the incarnation of *Śiva*,[8] the estimation of the Alvārs and the Āchāryās as incarnations of *Viṣṇu* or his parts, and Umāpathi's *Guruvāda*[9] are all assimilations to the *Sufi* type. From them the idea spread all over India, so that a modern Hindu writer says, "nothing strikes as so peculiar in Hindu religious life as the high pedestal on which the spiritual teacher is placed and the implicit faith which the community has in him for weal or woe."[10] The *ācharyābhimāna-yoga* of the *Artha Panchika* and Rāmānuja system were loans then not from Christianity but from Islam.

The appearance of new ideas and the emphasizing of certain old ones in Southern India from the ninth to the fourteenth century is rather peculiar. Such things did not happen in the North, for all the early medieval reformers belonged to the South. If one of the reasons was not the influence of Islam

6 Asvalayana : Grihya Sūtras, III, 4, 4, S. B. E.
Āpastamba : Dharma Sūtras, 1, 1, 13-19, S. B. E.
Manu : Dharma Śāstra, II, 146, 148, II, 243-44, S. B. E.

7 Śvetāśvatara Upaniśad, Hume's translation.

8 Ānandagiri : Śankara Vijaya.

9 Pope : Introduction to Māṇikka Vāsahar.

10 Rājagopālāchariar : The Vaiṣṇava Reformers, p. 12.

steadily and increasingly exerted during this very period and in this very region till it was suddenly eliminated by the advent of the Europeans, it would be difficult to account for the phenomenon, still more so considering that the reforming shears were applied to the very parts anathematised by Islam, and that the new acquisitions were the very features which most prominently marked that religion.

Before leaving the South two more sects require consideration, in which the influence of Islam appears more clearly than in those considered so far. They are the Lingāyats or Jangamas and the Siddhārs.

The Lingāyats consider themselves an ancient *Śaiva* sect. Without disputing the fact of their ancient lineage from one of the many branches of *Śaivism* and admitting the probability that the *Ārādryas* made an early attempt to organise a reformed *Vaiṣṇava* faith, it may be taken for granted that the uncompromising Lingāyatism arose in the twelfth century. Who were the leaders of this movement? Basava and Channabasava, his nephew, are universally recognised by the Lingāyats. Dr. Fleet, on the strength of an inscription of about 1200 A.D. found at Ablur, associated *Ekānta* (or *Ekāntada*) Ramayya with Basava as the founder of the sect.[11] Some *Śaiva* poets who lived in the court of a Ballāl raja—Harīśvara, Rāghavaṇika, and Kereya Padmarāsa—are said to have espoused similar views.[12] Basava, however, whether he was the actual founder of the system or not, was its most powerful advocate and sponsor. It is not necessary to extricate all the details of his career from the conflicting accounts of the legendary historians. It is enough to know that he was the Minister of Bijjala, the Kalachūrī king who ruled at Kalyān, 1156—1167. The Jaina and Brāhmaṇa influences were strong at the court and in the kingdom, and Basava was an uncompromising enemy of both. A conflict in the circumstances was inevitbale and Bijjala and Basava were both simultaneous victims of mutual hostility. Basava's nephew

[11] Epigraphia Indica, Vol. V. p. 239.
[12] Wurth : J. Bo. Br. R.A.S., Vol.VIII, pp. 65—221,

Channabasava carried on the propaganda after the uncle's death. The movement started by Basava had wide and lasting effect. The power of the Kalachūrīs was completely undermined so that Kalyān soon after fell into the hands of the Hoysalas, from whom the kingdom passed to the Muslim conquerors from the north.

The system of Basava in its original form was one of resolute and wholesale opposition to the prevailing religious thought. It was revolutionary all along the line in doctrine, ritual and social custom, so much so, that in spite of all the attempts of the Lingāyats to tone down its daring originality they have not succeeded in completely obliterating its individuality or in assimilating it to orthodox Hinduism.

The Lingāyats are worshippers of one God (*Para Śiva*), the infinite, independent, invisible Being, the highest radiance, the supreme joy, the most excellent substance, exalted above all change and void of all materiality. He is the creator of souls and of nature which are conceived of as the self-diremption of the supreme Being. He manifests himself as the world-teacher (*Allama Prabhu*) and guide of the individual soul (*Śiva* the Redeemer). The human teacher, Basava, is the incarnation of the Redeemer, whose divinity passes to his successors and representatives. The first four among them are especially revered—Revān, Marūl, Ekorāma and Pandit. According to Brown they are analogous to the four *'pīrs'* of the Musalmans, the canonised spiritual guides, who "play the same part in the ceremony of making a Musalman *murīd* that the four *Ārādhyas* do in that of making a *Jangam*. They too are described in an apostolical succession."[13] The preceptor initiates the novice into the creed. "The rules regarding initiation are analogous to those used among Musalmans."[14]

Love is the first creation of God. *Bhakti* or faithful devotion is the means of attaining the goal of human life. It is an attraction towards God and there are three stages in the progress

13 & 14 Brown: Madras Journal of Literature and Science, January 1840, p. 146.

of the soul. The first is the stage of indifference which involves firm belief in God, the discipline of vows and restraints and the practice of rites and devotion; the second involves the renunciation of egoism, concentration in God, resignation and serenity; the third, the sharing the joys of blissful union and seeing God in oneself and in everything else.[15]

The practices of the Jangamas are summed up in the *ashta-varanam* (the eight environments), they are—(1) *guru* (preceptor), (2) *lingam* (phallus), (3) *jangama* (follower), (4) *vibhūti* (ashes), (5) *rudrākśa* (rosary), (6) *pādodaka* (water in which the preceptor's feet are washed), (7) *prasāda* (sacramental food), (8) *panchakśara* (five-syllabled formula).[16]

The preceptor is considered as 'superior even to the deity.[17] The *lingam* is the symbol of divinity embodied in the saints. The *jangam* represents the incarnation of the deity in the whole community. He is the passive principle, *Śiva* is the active, and the preceptor the intermediate link between the two. The formula (*namah Śivāya*) is the confession of faith and the remaining elements are the ritual of the sect.

There are no sacrifices, no fasts or feasts, no pilgrimages. "There is no river (purificatory ceremony) for a *Lingāyata*."[18] There is no caste, "even if a Pariah joins the sect, he is considered in no way inferior to a Brahman."[19] There are no distinctions based on differences of birth or sex. "All men are holy in proportion as they are temples of the great spirit."[20]

Marriage is voluntary, the consent of the bride before marriage is necessary and child marriage is considered wrong. Divorce is allowed. Widows are treated with respect, and they are permitted to marry again. The dead are not cremated but

15 Brown: Madras Journal of Literature and Science, January 1840, p. 150.

16 Bhandārkar: Op. cit., p. 136.

17 Thurston: Castes and Tribes of South India, Lingāyats, p. 280.

18 Ibid.

19 Ibid.

20 Brown: Op. cit., p. 146.

buried, the dying man is given a bath, no *śrāddha* or death ritual is prescribed. The theory of transmigration of souls or metempsychosis is not believed in. All *Lingadhāris* or wearers of the divine symbol eat together, intermarry and live in unity.

Lingāyats are devout, puritanical and warlike in their character.[21] They are found chiefly in the Kanarese and Telugu countries, constituting thirty-five per cent. of the total population in the Belgaum, Bijapur and Dharwar districts and ten per cent. in the Mysore and Kolhapur States.[22] They call themselves *Vīrśaivas*, the brave followers of *Śiva*.

Whence did they develop their peculiar doctrines and social institutions? Brown, although he noticed the resemblances with Muslim ideas inconsequentially came to the conclusion that "an observation of the Christian faith in the neighbouring country of Malayala may have led to his (Basava's) seeking a better creed."[23] This is, however, a mere fancy. There is no evidence for the existence of a Christian community on the Konkan coast. On the other hand, the whole of Western India from Cambay to Quilon was studded with Muslim colonies, established in the early centuries of the Muslim era. Nairn, after investigating the Musalman remains on the Konkan coast, arrived at the conclusion "that the Musalmans of this part, who differ so strongly from others of their religion in physical appearance, in dress, and in some of their customs, must be descended from sea-faring Arabs who settled on this coast, and not from the Musalman conquerors of India."[24] It is difficult to resist the inference that Lingāyatism was a result of the influence which these Muslims exerted in these parts of India. No other hypothesis appears sufficient to explain the revolutionary

21 Brown : Op. cit., p. 175.

22 Thurston : Op. cit.

23 Brown : Op. cit., p. 145.

24 Nairn : The Muslim Remains on Souuhern Konkan. Indian Antiquary, Vol. II, pp. 278, and 317; Vol. III, 181.

character of its doctrines and customs. The abandonment of such a deep-rooted Hindu idea as that of metempsychosis and of such customs as cremation and purificatory death ceremonial, the abolition of inequalities of caste and sex and the reform of marriage, the conceptions of the community of brave warriors led by their sanctified prepceptor, and of God (*Allama*) whose very name is probably of Muslim origin,[25] point unmistakably to the source of inspiration, that is, Islam.

It is easily comprehensible that after the downfall of their kingdom and the conquest of their lands by Muslim armies from the north at the end of the thirteenth century, the reformers, dismayed by the effects of the schism that they had started, attempted to bring about a reconciliation with the peoples surrounding them and professing more orthodox views, and, therefore, deliberately or compelled by force of circumstances or by sheer neglect, they mitigated the sharp outlines of their system and gradually permitted the reappearance of such features as caste to creep in. Thus the *Lingāyats* of today, although still distinct from other Hindu communities, are fast becoming identical with them. The memory of their earlier career and its vicissitudes is, however, still preserved in the prophecies of Channabasava who predicted that sixty years after the rule of the Kalachūrīs "the great Pitambar will be born by the blessings of *Śiva* among the Turks, and his house will reign over this country seven hundred and seventy years, demolish Kalyan and build Kalaburigī" and the country will be called *Turkānya.* But ultimately the great Vasantarāya will rise, who will drive out the foreigners, rebuild Kalyāna, take Channa as the Minister of his realm, and establish the faith.[26]

The following extracts from the *Vachanas* attributed to Basava illustrate the doctrines of the Lingāyats.[27]

[25] Brown : Telugu and English Dictionary.
Kittel : Kannada and English Dictionary.

[26] Wurth : Op. cit., p. 220.

[27] Halkathi, P. G. : Indian Antiquary, Vol. II, 1922.

There is One God

(1) Thou art the only Lord and Thou art eternal; this is Thy title. I proclaim it so that the whole world may know. There is no word beyond the Almighty God, the Almighty God *Pāśupati* is the only God in the whole universe. In all the heavenly world, the mortal world and the nether world, there is only one God, *O Kudalasangama Deva.*

(2) I did not see those so-called gods alive, when the four *yugas* and the eighteen cycles of those *yugas* were being destroyed; nor did I see them, when all was burning; nor do I see them now. Neither that day nor this day, do I see those gods, except *Kudalasangama Deva.*

How can I say that the god that, filled with lac, melts down, or the god that, being touched with fire, twists itself, is equal to Him? How can I say that the god that is sold, when the time comes, is equal to Him? How can I say that the god that is buried, when there is fear, is equal to Him? *Kudalasangama Deva* is the only one God whose state is natural, who is in union with truth, eternal, pure and chaste. O think: there is only one husband to a wife that loves. So there is only one God to the devotee that believes. Oh, do not seek the company of other gods. To speak of other gods is adultery.

God is Universal

Ah, wherever I look, there Thou art, O God! Thou Thyself art one with a universal eye. Thou Thyself art one with a universal mouth. Thou Thyself art one with universal arms. Thou Thyself art one with universal feet, *O Kudalasangama Deva.*

Thy width is as wide as the universe, wide as the sky, wide as the widest. Thy auspicious feet are far beyond the nether world, and Thy auspicious crown far far above the globe of the Universe. *O Linga,* thou art unknowable, immeasurable, impalpable, and incomparable, *O Kudalasangama Deva.*

Do Not Believe in Expiatory Ceremonies

O you who have committed sinful deeds! O you who have killed a Brahman! Say only once, "I yield myself to God." If you say once, "I submit," all sins break and fly away. Even mountains of gold will not suffice for expiations. Hence, say only once, "I submit," to that only one, our *Kudalasangama Deva*.

Do Not Sacrifice

Leave it alone, that Horse-sacrifice, leave it alone, that initiation into the *Ajapa Mantra*. Leave it alone, that offering in fire, and those countings of the *Gāyatri* spell. Leave them alone, those charms and incantations for bewitching people. But the company and the words of the servants of *Kudalasangama Deva,* mark, are greater than any of these.

With one who knows not the subtle path of God, the time of the eclipse is far superior to the twenty-four *tithis*. The fast day is far superior to *"Sankrānta"*. Sacrificial offerings and the daily rites are far superior to *Vyātipata*. But to one who constantly meditates on *Kudalasangama Deva,* such meditation is far superior to innumerable countings of *mantras* and the performance of severe penances.

Do Not Believe in Caste

Do they look for beauty in an enthroned king? Should they look for caste, when one is worshipper of God *Linga*? Why, it is the word of God that the devotee's body is His body.

None but the ancients can know it. O stop, stop. Only the devotee of God is of the highest caste. Hence no distinction of caste should be observed. He is neither born nor unborn. The servant of *Kudalasangama Deva* is limitless.

What, if he has read the four Vedas? He that has no *Linga* is a *Māhar*—what if he is a *Māhar*? He that has the

Linga is Benares. His clusters of words are good. He is holy in all the worlds. His *Prasād* is nectar to me. It is said, "My devotee is dear to me, even though he is a *Māhar*. He is acceptable to me. He should be worshipped even as I am." Since it is so said, then he that worships *Kudalasangama Deva,* and knows Him, is greater than the six philosophies and is pure in all the worlds.

The *Vedas* trembled and trembled; the *Śāstras* retired and stood aside; Logic became dumb; the *Āgams* went out and withdrew; for our *Kudalasangama Deva* dined in the house of Channayya, the *Māhar*.

What does it matter what caste he belongs to? He that wears the symbol of God is of the highest caste. It has been said, "The caste of him who is born from God is sacred and he is free from births. His mother is *Umā* and his father is *Rudra,* and certainly his caste is Īśvara." Since it is so said, I will accept the remains of their food and will give them my child in marriage. *O Kudalasangama Deva,* I place my trust in thy servants.

Work Without Desiring Anything in Return

Mere strings of words such as "God is the soul of all created beings" will never do instead of the work which is your duty. You ought to use up your body, mind and soul for *Guru,* the servants of *Kudalasangama Deva.*

The State of Sarana

Do not compare things that are incomparable. They are devoid of time and action, devoid of worldliness, Thy servants, *O Kudalasangama Deva.*

Is the sea great? It is bound by the earth. Is the earth great? It stand on the head-jewel of the Lord of serpents. Is the Lord of serpents great? He is only a signet-ring on the little finger of *Parvatī*. Is *Pārvatī* great? She is only one-half of the body of *Parameśvara*. Is *Parameśvara* great? He is confined on the edge of the top of the mind of the servants of our *Kudalasangama Deva*.

His origin is not like that of the creatures of the air. Thy servant is a creation of Linga. He sticks to one. His heart does not vacillate. He penetrates the mind. He forgets his bodily qualities and worships Thee. He is, as it were, Thine own reflection, *O Kudalasangama Deva*.

A State of Final Absorption

Ah, what can I say about the bliss I feel, when my body melts, like a hailstone in water, or an image of lac in fire? The waters of my eyes have overflowed their boundaries. Oh, to whom shall I speak of the happiness of uniting with *Kudalasangama Deva* in oneness of mind?

I know not the earth, the sky or the ten quarters. I do not understand them. They say, "The whole universe is contained in the centre of the *Linga*," but, like a hailstone, I fell into the midst of the ocean; I am overwhelmed in the happiness of the touch of the *Linga;* and am saying only, "God," knowing nothing whatever of duality.

The *Siddhārs* were a school of philosophical rhymists, who were *Yogīs* as well as medical men and alchemists. It is difficult to determine their age for all signs of the school have now completely disappeared and their writings have undergone much interested editing. Mr. Srinivasa Aiyangar, a Brahmana scholar, does not speak of them in terms of praise. He calls them impostors and plagiarists who assumed the great names of antiquity like Agastiyar, Kapilar and Tiruvalluvar to throw dust into the eyes of the people. According to him, they were eaters of opium, dwellers in the land of dreams, and full of unbounded conceit.[28]

[28] Srinivasa Aiyangar: Tamil Studies, p. 226.

It is manifest, however, that they did not like the Brahmanas. They ridiculed them in their writings and poured unlimited contempt on their social institutions, religious observances and sacred books. They were monotheistical quietists who retained the name of *Śiva* as that of God, but rejected everything in the *Śiva* system which was inconsistent with pure theism. Their *summum bonum* was to apprehend and approach that *Eternal Light* which they termed *Parāṇjoti, Peroli* or *Vetta veli.*[29]

Thou shalt adore the world's one Light,
Who at a thought this vast earth framed,
Made noble man, then, dawnlike, flamed
A priest (*Guru*) upon His sight.
No kin had he of mortal race;
Ascetic-wise hard deeds He wrought,
Then having made disciples (*Siddhās*), sought
The Unlimitable Place.[30]

God is "the Light whom earth and heaven and hell cannot contain,"[31] and He is my king, the King of Kings.[32] God is transcendent for He "stands far, far and far, beyond all beings, utmost pale,"[33] and yet within, "His sacred feet are in your heart.[34]

They believed in one God, in one true preceptor (*satguru*), in one way for all men, and rejected the theory of many births and the authority of the Hindu sacred scriptures.

God is one and the *Veda* is one;
The disinterested, true *Guru* is one, and his
initiatory rite is one,

29 Srīnivāsa Aiyangar : Tamil Studies.

30 Caldwell : Tamil Pŏpular Poetry, Indian Antiquary, 1872, Vol I, p. 203.

31 Ibid., p. 101.

32 Ibid., p. 179.

33 Ibid., p. 100.

34 Ibid., p. 179.

When this is obtained his heaven is one;
There is but one birth of men upon earth;
And only one way for all men to walk in.
But as far as those who hold four *Vedas* and six *Śāstras*.
And different customs for different peoples,
And believe in plurality of gods,
Down they will go to the fire of hell !"[35]

The denunciation of those who do not agree with them is quite Islamic in its fierce sternness.

The *Siddhārs* were followers of the path of devotion and of love. Tirumūlar says:

The ignorant think that God and love are different.
None knows that God and love are the same.
Did all men know that God and love are the same,
They would dwell together in peace, considering love as God.[36]

True worship does nor consist in bowing
To idols made of clay, or mud
Baked in the fire. No image made
Of stone or wood, no *linga* stump,
Built of earth and made by hand,
Could ever seem divine to one
Who knew he came from God.[37]

Or in the worship of gods and goddesses.

How many flowers I gave
At famous temple shrines !
How many *mantras* said !
Oft washed the idol's head !
And still with weary feet
Encircled *Śiva's* shrines !

[35] Caldwell: Comparative Grammar of the Dravidian Languages, Second Edition, p. 147.

[36] Ibid.

[37] Gover: Folk Songs of Souhern India, p. 162.

But now at last I know
Where dwells the King of Gods,
And never will salute
A temple made with hands.[38]

What then is true worship? Śivāvakyār replies :

My thoughts are flowers and ashes,
In my breast's fane enshrined,
My breath too is there in it
A *linga* unconfined :
My senses too, like incense
Rise and light bright lamps shine,
There too my soul leaps over
A dancing-God divine.[39]

Worship needs the guidance of the teacher, and therefore it is necessary to

"Be faithful to the glorious priest (*Guru*)
Who teaches truth. Receive from him
The heavenly light that shall make clear
What body is and what is soul.[40]

The *Siddhārs* did not believe in caste. Patirakiriyār asks the Brahmans,

O Brahmans, list to me
And answer if you can.
Do rain and wind avoid
Some men among the rest
Because their caste is low?
When such men tread the earth
Hast seen it quake with rage?
Or does the brilliant sun
Refuse to them its rays?[41]

38 Caldwell : Indian Antiquary, Vol. I, p. 170.
39 Ibid., p. 101.
40 Gover : Op. cit., p. 162.
41 Caldwell : Indan Antiquary, Vol. I, p. 168.

He deeply yearned for the coming of the brother of man,

> When shall our race be one great brotherhood
> Unbroken by the tyranny of caste ?[42]

But he has a firm faith that it will come,—

> O Brahmans list to me !
> In all this blessed land
> There is but one great caste,
> One tribe and brotherhood.
> One God doth dwell above
> And He hath made us one
> In birth and frame and tongue.[43]

It will be seen from the ample quotations given here that the *Siddhārs* were severely monotheistic, they had no use for *Vedas* and *Śāstras,* or for idolatrous practices, and they repudiated metempsychosis. The hymns of the *Siddhārs* remind one of the uncompromising severity of Islam. Their conceptions of God and absorption in Him are reminiscent of the teachings of the *Sufis,* for both describe the ultimate reality as Light and both give to Love a dominating position among universal forces. In regard to alchemy especially they were the disciples of the Muslims,[44] their attitude towards it was the same as that of Dhul Nūn Misrī[45] and of those who followed him. One last quotation will show how much they were imbued with *Sufi* phraseology :

> That highest one is not a beauteous rose
> Nor doth He hide Him in the sweet perfume.[46]

In short, the progress of religious thought in the south reveals a growing absorption of Muslim ideas into Hindu

42 Caldwell : Indian Antiquary, Vol. I, p. 102.

43 Ibid., p. 168.

44 Barth : Religions of India.

45 Nicholson : J.R.A.S., 1906.

46 Caldwell : Indian Antiquary, Vol. I, p. 177.

systems. The philosophies of Śankara, of Rāmānuja and others had their roots in the systems of the past, their presentation was original, but in the case of the latter it appears probable that they did not grow up utterly regardless of the new currents of thought which then flowed in the country. But if in their case it is only possible to give a judgment which must be largely conjectural, the evidence leaves almost no doubt that the *Vīrśaivas* and the *Siddhārs* were largely influenced by Islam.

THE ADVENT OF THE MUSLIMS IN THE NORTH

When the empire of Harṣa fell the North broke up into small principalities. Rajput clans starting from their original homes in the West spread north and east establishing the chieftaincies in the Himalayan regions, in the plains watered by the Ganges and the Jumna, and in the wide stretch of territory broken up by the Vindhya and Kaimur ranges between Gujarat and Orissa. Even those who had no title to the name of Rajput constructed imaginary pedigrees and affiliated themselves to the dominating race. The Rajputs thus were the masters of the destinies of India from the Panjab to the Deccan and from the Arabian Sea to Bengal before the Muslims appeared upon the scene.

Under their sway great changes came upon the social life and culture of Northern India. The old landmarks—racial, political and religious—were obliterated. The ancient tribes mentioned by Varāhamihira in the *Vrihat Samhita*[1] or those conquered by Samudra Gupta[2] in the fourth century, Lāṭās, Pānchālas, Arjunāyanas, Yādavas, Mālavas, Kośalas, Vatsas, Śakas, Ānartas, Videhas, Kurus, Matsyas, Chedis and innumerable others, disappeared; and their places were occupied by Gurjaras, Rāśtrakūtas, Gaharwārs, Kalachūrīs, Chandels, Chauhāns, Parihārs, Tomaras, Panwārs, and Solankīs. Feudal institutions swept away the ancient councils and assemblies and tribal kingdoms. The ancient imperialistic idea—the over-lordship extending from sea to sea—vanished, and a kind of balance of power, of alliance and counter-alliance of princes, took its place, making civil strife a daily habit and national unity a rare dream.

[1] Kern: Varāhamihira's Vrihat Samhitā. Verspreide Geschriften 1913-14.

[2] Vincent Smith: J.R.A.S., 1897, pp. 19, 859.

The ancient seats of culture and regions of busy and humming life changed. Magadha was no longer the cradle of empire; Pātaliputra and Gayā were in ruins, and in their walled cities there were few inhabitants; Vaiśālī, Kuśinagara (Kania), Rāmagrāma, Kapilavastu and Śrāvastī, the cities renowned in Buddhist history, were desolate. The scenes of political activity had shifted from the middle country to the west and the extreme east. Kanauj, Gwalior, Delhi and Anhilwaḍa, and Ajmer in the west and Gaur in the east had risen into prominence as centres of political life, art and literature.

In religious matters a vast transformation took place. The India of Harṣa was still mainly Buddhist or *Śaivite*. India in the eleventh century, as Alberuṇī saw it, was quite different. Buddhism or a mixture of Buddhism and *Śāktism* or *Tāntrism* was confined to one corner of the country, namely, Bengal; Jainism maintained its existence in the extreme west, Gujarat and Rajputana; but the dominant creed of India was Hinduism, and here *Viśṇu* or *Nārāyaṇa* is the first god in the pantheon of his (Alberunī's) Hindu informants and literary authorities, whilst *Śiva* is only incidentally mentioned, and not always in a favourable manner.[3] The transformation was due to the ascendancy of the Brahmans in the social life of India, an ascendancy which began in the Gupta period and was completed when the foreign immigrants were received into the Hindu social system. The Brahmans transformed the Scythians, the Huṇas, the Śakas and other foreigners, and the Gonds and Bhils and other indigenes into Rajputs; and the Rajputs paid the price of their elevation from barbarism to civilisation by accepting and confirming their claims of superiority. *Vaiśnavism*, at one time a heterodox system, had very early been appropriated by the Brahmans as peculiarly their own. *Śiva's* worship was, however, the religion of the common folk or semi-Hinduised peoples. The first recommended itself to them because the priest played such an important part in it, the latter's ritual might be performed

3 Sachau : Alberunī, Vol. I, p. xlvii.

without a priest. The Rajputs themselves were attached to *Śiva,* they built numerous temples in Gujarat, Rajputana and Bundelkhund, dedicated to him, but in deference to the views of their benefactors paid worship to *Viśṇu* and erected his temples and created endowments for their maintenance. Even today, however, the Rāṇās of Mewar consider themselves *Dīwāns* or vicegerents of *Śiva,* and when they visit the temple of *Ekalinga,* supersede the Brahman high priest in his duties and perform the ceremonies.[4] The information of Alberunī was, however, derived from his Brahman teachers, and he naturally received the impression that India was dominantly *Vaiśṇava.*

The impression was perhaps exaggerated but not wrong. The Guptas had encouraged *Viśṇu* worship, they had set up pillars to *Viśṇu* and proclaimed themselves in their title adorers of *Bhagwat.* Perhaps a setback was given to the spread of *Vaiśṇavism* in the period immediately succeeding their downfall. But the movement again became vigorous under Rajput princes. The Gurjara-Pratihār ruler of Kanauj, Mihira Bhoja (840—90 A.D.) posed as an incarnation of *Viśṇu,* Ādi Varāha, and his successor was obliged to surrender an image of *Viśṇu* to his powerful ally, Yaśovarman Chandel who built for it a splendid temple at Khajurāho.

About the same time the doctrines of *Bhakti* which were taught in the South by the *Alvārs,* travelled to the North and gave new strength to the *Vaiśṇava* movement. The *Bhāgwata Purāṇa* was the result of these religious upheavals. The *Ahetuki* (motiveless) *Bhakti* which the Purāṇa preached was based on monotheistic philosophy.

The *Bhāgwata Purāṇa* conceives of God as free, pure and omniscient. He is changeless, primeval, without constituents (*nirguṇa*). He is the soul. He beholds the intellect in the light of consciousness. He is absolute joy. He is the creator and protector. "Even as a cow suckles her ignorant calf and protects it from ferocious animals, so Thou deliverest persons

4 Tod : Rājasthān, Vol. II, p. 602 (edited by Crooke).

distressed."[5] He is ever loving towards His votaries and delights in their devotion; by His grace the devotees snap the consciousness of ego tied with actions, and "as the fire of greatly increased flames reduces pieces of wood into ashes so devotion unto Me consumes all sorts of sins."[6] God is absolute, but personal, and He incarnates upon earth for the welfare of man and the protection of His devotees. The *Bhāgwata Purāṇa* describes at length the events of the life of His complete incarnation, Kṛṣṇa, in order to stimulate the love of His votaries and to spread the doctrine of *Bhakti.*

The aim of *Bhakti* is described by Prahlāda, the exemplar of *Bhaktas.* He says, "I who know the result of the enjoyment of corporal beings am not desirous of having longevity, prosperity and wealth, and even the pleasures and privileges of *Viranchi* which contribute to the gratification of senses. Neither do I wish to possess the *Siddhis* (miraculous powers) ......Convey me besides Thine own servants."[7] In the path of devotion and love, expiatory ceremonies, rigid mortification, even knowledge of the *Śāstras* are of no avail. It demands a discipline of concentration of mind, practice of virtues, meditation and asceticism, friendship towards all, companionship of devotees, chanting the glories of the Lord, repeating His names, thrilling with joy begotten of love, surrendering the mind to *Hari,* to weep, laugh, dance and sing with joy.[8] The seeker after God, who desires to cleanse himself of all impurities and to escape from the meshes of mundane existence, should seek refuge with some ascetic as a preceptor, and "he should be shorn of malice and with reverence, devotion and love serve his preceptor considering him as identical with me."[9] The path is open to all, to a *Śudra* and a *Śupacha* or *Chandāla,* even the

[5] Dutt : Bhāgwata Purāṇa, Book IV, Chap. IX.

[6] Ibid., Book XI, Chap. XIV.

[7] Ibid., Book VII, Chap. X.

[8] Ibid., Book IX, Chap. III.

[9] Ibid., Book XI, Chap. XVIII.

leader of the elephant herd who appealed to the Lord for mercy was saved from the dread jaws of the alligator.[10]

The devotional religion of the *Bhāgwata Purāṇa* opened the way for the spiritual emancipation of the individual, it did not remove the chains of social slavery, it still demanded that the followers of *Bhāgwata*, "forsaking all desires should act in consonance with their castes."[11] Nor did it hold an uncompromising position regarding the external forms of worship. It regarded *Yoga*, knowledge, virtue, study of *Vedas*, asceticism, charity, sacrifice, vows, worship of deities, *mantras* (spells), journey to sacred shrines, self-control, as inferior to the companionship of the devotees, yet not quite dispensable to devotion.[12] It prescribed the worship of idols and symbols, and meditation upon the image of God according to Yogic methods.[13]

The *Bhāgwata Purāṇa* marked the transition from the ancient religion of books to the medieval religion of *Bhakti*. But the influence of the emotional elements in the faith was not strong enough to counteract effectually the growing rigidity of caste or the growing power of the priest. The period of Rajput ascendancy was one of division and conflict. Society was enfeebled by feudal anarchy and clannish pretensions on the one side and by religious dissensions and priestly selfishness on the other. But although political power suffered an eclipse, literature, art and science still continued to flourish.

Bhavabhūti, Rājaśekhara and Kṛṣṇa Miśra, the author of *Prabodha Chandrodaya*, continued the traditions of Kālidāsa. In mathematics, astronomy and other branches of science, Bhāṣkarāchārya succeeded Āryabhatta, Brahmagupta and Varāhamihira. The art of sculpture devoted to the service of Hindu gods was developed in diverse styles by many schools

[10] Dutt : Bhāgwata Purāṇa, Book VII, Chap. X.

[11] Ibid., Book XI, Chap. X.

[12] Ibid., Book XI, Chap. XII.

[13] Ibid., Book XI.

of artists, and architectural monuments were raised on a magnificent scale.

Upon this scene of petty Rajput feuds and glorious Rajput art the avalanche of the Muslim conquest burst. The Muslim advance from across Baluchistan into Sind, in the eighth century, was held up by the inhospitality of the country and the difficulties of maintaining communications with far off Baghdad, especially when rebel chiefs blocked the ways which led from the centre of the Caliphate to its outlying territories. Nearly three centuries passed till attacks were resumed but now they proceeded from a different quarter. Subuktagīn and Mahmūd undertook their annual forays from the north-west. Their effect was not great, some temples were plundered and a few cities were sacked, the Hindu-Shāhīya dynasty and with it the Hindu dominion disappeared from the Panjab, otherwise things remained as heretofore. Permanent conquest in India was not the aim of the Ghaznavides, who looked for empire towards the west. Another century passed, during which the disturbances created in Central and Western Asia by the rise of the Turks turned the attention of the Ghorī rulers of Afghanistan definitely in the direction of the east.

Here the victim was ready for the sacrifice. India on the eve of Muslim conquest resembled Greece before the rise of Macedonia into power. There was the same incapacity in both regions to create a political union, and there was the same keenness and brilliance in the pursuit of science, literature and art. The analogy went further, for if the Macedonian was the semi-hellenised Greek, the Turk, who swept over India, was the non-Hinduised Rajput.

The thirteenth century had hardly begun when the conquest of Northern India was completed. Within a quarter of a century the Muslim armies had overrun the country from the Panjab to Assam and from Kashmir to the Vindhyas. The Rajput princes offered scarcely any resistance, they were all taken by utter surprise. Each one fought singly, bravely, but no one showed any particular foresight, and collectively they showed complete lack of cohesion and power of combination. The story of Lakśmana Sena, the last ruler of Bengal, may not be accurate history; nevertheless, it is true history. If the Muslim generals were at all in the habit of writing despatches, if they needed a motto for their reports, they might have done worse than choose the victorious announcement of Julius Cæsar—they came, they saw and they conquered. A hundred years more and India down to Mysore lay within their grasp.

The Muslim conquest had a tremendous effect upon the evolution of Indian culture. Superficially, it upset everything: the Hindu religion received a terrible blow, the state patronage of the priest and Pandit ceased, the Hindu monuments were destroyed, literature received no royal encouragement and languished; to all outward appearances political conquest was synonymous with cultural death. Fundamentally, it had a different effect. The Muslim kings displaced the Hindu Rajas in the important principalities. Delhi, Kanauj, Gwalior, Anhilwaḍa, Deogir and Gaur passed into their hands; not so the outlying countries. Then, too, the new ruler was master of the immediate lands within striking distance of his cavalry encampment; beyond, the petty landholder with his retinue was safe within his mud castle and defied the sovereign power. To reduce these small chieftains was a task of Sisyphus. Every energetic ruler of the many dynasties that sat upon the throne of Delhi from the time of Qutb-ud-din Aībak to the spacious days of Akbar had to carry out annual *razzias* to keep them under control or to collect revenue. In fact the imperial authority masked a surprisingly extensive system of local autonomy which tended continually to break out into anarchy when not kept in check by a Balban, an 'Alā'uddīn Khiljī or a Muhammad Tughlaq.

Muslim authority was not only restricted in these two ways, it had also to impose upon itself other restraints. The employment of the Hindus was a necessity of their rule. Mahmūd of Ghazni had a numerous body of Hindu troops who fought for him in Central Asia, and his Hindu commander Tilak suppressed the rebellion of his Muslim general Niyāltigīn. When Qutb-ud-din Aibak decided to stay in Hindustan, he had no other choice but to retain the Hindu staff which was familiar with the civil administration, for without it all government including the collection of revenue would have fallen into utter chaos. The Muslims did not bring with them from beyond the Indian frontiers artizans, accountants and clerks. Their buildings were erected by Hindus who adapted their ancient rules to newer conditions, their coins were struck by Hindu goldsmiths, and their accounts were kept by Hindu officers. Brahman legists advised the King on the administration of Hindu law and Brahman astronomers helped in the performance of their general functions.

The Muslims who came into India made it their home. They lived surrounded by the Hindu people and a state of perennial hostility with them was impossible. Mutual intercourse led to mutual understanding. Many who had changed their faith differed little from those whom they had left. Thus after the first shock of conquest was over, the Hindus and Muslims prepared to find a *via media* whereby to live as neighbours. The effort to seek a new life led to the development of a new culture which was neither exclusively Hindu nor purely Muslim. It was indeed a Muslim-Hindu culture. Not only did Hindu religion, Hindu art, Hindu literature and Hindu science absorb Muslim elements, but the very spirit of Hindu culture and the very stuff of Hindu mind were also altered, and the Muslim reciprocated by responding to the change in every department of life.

The effect of Islam upon Hindu sects in the South has been traced in a previous chapter. The movement which started there continued to develop in the North. The religious leaders in Mahārāśtra, Gujrat, the Panjab, Hindustan and Bengal from the fourteenth century onwards deliberately reject certain elements of ancient creeds and emphasize others and thus attempt to bring about an approximation between the Hindu and Muslim faiths. At the same time Muslim Sūfī orders and Muslim writers and poets show a strong tendency to assimilate Hindu practices and doctrines, in some cases going so far as to adopt even the adoration of Hindu gods.

The Indian architecture of the period exhibits the same synthetic tendency. The Hindu palaces, temples and cenotaphs are no longer built on the lines of the pure styles of the preceding period; they not only employ the Muslim elements of architecture, but they also breathe a new spirit which demonstrates how much the ancient æsthetic values have changed. Again, the influence is not confined to any particular part of the country, it appears most strongly among the Hindu principalities of Rajputana and Central India, in holy places like Mathura, Brindāban and Benares, and it is felt in far off Khatmandu and distant Madura. The mosque, the tomb and the palace of the Muslim are equally Indian. The Musalman borrows certain definite features from the styles of the so-called Arab and Persian architecture, but evolves a new style in India or rather a number of new styles, which continue the traditions of Hindu styles. As a matter of fact the architectural schools of the period, whether Hindu or Muslim, are really two branches of the same tree for both spring from the same root. Their purpose differs but the significance of their form remains the same.

Indian painting, Mughal or Rajput, is like Indian architecture. In fact here, even more than in architecture, one æsthetic law governs the form. The difference between the style of Ajanta and that of Delhi or Jaipur is great; line, colour and rhythm have all changed. But the difference between Delhi and Jaipur or Kāngḍā is just the difference between two individual artists of the same school and hardly more. The influence of Central Asian and Persian art is evident; but Indian art, whether produced in the courts of Mughal emperors and Nawabs or those of Hindu princes of Rajputana or Tanjore, does not imitate slavishly the foreign models. It has an individuality all its own, and it can only be described by the term Muslim-Hindu art.

In literature, Sanskrit no more provides the medium for the most vital needs of the people. Thought creates new instruments of self-expression. In the north Hindi, in the west Marāthī, and in the east Bengālī develop into literary languages, and Hindus and Musalmans share in the glory of their achievements. Above all, a new linguistic synthesis takes place: the Muslim gives up his Turkish and Persian and adopts the speech of the Hindu. He modifies it like his architecture and painting to his needs and thus evolves a new literary medium—Urdu. Again both Musalmans and Hindus adopt it as their own; and a curious phenomenon occurs, Hindī Bhāṣā is employed for one kind of literary expression, Urdu for another; and thus whenever the creative impulse of the Muslim or the Hindu runs in one channel, he uses Hindi and when it drives him into the other he uses Urdu.

Moulavī Muhammad Husain Āzād in comparing Hindi and Urdu composition lays bare the secret. The first lends itself to the creation of a natural, direct, simple, sweet, unperiphrastic and non-exaggerated style, which is racy of the associations, traditions and emotions of its native soil. The second is involved, subtle, high-flown, throbbing with the energy of rhythm and the power of words, the pomp of imagery and the splendour of diction, and drawing its metaphors and similes from Persia and Turkestan.[14] Another writer, Mīr Ghulām 'Alī Āzād of Bilgrām says, "The creators of significance in Arabic and Persian have drawn blood from the arteries of thought, and raised the style of subtle thought to the highest stage. The magicians of India have not remained behind in this valley; on the other hand, in the art of *Nāyekā Bheda* (descriptions of heroines) they place their magic-making steps far in advance of them. Whoever has acquired both Persian and Hindi and fully cultivated a taste to distinguish between what is white and what is black, will endorse the words of the *fakīr* (the writer).[15]

[14] Muhammad Husain Āzād: Āb-i-Hayāt, pp. 27—68.

[15] Mīr Ghulām 'Alī Āzad: Maāsir-ul-Kiram, p. 352.

Of the numerous Muslim poets of Hindī and of the Hindu poets of Urdū space forbids a lengthy notice. The history of Hindi literature written by Pandit Shyām Bihārī Miśra and his brothers furnishes a list of the first and any Tadhkira—Munshi Śrī Rām of Delhi is responsible for the latest,—gives that of the latter. Mīr Ghūlam Alī Āzād mentions the names of eight Muslim poets of Bilgrām who wrote in Hindi and quotes extensively from their works.[16] Muslim influence upon Hindi[17] as such was deep and is seen in its vocabulary, grammar, metaphor, prosody and style; what is true of Hindī is true of Marāthī[18] and Bengālī [19] and more so of Panjābī[20] and Sindhī.

In science the Hindus had inherited highly developed systems of mathematics, astronomy and medicine and they had laid the Arabs under obligation to them in these departments of knowledge. But the Arabs borrowed from Greece a great deal and on the combined basis of Hindu and Greek ideas built up original structures of their own. When, therefore, the Muslims came into India, they brought with them their own scientific systems, which were not inferior to those of the Hindus, and possessed some novel features. The Hindus did not disdain to incorporate what they found new with their own systems. Thus the Hindu astronomers took from the Muslims a number of technical terms, the Muslim calculations of latitudes and longitudes and various other items of the calendar (*Zīch*) and in horoscopy a whole branch which they called *Tājīk*. Maharaja Jai Singh (1686—1743) occupied himself with

16 Mīr Ghulām 'Alī Āzād : Op. cit.

17 Muhammad Husain Āzād : Op. cit.

18 'Abdul Haq : The Influence of Persian on Marāthī. Urdū, a quarterly magazine of the Anjuman-i-taraqqī-i-Urdū (April 1921).

19 Dinesh Chandra Sen : History of Bengālī Language and Language.

20 Newton, E. P. : Grammar of the Panjābī Language;
Grierson, G. A. : Linguistic Survey, Panjābī.

the reform of the Hindu calendar. He established observatories at Jaipur, Mathura, Delhi and Benares. His Pandits translated the *Al-Majistī* (Almagest) from Arabic into Sanskrit, and in the preparation of his *magnum opus*, the *Zīch Muhammad Shāhī*, he used the astronomical tables of Uḷugh Beg, Nāsir-ud-dīn Tūsī, al Gurgān (Ilkhānī), Jamshed Kāshī (Khāqānī), and others. Hindu medicine borrowed from the Muslims the knowledge of metallic acids ant many psocesses in iatro-chemistsy and arts. Of the many crafts and arts that the Muslims introduced in India mention may be made of the manufacture of paper, of enamelling and faience, many woven stuffs and damascening. If in the economic life of India the changes produced were considerable, in the social and political life they were great. The Islamic outlook upon social life was democratic, it set little value upon birth and heredity, and its influence quickened in Hinduism the feeling of social equality and tended to break down social barriers. Politically, pre-Muslim India was feudally particularistic; each small tribe cherished its autonomy and acknowledged grudgingly the suzerainty of the Emperor. The State was a kind of feudal hierarchy of chiefs of tribes and clans, of province, district and village, and suffered from all the evils of such a system. Muslim domination tended to break up the far too many centres of independent power, and to suppress the series of lords and chieftains who interposed between the Central Government and the individual, and thus to create a political uniformity, and a sense of larger allegiance.

It is hardly possible to exaggerate the extent of Muslim influence over Indian life in all departments. But nowhere else is it shown so vividly and so picturesquely, as in customs, in intimate details of domestic life, in music, in the fashions of dress, in the ways of cooking, in the ceremonial of marriage, in the celebration of festivals and fairs, and in the courtly institutions and etiquette of Marāthī, Rajput and Sikh princes. In the days of Bābar the Hindu and Muslim lived and thought so much alike that he was forced to notice their peculiar

"Hindustānī way"[21]; his successors so gloriously adorned and so marvellously enriched this legacy that India might well be proud today of the heritage which they in their turn have left behind.

21 Beveridge : *Memoirs of Bābar.*

RAMANANDA AND KABIR

Rāmānanda was the bridge between the *Bhakti* movement of the south and the north. There is a great deal of uncertainty with regard to the dates of his birth and death. According to Bhandārkar[1] and Grierson,[2] he was born in 1299 A.D. Macauliffe[3] places him between the end of the fourteenth and the first half of the fifteenth centuries, and Farquhar[4] agrees with him. Nābhājī does not give any dates; the Agastya Samhita[5] gives the date of birth as 1299 A.D. (1356 Samvat); and a Sanskrit commentary of *Rahasyatrayi* by Agraswāmī, 1299 A.D.[6] Bhandārkar and Grierson both consider that Rāmānanda was the fourth in spiritual descent from Rāmānuja. This, however, does not seem to be borne out by tradition. Nābhājī only says, "The immortal glory of Rāmānuja's system prevailed upon earth. Devāchārya (was the first) and Hariyānand the second greatly renowned (teacher), from him Rāghvānanda came who gave great joy to the devotees......From him was manifested Rāmānanda who incarnated for the joy of the world."[7] Nābhāji here only mentions the names of some specially famous saints who were in the direct line of descent from Rāmānuja but does not name all of them. Sītārām Bhagwān Prasād[8] definitely states that Rāmānanda was twenty-second in descent, Devāchārya (or Devādhīpa Āchārya) being sixth from Rāmānuja, Hariyānanda fifteenth from Devāchārya, and Rāmānanda next

1 Bhandārkar: Vaiśnavism and Śaivism.

2 Grierson: J.R.A.S., 1920.

3 Macauliffe: The Sikhs, Vol. VI.

4 Farquhar: Outline of the Religious Literature of India, p. 323.

5 Sītārām Śaran Bhagawān Prasād: Bhakta Māla, p. 264.

6 Ibid.

7 Ibid.

8 Ibid.

to Hariyānanda. If Rāmānuja's date of death was 1137 A.D. and twenty teachers followed him before Rāmānanda then it is more likely that he was born about the end of the fourteenth rather than that of the thirteenth century.

The date of his death again is difficult to determine. Bhandārkar puts it at 1411 A.D. (1467 Samvat), Farquhar at 1470 A.D. and the Sanskrit commentary at 1448 A.D. (1505 Samvat). The date of Bhandārkar is obviously unacceptable; it is incompatible with the date of his birth and the dates of his disciples. The date of Agraswāmī gives him nearly fifty years of life but raises no great difficulty with regard to the dates of his disciples. Farquhar's date fits all the facts easily but it does not appear on what authority it is based. The authors of the history of Hindi literature, *Miśra Bandhu Vinoda,* vaguely suggest that Rāmānanda lived about 1456 A.D.[9] His career may provisionally be accepted to lie in the last quarter of the fourteenth and the first half of the fifteenth centuries.

Rāmānanda was born at Prayāg (Allahabad) in a Kānyakubja Brahmin family. He was educated partly at Prayāg and partly at Benares. His first teacher was a *Vedantist* of the monist school, but he became later the disciple of Rāghavānanda who belonged to Rāmānuja *Śrī* sect. He had an independent mind, he travelled about the country broadening his outlook, and, according to Macauliffe, "it is certain that Rāmānanda came in contact at Benares with learned Musalmans."[10]

The result of his experiences and discussions was that he made a bold departure from the doctrines of the school to which he belonged. In theological belief he substituted the worship of *Rāma* for that of *Viṣṇu* and his consort, and he taught the doctrine of *Bhakti* to all the four castes without prejudice. He rejected the regulation of Rāmānuja with regard to the preparation and partaking of meals, and admitted to his new sect disciples from all castes, from both sexes and even from among

9 Miśra Bandhu Vinod : Rāmānanda.

10 Macauliffe : The Sikhs, Vol. VI, p. 102.

the Musalmans. The names of his twelve disciples who became famous were Anantānanda, Kabīr, Pīpā, Bhāvānanda, Śukhā, Sursura, Padmāvatī, Narharī, Raidāsa, Dhanā, Saina and the wife of Sursura.

Rāmānanda's teaching gave rise to two schools of religious thought, one conservative, and the other radical. The first remained true to ancient beliefs and allowed only slight changes in doctrines and rites, the other struck out a more independent path and attempted to create a religion acceptable to men of different creeds—especially Hindus and Musalmans. The greatest name in the first class is that of Tulsīdāsa and in the second that of Kabīr. These two indeed are undoubtedly the most remarkable men that the middle age of India produced. Tulsīdāsa is unrivalled as the saintly singer of *Rāma Bhakti*. He combines profound philosophy with passionate yet chaste and ethical emotion. He delves into the deepest recesses of the human heart but never completely exposes their mystery to the common gaze. Yet he knows the varying moods of man and nature and by his directness and simplicity appeals to all, young and old, ignorant and learned. He is essentially humble and therefore touchingly humane. He is completely wrapped up in his devotion and utterly lacking in self-conscious or self-righteous sentiment. He is like a natural perennial mountain-spring which bubbles with the waters of pure sweet joy and slakes the thirst of those who are weary and heavy-laden with the sorrows of the world.

Kabīr is a genius of a different order. He has gazed into the mystery of life and seen the vision of the ineffable light. He brings from the world of beyond a new message for the individual and for society. He dreams of a future purified of insincerities, untruths, uglinesses, inequalities; he preaches a religion based on the only foundation on which faith can stand, namely, personal experience. He brushes aside unhesitatingly the whole paraphernalia of dogma and authority, for his soul is sick of the sorry spectacle of the quarrels of creeds and the worship of empty shells of formal religions. He tolerates no shams and demands reality in the search after God. Kabīr is no retiring ascetic who has abandoned the world in despair, nor is he an idealiser who finds good in all things, he is eager to lift the sword in the moral struggle of the world and strike a doughty blow for the victory of righteousness, and he is not afraid of administering stern even harsh rebuke to all infringements of rational conduct and all degradations of human dignity. He is a mighty warner, an intrepid pathfinder, the great pioneer of the unity of the Hindu and Muslim communities of India and the apostle of the faith of Humanity who taught that "the divine disclosed itself in the human race as a whole."[11]

Kabīr's life is shrouded in obscurity. Different writers give different dates of his birth and death. According to Macauliffe,[12] whose date is accepted by Bhandārkar, he was born in 1398 A.D. (1455 Samvat); but according to Westcott,[13] who is followed by Farquhar, Burns and others, the date of his birth was 1440 A.D. The Hindi authors do not give clear guidance. The editor of the *Santa Bāṇī Sangraha*[14] gives 1398 A.D. as the date of birth and 1518 as that of death. Sītārām Śaraṇ Bhagvān Prasād[15] quotes a *Doha* which gives 1492 A.D. (1549 Samvat) as the date of death and says that Kabīr lived for a hundred and one years. Excepting the last writer most of the others agree in assigning 1518 as the date of death. There is however no adequate reason for preferring 1518 to 1492. If the latter date is accepted as that of death, and 1398 A.D. as that of birth, the total length of life comes to ninetyfour years which is unusual but not impossible. These dates however make Kabīr a contemporary of Rāmānanda, and in this respect contradict the tradition according to which he was a

11 Evelyn Underhill: The Mystic Way, p. 25.

12 Macauliffe: Op. cit., Vol. VI.

13 Westcott: Kabīr and Kabīr Panth.

14 Sant Bāṇī Sangrah, Vol. I, p. 1.

15 Sītārām Śaraṇ Bhagwān Prasād: Bhakta Māla, p. 474.

mere youth when he became the latter's disciple. In any case it is difficult to hold to the year 1398 as that of Kabīr's birth. If Kabīr was about eighteen years of age at the time of his initiation and remained under the tutelage for three or four years—which may be surmised from the fact that Rāmānanda passes out of Kabīr's legends quite early and leaves only a shadowy impression upon the development of his ideas, the year 1425 may be fixed as much as any other for the date of his birth. This subtracted from the year 1492 gives a life of sixty-seven years which is eminently reasonable, or from the year 1518 it gives him ninety-three years.

Kabīr was the son of a Brahmin widow who in order to hide her shame left him on the side of a tank in Benares. He was found by a weaver Nīrū and his wife Nīmā who adopted him. Kabīr spent the years of his childhood in the house of his Muslim parents, who were very poor and were unable to give him regular education. He was left more or less to his own devices, except that he learnt his father's profession. In the city of Benares, surrounded by the Hindu atmosphere and endowed with a keen and enquiring mind, he early became familiar with both the Hindu and the Muslim religions. It is related that even as a boy he showed such freedom from bias, that both Hindu and Muslim boys misunderstood him and persecuted him. He soon began to seek for a teacher, and, according to Dabistan Musin Fnī, "at the time when he was in search of a spiritual guide, he visited the best of the Musalmans and Hindus, but did not find what he sought, at last somebody gave him direction to an old man of bright genius, the Brahman Rāmānanda."[16] Thus he became the disciple of Rāmānanda. Kabīr himself says, "I was revealed in Kāśī, and was awakened by Rāmānanda."[17] He initiated him in the knowledge of Hindu philosophy and religion.

[16] Troyer and Shea: Dabistān-i-Mazâhib, p. 186.

[17] Kabīr: Bījak, Rāmāiṇi, p. 77.

It appears however that he did not remain long with his teacher, for tradition finds him soon after wandering from place to place and associating with ascetics and saints. He spent considerable time in the company of Muslim Sūfīs. On this he speaks in a *Rāmāiṇī*, 'Mānikpur was the dwelling place of Kabīr, where far long he listened to Shaikh Taqī. The same (teaching) he heard at Jaunpur, and at Jhūsī (near Allahabad) he learnt the names of the *Pīrs* (Muslim preceptors). In that place they have a record of twenty-one *Pīrs* who read the prayers (khutbā) in the name of the Prophet."[18]

The knowledge which Kābīr acquired from his teachers was all imparted by word of mouth. It is almost certain that he never learnt to use books and he does not display acquaintance with the learned languages, Persian or Sanskrit, although he uses freely the technical terms of Sūfīsm and Hindu philosophy. However, learning and scholarship have not been the objects which men, drunk with the love of God, have principally placed before themselves; and Kabīr, whose mind was saturated with Hindu and Muslim traditions and theories of knowledge, could not accept learning as an end. He was a seeker after higher knowledge (*parā vidyā*), gnosis (*m'arifat*), which he later became satisfied he had attained. History has kept records of the struggles and achievements of an ancient predecessor of Kabīr, viz., Buddha, but is entirely silent regarding him. It is under the circumstances impossible to give a consecutive account of the various events of his life.

After the period of his apprenticeship was over he settled down as a teacher at Benares. His teaching was of so independent a character that both Hindus and Muslims were greatly offended, and they tried to suppress him by all the means which priestcraft with its vested interests has employed in all the ages. There were in the beginning bitter and prolonged discussions and petty persecutions, and when they failed, the aid of the State was invoked. Legend has thrown

[18] Ibid., Kabīr Bījak, Rāmāiṇī, p. 48.

a veil woven of marvellous occurrences and miraculous escapes round the actual facts but this much may be probable that Sikandar Lodī (1488–1517), impressed by the simple earnestness of Kabīr, allowed him to get out of the hands of the Pandits and Maulvis persecuting him by a temporary exile. Kabīr's teaching was so much akin to the then prevailing *Sūfī* antinomianism that it could have hardly appeared to him deserving of severe punishment. He soon returned to Benares and was not molested any further. He won many followers among both communities and his fame spread all over the land. The private life of Kabīr was a simple householder's (*grihastha*). He did not believe in extreme asceticism and abstraction from the world. He married a girl named Loī whom he met on the banks of the Ganges in the hermitage of a *Virāgī*, and by her he had one son named Kamāl, and one daughter Kamālī. He continued his profession of weaving and his pictures represent him sitting by the loom instructing his disciples. Some of the finest illustrations for his teaching are drawn from this art in which he was engaged, and by which he earned his living.

His departure from the world was characteristc of the man. When he felt that his end was approaching he left Kāśī, the city whose holiness was considered so great as to confer paradise on those who died there, and migrated to Maghār where death entailed rebirth as an ass. This gesture of supreme contempt for ignorant superstition was the last act of his strenuous life. It is related that on his death Hindus and Muslims quarrelled as to the method of disposing of the body—Muslims desiring to bury him and Hindus to cremate. The quarrel is significant, for it shows that Kabīr's faith was so broad and impartial that Hindus and Muslims could both claim him as their own; it also shows that although both reverenced and admired the man both failed to rise to his message. But where have not the disciples betrayed their Master?

What was Kabīr's message? In the words of Nābhājī, "Kabīr refused to acknowledge caste distinctions or to recognise the authority of the six schools of Hindu philosophy, nor did he set any store by the four divisions of life prescribed by Brahmins. He held that religion without *Bhakti* was no religion at all, and that asceticism, fasting and alms-giving had no value if unaccompanied by *Bhajan* (devotional worship). By means of *Rāmāiṇī, Shabdas* and *Sākhīs* he imparted religious instruction to Hindus and Musalmans alike. He had no preference for either religion, but gave teaching that was appreciated by the followers of both. He spoke his mind fearlessly and never made it his object merely to please his hearers."[19]

The mission of Kabīr was to preach a religion of love which would unite all castes and creeds. He rejected those features of Hinduism and Islam which were against this spirit, and which were of no importance for the real spiritual welfare of the individual. He selected from both religions their common elements, and the similarities between them. He found analogies in their philosophic ideas, their dogma and ritual. He used both Sanskrit and Persian terms and both forms of the vernacular, *Rekhta* and Hindi *Bhāśā*. He placed the greatest value upon the inwardness of religion and impartially condemned the external formalism of both. He deliberately abandoned the divisions between the two faiths and taught a middle path.

"The Hindu resorts to the temple and the Musalman to the mosque, but Kabīr goes to the place where both are known. The two religions (*dīn*) are like two branches in the middle of which there is a sprout surpassing them. Kabīr has taken the higher path abandoning the custom of the two. If you say that I am a Hindu then it is not true, nor am I a Musalman; I am a body made of five elements where the Unknown (*ghaibī*) plays. Mecca has verily become Kāśī, and Rāma has become Rahīm."[20]

Kabīr was conscious of his apostolic mission and his life and teaching followed the line which is analogous to that of

19 Sītārām Śaraṇ Bhagwān Prasād: Bhakta Māla, p. 465.

20 Yugalānand: Kabīr Sāhib Kī Sākhi, Madhya Ka Anga.

the *Imāms* and *Shaikhs* of Shī'ah and Sūfī sects "I am the servant of the Absolute (*avigat*) God and I have come to save the devotees (*haṃsa*). I have taoght to the world by word of mouth the knowledge which has the true stamp. I was sent here because the world was seen in misery, all were bound in chains of birth and death and no one had found the lasting home. The Almighty sent me to show clearly the beginning and the end."[21] After discussing the creation of the world from *Śruti,* he says, "I came after that in order to spread the true word...... I have taught the word from house to house. Those who will not listen to me, they will surely be drowned in the ocean of existence, in the midst of eighty-four lakh currents.... This, says the awakened teacher Kabīr, is the decree (*farmān*) of the Almighty."[22] And again, "Those who will not listen to my teaching will go to the gates of Yamā, but those who will listen they will come to my abode (salvation)."[23] Dharam Dāsa, his immediate disciple, completes the similarity by deifying Kabīr, "He is an incarnation of the Absolute, who revealed himself to the world."[24]

The expression of Kabīr's teachings was shaped by that of Sūfi saints and poets. In the Hindi language he had no precursor, and the only models which he could follow were Muslim ones, e.g., *Pandnāma* of Farīd-ud-dīn 'Attār; a comparison of the headings of the poems of both brings that out clearly. He must also have heard the poems of Jalāl-ud-dīn Rūmī and Sa'dī besides the teachings of other Sūfis, for there are echoes of them in his works. For instance, "when you came into the world the people laughed but you wept, do not conduct yourself in a manner that after your (death) people should laugh at you,"[25] is a paraphrase of the well-known lines of Sa'dī. And further he says:

21 Kabīr: Siddhānt Dīpikā, Ādi Mangal.
22 Ibid.
23 Ibid., p. 81.
24 Dharam Dāsa: Aśtānga Yoga
25 Yugalānand: Op. cit., p. 72.

"This always is a bubble (*hubāb*) on the motionless sea, the bubble is essentially the sea, although seemingly the waves, the sea and the vision are separate. It is a bubble when it rises, but in its mingling its aim is God. Both the bubble and the sea are Kabīr, and all other names are unmeaning."[26]

"I am not the follower of law (*dharma*) nor am I without law; I am not an ascetic nor a devotee of desire. I am not a speaker nor a listener, I am not a servant nor a master. I am not bound nor am I free, nor am I engaged in worldly pursuits, I never parted from any nor am I a companion of any. I do not go to hell nor do I proceed to heaven. I am the doer of all actions, yet I am different from them."[27]

"There is no place to go to nor is there room to stay."[28] He often compares the relation of the individual with God as that of waves and the sea, and he uses the same simile to represent the essential oneness of the Universe and the Absolute which Jīlī and other Muslim mystics have used. "As ice is made from water, and as ice will become water and vapour, so is the reality from that, and therefore this and that are the same."[29] He frequently speaks of the wine and the cup of love,[30] of the lover (*'āshiq, habīb*) and the beloved (*ma'shuq, mahbūb*),[31] of the rose and the garden,[32] of the path, its stations (*muqām*) and its difficulties, of the traveller (*musāfir*) and of his goal.

All these quotations prove that he was greatly indebted to Sūfī literature, but if his writings do not show more coincidences in phraseology, it is not due to the fact that his familiarity with

[26] Kabīr : Gyān Gudṛī and Rekhta, No. 48.

[27] Kshiti Mohan Sen : Kabīr, Vol. III, pp. 66, 67.

[28] Yugalānand : Op. cit., Sūkśma Mārg Kā Anga.

[29] K. M. Sen : Op. cit., Vol. II, p. 74.

[30] Gangā Prasād Varmā : Bījak, Kabīr, Śabda, 12.

[31] Kabīr : Gyān Gudṛī and Rekhta, No. 54.
Kabīr : Siddhānt Dīpikā, p. 69.

[32] Kabīr : Gyān Gudṛī and Rekhta, No. 53, 55.

their thought was less, but because he was not a man of learning and therefore while he absorbed the ideas he could not retain the Persian lines complete in his mind. Yet Ahmad Shāh, the translator of his *Bījak,* found over two hundred Arabic and Persian words in the work, and an analysis of these words shows how deeply his mind was imbued with Sūfī doctrines. The main proof of Muslim influence on Kabīr, however, lies in his teaching and to that it is necesasry to advert.

Kabīr left behind him a vast mass of poetry in many metres. His compositions were all orally commhnicated; "he did not touch ink or paper and never held a pen."[33] In such circumstances many others added to the great teacher's words, and therefore it is difficult to say how far his works exactly represent his teaching. The *Bījak* (the invoice or seed) was compiled by Bhāgo Dāsa, and *Sukh Nidhān* by Surat Gopāla Dāsa. In the headquarters of the Kabīr Panthīs at Kabīr Chaurā at Benares there exists a collection of twenty-one books called *Khās Granth* (The Special Book, or The Book). The correct list of books is given by Wilson, but Westcott has swollen their number to eighty-two, by counting some twice over and by including modern compilations. Kabīr used the *Bhāśā* in preference to Sanskrit, for he wanted his teaching to spread among the masses, and any work composed in the learned language could reach only the few. He felt however the need to justify his departure and so said, "Sanskrit is indeed the water of the well, but Bhāśā (the Hindī language) is like the running river."[34] He employed, however, both forms of the *Bhāśā,* i.e., the Sanskritised Hindī and the Persianised Urdū, and some of his works are in the latter, for example, *Rekhta.*

Kabīr is not a systematic philosopher but a poet and mystic and his language is not always clear. There is therefore some difficulty in analysing his thought, but the main lines are clear. His central theme is God, whom he indifferently calls by many

33 Vishwanath Singh : Bījak Kabīr Dās Satīk, Sākhī 187.

34 Yugalānand : Kabīr Sākhī, Bhāśa Ka Anga.

names—*Rāma, Hari, Govinda, Brahma, Samrath, Sā'īn, Sat-puruśa, Bechūn* (the Indescribable), *Allah, Khudā*, but his favourite name is *Sāhib*. His conception of God is extremely subtle; according to him God is transcendent and immanent, impersonal and personal, infinite and finite, without qualities and qualified, the non-being and the being, the unconscious and the conscious, neither manifest nor hidden, neither one nor two, both within and without and yet above and beyond all pairs of opposites. It is this difficulty of adequately expressing God's nature which makes him exclaim:

> "Oh, how may I ever express that secret word?
>
> Oh, how can I say He is not like this, and He is like that?......
>
> There are no words to tell that which He is."[35]

This inadequacy of the ordinary human consciousness to hold in one moment the entire view of the total reality does not drive him to despair, for his mind has attained certainty through a direct vision in the unitive state, when his expanded consciousness saw "the Lord in me and in you" and in all things and beyond in one magistral survey in which the logical antinomies fused and were transcended.

> "Between the poles of the conscious and the unconscious there has the mind made a swing;
>
> Thereon hang all beings and all worlds, and that swing never ceases its sway.
>
> Millions of beings are there; the sun and moon in their courses are there.
>
> Millions of ages pass and the swing goes on,
>
> All swing! the sky and the earth, and the air and the water.
>
> And the Lord Himself taking form."[36]

35 Rabindra Nath Tagore: Kabir's Poems, IX.
36 Ibid., XVI.

His vision of dynamic reality is vouchsafed to few. It is impossible to see it by the light of ordinary reason, for the analytical intellect is the cause of separation, and "the house of reason is very far away."[37]

It is necessary however to give to the ordinary man partial views separately and lead him on by demonstrating their inadequacy and the intellect's futility to the ecstatic condition in which the reality is fully known. This explains why Kabīr speaks of God sometimes as transcendent. "The Absolute (*Pāra-Brahma*), the Supreme Soul (*Puruśa*) dwells beyond the beyond,"[38] or as Pure Essence (*Pāk Ḍhāt*),[39] at other times as identical with all beings. "He Himself is the true, the seed and the germ, He Himself is the flower, the fruit and the shade. He Himself is *Brahma*, creature and Māyā"[40] and again as existent within every heart, "in every vessel He is revealed."[41] But more usually he holds that the nature and essence of God is Light, herein betraying his deep debt to the Sūfīs. "See the ocean-filling One Light (*nūr*) which spreads in the whole creation,"[42] and, "Thy Light (*nūr*) fills all,"[43] and, "The Light is covering, the Light is the seat, the Light is the pillow." Says Kabīr, "hear, O brother saints, the True Teacher (God) is completely Light (*nūr*)."[44]

Kabīr gives several accounts of how the universe came into existence. Some of these accounts are based on ancient Hindu cosmogonies, others are apparently taken from Islam. Of the first set one example is in the first *Rāmāiṇī*, a slightly

[37] Rabindra Nath Tagore: Kabīr's Poems, XCVII.

[38] Kabīr: Rekhta, No. 36.

[39] Ibid., No. 41.

[40] Rabindra Nath Tagore: Op. cit., VII.

[41] K. M. Sen: Op. cit., Vol. II, p. 105.

[42] Kabīr: Rekhta, No. 35.

[43] K. M. Sen: Op. cit., Vol. II, p. 66.

[44] Ibid., Vol. III, p. 55.

modified one in the second *Rāmāiṇī,* and a fully developed one in the *Ādi Mangal.* The first *Rāmāiṇī* may be rendered thus:

In the beginning *Jīva* (soul) existed. The Internal light illuminated it. Then was manifested will (*ichchhā*) which was called *Gāyatrī.* That woman produced *Brahmā, Viśṇu* and *Maheśa.* Then Brahmā asked the woman who was her husband, and whose wife she was. She replied, "Thou art I, I am thou, and there is no third. Thou art my husband, and I am thy wife." The father and son had a common wife, and one mother has a twofold character; there is no son who is a good son and who will endeavour to recognise his father.[45]

In the second *Rāmāinī* after Brahmā is created, he carries on the next stages of creation by bringing into being an egg from which the fourteen regions are developed, and then *Brahmā, Viśṇu* (*Hari*) and *Maheśa* (*Hara*) preside over the universe. In the *Ādi Mangal,* in the Almighty, who in the beginning was alone, first appears knowledge (*śruti*), from this comes the word (*śabda*) and from *Śabda* five *Brahmans* and five breaths and from them the whole creation according to the *Sānkhyan* system.

The first *Rāmāiṇī* has a curious resemblance with similar notions of Jīlī and Badruddīn Shahīd.[46] Both Kabir and Jīlī seem to mean, that soul (*Jīva* or *rūh*) is the object of divine knowledge, God as the centre of the soul is the father, yet God becomes the object of knowledge and therefore the son of soul. The account of the sacred *Rāmāinī* may be compared with Jīlī's cosmological myth. Kabīr and Jīlī start with one God who was Himself before creation. Then He created the idea of ideas (*haqīqat-al-haqaīq*) or word (*śabda*). From *Śabda* comes *Brahma* who creates an egg (the white chrysolite of Jīlī), from which evolves the fourteen regions (the seven heavens and seven earths).[47]

[45] Kabīr : Bījak, Rāmāiṇi, I.

[46] Nicholson : Studies in Islamic Mysticism.

[47] Kabīr : Bījak, Rāmāiṇi II.

In other places Kabīr makes an attempt to reproduce the scheme of nine spheres through which creation develops in accordance with Muslim philosophy. The *Panjī Mangal* gives the list of nine regions and their presiding forces, but does not mention the names of the planets or regions. Sometimes he speaks of creation in such terms: "In the sky He was seated meditating behind closed doors, then He saw his own image and thereby the three became pleased."[48] This seems like an echo of Ibn Sīnā's theory. Two other speculations occur in the *Siddhānta Dīpikā*, in one everything is created from water, "The whole universe is bodied forth from water, out of the essence of water it is kneaded. The seven heavens and fourteen regions all are sieved out of water and dissolved in it. The ten *Avatārs, Pīrs* and *Paighambars* (prophets) are all made of water."[49] In the other, creation is likened to a mechanical process, "the Artisan is a wonderful smith, who has made innumerable things."[50]

The individual soul was in the Supreme Being before creation, it came into existence when His Light illumined it. The first created was the female principle *Śabda* whose offspring were distinct individuals. This distinction however is unreal, "I and thou are of one blood and are one life."[51] Kabīr recognised individuality and yet did not forget the unity that lies behind and thus he avoided an atomic view of personality. He says:

"O friend, this body is His Lyre;
He tightens its strings, and draws from it the melody of *Brahma*,
If the strings snap and the keys slacken, then to dust must the instrument of dust return;
Kabīr says: none but *Brahma* can evoke its melodies."[52]

48 Yugalānand: Op. cit., Jyotī Kā Anga.
49 Kabīr: Siddhānta Dīpika, p. 44.
50 Ibid., p. 46.
51 Kabīr: Bījak, Rāmāiṇi, II.
52 Rabindra Nath Tagore: Op. cit., XXXIX.

The destiny of the individual, according to Kabīr, is ultimate realisation of union with God. Nothing short of it is adequate, paradise will not satisfy him, for

"As long as you expect paradise (*vaikuṇṭha*)
So long will you delay dwelling at the feet of
the Lord[53]

and, "Paradise and hell are only for the ignorant, not for one who knows *Hari*."[54]

For the attainment of the goal it is of the utmost importance to select a teacher (*guru*). In the *Pantha* (way, sect) of Kabīr, the *Guru* holds the same position as in any other Sūfī order. If it is true of the Sūfīs that 'among them the worship of God is the same as the worship of man,' it is equally applicable here, for says Kabīr,

"Consider the *Guru* as Govinda (God)"[55];

nay more,

"If Hari becomes angry still there is some chance, but if the Guru is angry then there is no chance whatever."[56]

And as among Sūfī orders so in *Kabīr Pantha*:

"The real meditation (*dhyāna, dhikr*) is of the *Guru's* form, the real worship is of the *Guru's* feet. The real boat is the *Guru's* word, which in essence and feeling is true,[57] and "in the three worlds and nine regions none is greater than the *Guru*."[58]

[53] Kabīr : Siddhānta Dipikā, p. 54.

[54] K. M. Sen : Op. cit., Vol. II, 12.

[55] Yugalānand : Op. cit., Guru Deva Kā Anga. p. 4.

[56] Ibid., p. 6.

[57] Ibid., p. 8.

[58] Yugalānand : Op. cit., Guru Śiśya Parakh, p. 8.

It is essential then to exercise the greatest discretion in selection: "The *Guru* should be a polisher (*siqlīgar*) who would polish the mind, and who would clear away the stains and make the heart a mirror."[59] If the *Guru* is not of the right sort then it is a case of 'the blind pushing the blind and of both falling into the well.'[60] While those who have no *Guru*, 'their efforts will be of no avail,'[61] and 'they will be washed away by the current who do not take hold of the arms.'[62]

The teacher directs the devotee upon the path which is the discipline of the soul. The end of the discipline is to die to self in order to live in God. "He is a rare saint who dies when living."[63] There are then two aspects of the contemplative life of the mystic. First, he must die to the things of the world, and gain complete control over passion and desire. His mind must cease to be the monkey of the soul, and his self must cease to be a 'prostitute devoted to many men.' The preliminary step is complete trust in God. His heart is like wax. He is merciful (*dayālu*), and gracious (*miharbān*), and therefore he who seeks His protection (*śaraṇ*) is never disappointed. Then by constant repetition of His name, not merely 'by revolving the rosary in the hand, but by revolving the beads of the mind,'[64] by indifference, 'feeling neither pain nor pleasure,' by suppressing the five evil tendencies of the mind, by abandoning anger and pride, by the acquisition of humility, poverty, patience and discrimination, the self is effaced.

The dying to self did not mean to Kabīr complete retirement from the world and betaking to hills and forests. "O Saints, he who brings self-forgetfulness into his house, I like that man. Both meditation (*Yoga*) and pleasure (*Bhoga*) are in the house (householder's life), one need not abandon the

[59] Yugalānand: Op. cit., Guru deva Kā Anga, p. 5.
[60] Yugalānand: Op. cit., Satgur deva Kā Anga, p. 9.
[61] Yugalānand: Op. cit., Nirguṇ Kā Anga, p. 23.
[62] Ibid., p. 24.
[63] K. M. Sen: Op. cit., Vol. II, p. 19.
[64] Yugalānand: Op. cit., Smaraṇ Kā Anga, p. 31.

house in order to go to a forest."[65] Kabīr himself stayed at home and worked as a weaver. The dying to self meant waging a constant war with one's senses. Kabīr calls upon the devotee—

> "Lay hold on your sword, and join in the fight,
> Fight, O my brother, as long as life lasts......
> In the field of this body a great war goes forward
> against passion, anger, pride and greed.
>
> It is in the kingdom of truth, contentment, and purity that this battle is raging, and the sword that rings forth most loudly is the sword of His name."[66]

The end of the struggle is thus described:

> "The man who is kind and who practises righteousness,
> who remains passive amidst the affairs of the world,
> who considers all creatures on earth as his own self,
> He attains the immortal being, the True God is ever with him."[67]

The other aspect of the discipline is living in God. The devotee must realise, "one love it is that pervades the whole world."[68] He must realise that God is near.

> "Where dost thou seek me, O slave. I am indeed near thee, I am not in the temple, nor in the mossue, neither in *Ka'ba,* nor *Kailāś*. If thou art a true seeker I shall meet thee immediately in a moment's search. Says Kabīr, hear, ye *Sādhūs,* He is in the breath of breaths."[69]

He must realise that God is not *Hari* or *Rām* or *Krisṇa;* He transcends all conception. He is without body or form, yet

[65] K. M. Sen: Op. cit., Vol. I, 65.
[66] Rabindra Nath Tagore: Op. cit., XXXVII.
[67] Ibid., LXV.
[68] Rabindra Nath Tagore.
[69] K. M. Sen: Op. cit., Vol. I, 13.

He is most intimate of Beings. He is the Supreme Painter (*rangrezwā*), the world is His picture; He is the great sportsman, the universe is His sport; but above all He is the Father, the Lover and the Husband (*pītam*). The individual must seek Him as the son, the beloved or the spouse, and he must not rest till he has attained union with Him.

If the Muslim mystic speaks of God as the tender maid and the wine-giver (*Sāqī*), and of the dark hair, the shapely neck, the gazelle eyes and the lovely gestures which all symbolise His surpassing beauty, Kabīr thinks of Him as the Spouse, for whom the wife abandons her home, her name and honour, goes out in the night though it may be ever so dark and though storm and rain may impede her path. Like the Sūfī he too invites his fellow-travellers to inebriate themselves with the wine of love and throw worldly discretion to the winds.

The devotee who desires the mystic union must firmly set forward upon the path. It is like walking on the keen edge of a sword. There are many disappointments, and terrible obstacles. 'The clouds gather, the evening falls, the rain pours down, the fourfold blanket becomes wetter and wetter and the burden gets heavier and heavier'[70] and 'walking, walking the feet are aching.'[71] Kabīr experienced all the conditions (*hāl*) which the Sūfīs describe: contrition (*pachhtāwa*) and sorrow (*dukh*), hope (*āśā*) and fear (*durāśā*), intimacy in contemplating His beauty (*jamāl*) and awe at His majesty (*jalāl*), violence (*qahr*) and kindness (*mihr*), separation (*virahā*) and union (*milan*), absence (*ghaibat*), and presence (*hudhūr*), amazement (*hairat, chigūngī* or *bharam*), and satisfaction (*bharam vidhwans*). He describes the journey of the self within the self in the very terms which Mansūr al Hallāj used so early as the tenth century. Says he, "Abandoning the actions pertaining to humanity (*nāsūt*), one sees the sphere of the angels (*malakūt*); then leaving even the sphere of majesty (*jabarūt*) one gets the vision of divinity (*lāhūt*); but when these four are left behind

70 Kabīr: Bījak, Rāmāiṇi 15 (Armad Shah's translation).
71 Ibid., 16.

then comes *hāhūt,* where there is no death or separation and where *Yama* finds no entrance."[72] He knew the correct significance of each one of these terms and he expresses it in two terse lines:

> "Humanity (*Nāsūt*) is darkness, *Malakūt* is angelic, in *Jabarūt* shines the Majestic Light (*Nūr Jalāl*), in *Lāhūt* one finds the Beautiful Light (*Nūr Jamāl*) and in *Hāhūt* is the dwelling place of Truth (*Haq*).[73]

In the *Das Muqāmi Rekhta* (the poem describing the ten stations), Kabīr in his own way reproduces the whole story of Muhammad's *Mirāj* as developed in later Muslim tradition. It is, of course, symbolic of the path which the saint follows in his inward flight towards the ineffable goal "like the butterfly towards the light." This goal has been described in many beautiful poems by Kabīr; just one may be given here in the rendering of Rabindranath Tagore to illustrate his conception of the mystic regions to which the saint rises.

"There falls the rhythmic beat of life and death;
Rapture wells forth, and all space is radiant with light,
There the unstruck music is sounded; it is the
music of the love of three worlds.
There millions of lamps of sun and moon are burning,
There are drum beats, and the lover swings in play,
There love-songs resound, and light rains in showers;
And the worshipper is entranced in the taste of the
heavenly nectar.
Look upon life and death; there is no separation
between them.
The right hand and the left hand are one and the same
Kabīr says, There the wise man is speechless; for
this truth may never be found in Vedas or in books."[74]

72 Kabīr: Rekhta, No. 22; Siddhānta Dīpikā, p. 15.

73 Kabīr: Siddhānta Dīpikā, p. 14.

74 Rabindranath Tagore: Op. cit., XVII.

In this sorrowless region, Spring, the lord of seasons, reigns, the woods are ever a-bloom and the fragrant scent "He is I" is borne on the wind. There the Lord stands self-revealed and the goal of the long and weary search is at last reached.

Thus did Kabīr turn the attention of India to a religion of the universal path; a road was laid out which both could tread together. No Hindu or Muslim could take exception to such a religion. This was the constructive part of Kabīr's mission. But it had a destructive side also. It was impossible to build a new road without clearing away the jungle which obstructed the ancient footpaths. Kabīr therefore attacked with fearless indignation and in trenchant language the whole apparatus of externalia which obscured the truth or separated the Indian communities from one another. He spared neither the Hindu nor the Musalman.

He asked the Hindus to give up what every reformer since the days of Buddha had insisted upon—ceremonial, sacrifice, lust for magical powers, lip worship, repetition of formulæ, pilgrimages, fasts, worship of idols, gods and goddesses, Brahmin supremacy, caste differences, prejudices concerning touchability and food. He openly condemned the doctrine of incarnations: "The Creator did not marry Sītā nor did He make a stone bridge across the waters"[75], and "they say the Lord of the world finding inequalities of the weak and the strong came as Rāma. But Kabīr says, before such a one (*Rāma*) who took birth and died, I cannot bend my head."[76] Again, "the ten incarnations that people talk about do not concern me, they are merely the reapers of the fruits of their actions, but the Creator is some one else."[77]

It is difficult to say how far he was attached to the theory of metempsychosis. There are many passages in which he

[75] Kabīr: Śabda 8.

[76] Yugalānand: Op. cit., Avatār Kā Anga.

[77] K. M. Sen: Vol. II, p. 37.

appears to have repudiated it—"the soul (*jiyarā*) is a guest which will not come a second time,"[78] and, "birth as man is not easy to obtain, it does not happen a second time, when the ripe fruit falls it does not again get attached to the tree."[79] Again, "all go from this side taking their burdens with them, no one returns from the other side, who could tell the tale."[80] There are other passages where he speaks of the eighty-four lakhs of births, and of unceasing coming and going. It appears, however, that he uses the fear of death (*yama* and *kāla*) and of remorseless chain of birth and death, more or less, as warnings for men to deter them from their ungodly lives. He does not expatiate on the doctrine of *Karma* which is indissolubly linked with metempsychosis, and his whole attention seems to be concentrated upon the here and now, rather than on the hereafter and future.

He asks the Musalmans to give up their exclusiveness, their blind trust in one Prophet and his book, their externalism in the performance of rites—pilgrimage to Mecca, fast and regulated prayers, their worship of saints (*auliā* and *pīrs*) and prophets (*paighambars*).

He asks both Hindus and Muslims to have reverence for all living creatures and to abstain from bloodshed. He asks them both to give up pride whether of birth or position, to give up extremes of asceticism and worldliness, and to consider life as a dedication:

> "I shut not my eyes, I close not my ears, I do not mortify my body;
> I see with eyes open and smile, and behold His beauty everywhere.
> Whatever I do, it becomes His worship.
> All I achieve is His service."[81]

[78] Kabīr: Bījak (Gangā Prasād Varmā's Edition), Sākhī 10.
[79] Ibid., Sākhī 115.
[80] Ibid., Sākhī 226.
[81] K. M. Sen: Op. cit., Vol. I, p. 76.

He repeats again and again that Hindus and Muslims are one, they worship the same God, they are children of the same Father, and they are made of the same blood. "All the men and women that are created are Your form, Kabīr is the son of *Allah* and *Rāma.* He is his *Guru* and *Pīr.*"[82] And, "The Hindu and Turk have one path which the True Teacher has pointed out; says Kabīr, hear, ye saints, say *Rāma* or say *Khudā.*"[83] And, "the religion of those who understand is one, whether they are *Pandits* or *Shaikhs.*"[84] Naturally it pains him to find "Hindus call upon *Rāma,* the Musalmans on *Rahmān,* yet both fight and kill each other, and none knows the truth."[85]

Kabīr's was the first attempt to reconcile Hinduism and Islam; the teachers of the south had absorbed Muslim elements, but Kabīr was the first to come forward boldly to proclaim a religion of the centre, a middle path, and his cry was taken up all over India and was re-echoed from a hundred places. He had numerous Hindu and Muslim disciples, and today his sect numbers a million. At Kabīr Chaurā in Benaras they gather every year, and at Maghar the Muslim followers congregate to keep fresh his memory. But it is not the number of his following which is so important, it is his influence which extends to the Panjab, Gujarat and Bengal and which continued to spread under the Moghul rule, till a wise sovereign correctly estimating its value attempted to make it a religion approved by the State. Akbar's *Dīn-i-Ilāhī* was not an isolated freak of an autocrat who had more power than he knew how to employ, but an inevitable result of the forces which were deeply surging in India's breast, and finding expression in the teachings of men like Kabīr. Circumstances thwarted that attempt, but destiny still points towards the same goal.

82 K. M. Sen: Op. cit., Vol. III, p. 23.

83 Kabīr: Bījak, Śabda 10.

84 Yugalānand: Op. cit., Parīchha Kā Anga.

85 K. M. Sen: Op. cit., Vol. I, p. 6.

GURU NANAK

THE Panjab was on the highway along which Muslim arms and culture passed into India. In the fifteenth century the province had longer been under Muslim rule than any other. Its towns and villages were honeycombed with Muslim saints and *faqīrs*. Pānīpat, Sirhind, Pākpattan, Multān and Uchh were places where famous Sūfī Shaikhs had spent their lives, and the names of Bābā Farīd, 'Alā-ul-Haq, Jalāl-ud-Dīn Bukhārī, Makhdūm Jahāniyān, Shaikh Ismā'īl Bukhārī, had become household words for piety and devotion. The ferment in the minds of men set up by them prepared the intellectual *milieu* in which a synthesis of ideas could take place.

In the district of Gujrānwālā, in the subdivision of Shaikhupura, is the small village of Talwandī which is situated on the bank of the river Ravi. Rāi Bulār, a Bhattī Rajput, was the lord of this village, and he had a Bedī Khatrī as an accountant whose name was Mehta Kālū Chand. The accountant was held in respect by the villagers and also by the Rāi. On the full-moon day of Kartik (November) 1469 A.D. the Mehta was blessed with a son. His family priest gave him the name of Nānak, a name common to both Hindus and Musalmans. At the age of seven he was sent to school to learn Hindi, two years later to study Sanskrit, and shortly after to Mullā Qutb-ud-Dīn to learn Persian. It is difficult to say how much he profited by the teaching of the Pandit and the Mullā. Tradition relates the usual kind of miraculous story regarding the precocity and astonishing wisdom of the child. It may, however, be presumed that the son of the accountant who was destined by his father for government service acquired some working knowledge of Hindi and Persian. It is also likely that he did not show any violent desire for learning, and therefore he was tried on many odd jobs like agriculture, cattle-tending and shop-keeping with equal fruitlessness. Nānak was a moody, meditative child more given to reverie and day-dreams than energetic practical pursuits. He was unmindful of his personal needs and careless of his appointed tasks. Some thought he was possessed by an evil spirit, others that he had lost his senses. The efforts of the exorcist and the doctor failed to do any good or to render any harm. His father failed to understand him, but his sister, with the discerning sympathy and the sure instinct of a woman, perceived the true nature of her brother's ailment. She was married to one Jai Rām, a Dīwān in the service of Nawāb Daulat Khān Lodī, a relation of Sultan Buhlūl, the Emperor of Delhi. The Nawāb held an extensive *jāgīr* in Sultānpur near Kapūrthalā. She sent for the young Nānak and obtained for him a post in the Nawāb's service as the keeper of his storehouse of charities. Here he remained till 1499.

Nānak was married at the age of eighteen, to Sulākhin and had two sons—Śrīhand, who later founded the order of *Udāsīs*, and Lakhmī Dās. When he was thirty, he renounced home and service and became a *faqīr*. Mardāna, the Muslim minstrel of Talwandī and later, Bhāī Bālā, joined him and they commenced their wanderings over many lands, interviewing saints and gathering spiritual experience and, if any credence can be placed upon the legends, Nānak visited all the holy places and towns of importance in India, Ceylon, Persia, and Arabia during four series of travels in the remaining forty years of his life. He is said to have had long intercourse with Shaikh Sharaf of Pānīpat, the *Pīrs* of Multan, Shaikh Brahm (Ibrāhīm), the successor of Bābā Farīd at Pākpattan, and several others. He preached his own ideas wherever he went and never hesitated to uphold by action what he spoke by word of mouth. At last the wanderings were over, the message was delivered, and the day had arrived when the earthly journey was to end. "The *Guru* drew a sheet over him, uttered *Wāhguru,* made obeisance to God, and blended his light with Guru Angad's. The *Guru* remained the same. There was only a change of body produced by a supreme miracle."[1] The Hindu and Muslim disciples had a controversy over the disposal of the body, the *Guru* decided the difficulty, for when the sheet was lifted, the body had disappeared and there were only flowers there. They were divided, the Hindus erected a shrine and the Musalmans a tomb over them, but both were washed away by the flood of the Ravi river.

The mission of Nānak was the unification of the Hindu and the Musalman. He realised that in order to heal the wounds of society it was essential to end the conflict of religions. He says:

"When one remains and one is removed then alone is it possible to live with ease; but as long as the two remain established there is struggle and confusion. The two had failed, then God gave orders; for many had gone taking with them the *Furqān* (Qorān) in order to unite, but they had failed to unite. Thou art my son, go into world, all have gone astray from the path, direct them upon the right path. Go thou into the world, and make them all repeat the one name; Nānak, go thou as the third over the head of both. Establish the religion of truth and remove evil, whoever comes to you from the two receive him, let not life be taken unnecessarily, protect the poor, remember that God pervades the eighty-four lakhs of species."[2]

He regarded himself as the prophet of God, who had come from the divine court, and "received from His door-step the signs (*ā'itān*), the chapters (*sūrahs*), and the traditions (*hadīth*) of the prophet."[3] He taught that "there is one God in the world and no other, and that Nānak the Caliph (or son) of God speaks the truth."[4]

[1] Macauliffe: The Sikh Religion, Vol. I, p. 190.

[2] Khazān Singh: The History and Philosophy of Sikhism, Vol. II, p. 348.

[3] Ibid., p. 350.

[4] Ibid., p. 350.

It is clear that Nānak took the prophet of Islam as his model, and his teaching was naturally deeply coloured by this fact. He was a mystic in the sense tnat he had a lively realisation of the presence of God, but he was not an enwrapt visionary like Kabīr. His spirit took occasional flights to the sorrowless and where 'the Divine palace is illumined by His light which exceeds the light of millions of moons, lamps, suns and torches, and where from behind the curtain of the Unknown (*ghaibī*) the sound of bells is heard,'[5] but he does not revel in the transcendent joys of that illumined abode. His spirit draws its inspiration from that vision, but it is far too deeply interested in the fate of his fellow-beings upon earth to linger long in the rare mystic regions.

Nānak's conception of religion was severely practical and sternly ethical. His God is exalted above all. He "is inaccessible, unfathomable, altogether distinct from His creation."[6] At "His treshold millions of *Muhammads, Brahmās, Viṣṇūs, Maheśas, Rāmas* are lauding Him in millions of ways and millions of forms."[7] "He is incomprehensible, endless, incalculable, independent, immortal, actionless. He has no caste. He is not born nor does He die, He is self-existent, He has no fear, and no doubts. . . . He has no family, He has no illusion, He is beyond the beyond, the whole Light is Thine."[8] Yet he admits that He is immanent in all, "within each body the Absolute (*Brahma*) is concealed, and within each vessel the whole light is His."[9] God is husband (*khasam*) and bridegroom, and thus intimately related to the human soul. But in his more permanent mood Nānak looks upon God as the One Lord of all, the Commander (*Hākim*) according to whose pre-ordained will man ought to walk, for obedience to Him

5 Khazān Singh : Op. cit., Vol. II, p. 396.

6 Macauliffe : Op. cit., Vol. I, p. 363.

7 Khazān Singh : Op. cit., Vol. II, p. 393.

8 Ibid., p. 394.

9 Macauliffe : Op. cit., Vol. I, p. 171.

brings wisdom, knowledge, security from punishment, freedom from *Yama,* and salvation."[10] Nānak has no use for any anthropomorphic Being, nor does he dwell much upon His personal humane qualities; to him He is the great and high, formless (*nirankār*), light (*niranjan*), and from the viewpoint of personality the true teacher (*Satguru*). But he is far too much impressed by His power and His irresistible will to develop greatly the latter aspect.

As Creator He brings the universe into existence out of darkness:

"In the beginning there was indescribable darkness;
Then was not earth or heaven, naught *but God's* unequalled order.
Then was not day, or night, or moon, or sun; *God* was meditating on the void.
The Imperceptible God was himself the speaker and preacher;
Himself unseen He was everything.
When He pleased He created the world;
Without supports He sustained the sky.
He created *Brahmā, Viṣṇu* and *Śiva,* and extended the love of mammon.
He communicated the Guru's words to some few persons.
He issued His order and watched over all.
He began with the continents, the universe, and the nether regions, and brought forth what had been hidden.
His limit no one knoweth."[11]

The universe is the domain of the Lord. The creation is His play, His motiveless activity; but sometimes he speaks of it in other phrases, "Thou didst effect the expansion of the world"[12]; again, "from its brilliance everything is brilliant"[13]

[10] Macauliffe: Op. cit., Vol. I, p. 195.

[11] Ibid., pp. 165—67.

[12] Ibid., p. 205.

[13] Ibid., pp. 82, 83.

and "all is illumined by the light of His appearance."[14] Over the universe the Lord has established a system of government of His own.

"The Hindu and Muslim saints are the *dīwāns* in attendance upon the Preserver (*parvardigār*), the great *Pīrs* are magistrates (*siqdārs*) and collectors (*karorīs*), the angles are accountants and treasures (*fotedārs*). The gentleman trooper (*ahadi*) 'Izra'īl binds and arrests, and degrades the ignorant and beastly men."[15]

Such a conception of God and His relationship with creation lays greater emphasis upon the transformation of human will than upon his intellect or feeling. Nānak demands of his followers, like the Prophet of Islam, a complete surrender to the Lord.

"Nānak maketh one application.
Soul and body are all in Thy power.
Thou art near, Thou art distant, and Thou art midway
Thou seest and hearest; by Thy power didst Thou create the world,
Whatever order pleaseth thee, saith Nānak, that is acceptable."[16]

and again:

"Whatever the Lord does, consider it is for your
Good, wisdom consists in obeying His order.
Whatever the King commands obey with all your body and mind, such should be our reverence for Him.
Lose yourself and then you will find the King, no other wisdom avails."[17]

Nānak is impressed with the utter worthlessness of man, and there is a deep note of contrition and humility in the consciousness of his own sin. Says he:

'My sins are numerous as the waters of the seas and the ocean.

14 Khazān Singh : Op. cit., Vol. II, p. 397.

15 Ibid., p. 404.

16 Macauliffe : Op. cit., Vol. I, pp. 35-36.

17 Khazān Singh : Op. cit., Vol. II, p. 419.

Bestow compassion, extend a little mercy, save me who am like a sinking stone."[18]

And adds:

"I utter calumny night and day;
I am base and worthless, I covet my neighbour's house.
Lust and anger which are pariahs, dwell in my heart......
I am a cheat in a country of cheats.
I deem myself very clever, and bear a great load of sin.......
Ungrateful that I was, I did not appreciate what Thou didst for me,
How can I, who am wicked and dishonest, show my face?"[19]

Such a person who dares to tear so rudely aside the curtain of self-complacency and egotism which hides the ugliness behind will hardly tolerate the shams and falsehoods which masquerade in the guise of religion. Nānak shows little mercy to himself and he is naturally not very tender when he deals with others. With a mind definite, clear cut and keenly alive to the sharp distinctions between good and evil he condemns with Semitic vehemence the superstition and formalism of Hinduism and Islam. He says:

"Cooking places of gold, vessels of gold,
Lines of silver far extended,
Ganges water, firewood of the *Karanta* tree,
Eating rice boiled in milk—
O my soul, these things are of no account
Until thou art saturated with the true Name.
Hadst thou the eighteen *Purāṇas* with thee,
Couldst thou recite the four *Vedas*,
Didst thou bathe on holy days and give alms according to men's castes,
Didst thou fast and perform religious ceremonies day and night;
Wert thou a *Qāzī*, a *Mullā*, or a *Shaikh*,
A *Jogī*, a *Jangam*, didst thou wear an ochre-coloured dress,

[18] Macauliffe : Op. cit., Vol. I, p. 30.

[19] Ibid., p. 184.

Or didst thou perform the duties of a householder—
Without knowing God, Death would bind and take all
men away."[20]

Also,

"He who worshippeth stones, visiteth places of pilgrimage,
dwelleth in forests,
And renounceth the world, wandereth and wavereth
How can his filthy mind become pure?"[21]

He rejects the doctrine of incarnations; says he
"Nānak, God is independent; Rām could not erase his
destiny."[22]

And the inequalities of caste:
"I belong not to any of the four castes."[23]

And adds:

"Nānak is with those who are low-born among the lowly,
Nay, who are lowest of the low; how can he rival the great?"
"Where Thou, O Lord, watchest over the lowly, Thy look
of favour shall be their reward."[24]

To the Musalman he says:

"Make kindness thy mosque, sincerity thy prayer carpet,
what is just and lawful thy *Qorān,*
Modesty thy circumcision, civility thy fasting, so shalt thou
be a Musalman;
Make right conduct thy *Ka'bah,* truth thy spiritual guide,
good works thy creed and thy prayer,
The will of God thy rosary, and God will preserve thine
honour, O Nānak,"[25]

20 Macauliffe : Op. cit., p. 133.

21 Ibid., p. 339.

22 Ibid., p. 382.

23 Ibid., p. 43.

24 Ibid., p. 186.

25 Ibid., p. 38.

What should a man do then to attain salvation, or to blend the light of soul with that of God? Four things are necessary. Fear God, do the right, trust in the mercy of His name, and take a guide to direct you upon the path which leads to the goal. Regarding the first Nānak says:

"Be in fear of that day when God will judge thee,"[26]
"Put the fear of God into thy heart, then the fear of Death shall depart in fear."[27]

Regarding the second, his works are so full that it is difficult to make a choice. He is never tired of harping upon two themes—praise of virtue and condemnation of vice. He is careful, however, to remember that a mere catalogue of commands and inhibitions is not enough and that essentially moral conduct is the proper attitude of the inward soul. He also knows that men and women have to live in the world and work in their professions and a religion which suits merely the *faqīr* and the *sādhu* who has renounced the world cannot be the faith of an active community engaged in social pursuits. He, therefore, advocates a middle path between extreme asceticism and heedless satisfaction of sense, or rather he advocates an asceticism of the heart combined with the fulfilment of the wordly functions of body and mind. Here is one of the shorter catalogues of virtues:

Practise humility, renounce pride, restrain the mind, remember God,
Be honest, watch, restrain the five evil passions, be contented.[28]

Nānak loved to draw illustrations for human virtues from the daily occupations of men, for example:

"Make continence thy furnace, resignation thy goldsmith,
Understanding thine anvil, divine knowledge thy tools,
The fear of God thy bellows, austerities thy fire.

26 Macauliffe: Op. cit., p. 14.

27 Ibid., p. 78.

28 Ibid., p. 13.

Divine love thy crucible, and melt God's name therein.
In such a true mint the Word shall be coined.
This is the practice of those on whom God looked with an eye of favour.

Nānak, the kind One by a glance maketh them happy."[29]

Nānak was a believer in the transmigration of soul, and he taught that the doers of evil will continue to suffer from repeated births and deaths, till they turned their hearts towards Truth. Transmigration, however, did not apparently satisfy him as a sufficient deterrent from sin, and so he threatened those who would not walk along the path of virtue with the diret punishments. Says he:

"The sinners who have committed transgressions are bound and led away.

Their luggage of sins is so heavy that they cannot lift it.

The steep road ahead is dark, while the executioner walketh behind them.

In front is a sea of fire; how shall they cross it?

Ravens stand on men's skulls, and peck at them fast as a shower of sparks.

Nānak, where shall men escape when the punishment is by God's order?"[30]

And he goes on to describe the horrible fate that is in store for them. It is too gruesome to describe. From such a fate only the mercy of God can save man. Fortunately He is ever ready to help, "If for a moment thou restrain thy mind, God will appear before thee,"[31] and "God bestoweth gifts on whom He looketh with favour and mercy,"[32] and "the mere repetition of His name can confer salvation." His gifts are priceless, and his marks priceless, priceless his mercy and priceless His ordi-

[29] Ibid., Vol. I, p. 217.

[30] Macliffe: Ibid., p. 125.

[31] Ibid., p. 177.

[32] Ibid., p. 208.

nances. Good deeds, approved charities, penances and *yoga*, study of scriptures and meditation, "Nānak, these devices would be of no avail; true is the mark of grace."[33]

Like all Sūfīs Nānak taught that in the soul's journey towards God it was necessary to be guided by a *Guru* In his system the preceptor occupies the same position as in that of Kabīr. Muhsin Fānī, who was an earnest student of the religions of India and a contemporary and friend of many Hindu saints of the seventeenth century, describes accurately the Sikh belief. Says he: "When Nānak eypired, his spirit became incarnate in the person of Angad, who attended him as his confidential servant. Angad, at his death, transmitted his soul into the body of Amaradāsa; and this *Guru*, in the same manner, conveyed his spirit into the body of Ramadāsa, whose soul transmigrated into the person of Arjun Mal; in short, they (Sikhs) believe that with a mere change of name, Nānak the First became Nānak the Second, and so on to the fifth, in the person of Arjun Mal."[34] The *Guru* directed the disciple upon the path which has four stages–*Śaran Khand, Jñān Khand, Karam Khand* and *Sach Khand*, which, according to the author of *Nānak Prakāś*, correspond with the Sūfī *Sharī'at, Ma'rifat, Tariqat* and *Haqiqat*.[35] The path ultimately leads to the goal so dear to the soul of the devotee, where the fear of death is no more, the wheel of birth and death ceases to revolve, where man at last becomes united with the Light from which he emanated.

How deep Guru Nānak's debt is to Islam, it is hardly necessary to state, for it is so evident in his words and thoughts. Manifestly he was steeped in Sūfī lore and the fact of the matter is, that it is much harder to find how much exactly he drew from the Hindu scriptures. His rare references to them lead one to imagine that Nānak was only superficially acquaint-

[33] Ibid., p. 229.

[34] The *Dabistan* by Shea & Troyer (Jacksons edition), p. 287.

[35] Macauliff, op. cit., Vol. I, p. 13 *n* 2.

ed with the *Vedic* and *Purāṇic* literature. Be that as it may, it is certain that in his own mind he was clear that he had come upon earth with one purpose which was to proclaim that:

> "There is only one path to the Divine Court which is presided over by the one eternal Lord."[36]

The religious movement started by Nānak continued to gather momentum under his successors. Its stern ethical tone and its definite puritanism were elements which distinguished it from similar movements in India. Its spirit of non-compromise carried within it possibilities of martyrdoms and the seeds of an organised church. The unsettled political conditions of the later period of the Moghul Empire gave these possibilities their opportunity, and the seed bore fruit. The later *Gurus* were inevitably drawn into the whirl of politics and they transformed the Church into a militant society. But although the Sikhs changed their organisation their religion retained almost unaltered the impress of Guru Nanak's teaching.[37]

[36] Gurumukh Singh: Nānak Prakāś, pp. 215–16.

[37] Khazan Singh, Op. cit., Vol. II, p. 527.

KABĪR and Nānak were leaders of the radical school of thought. They had many supporters among their contemporaries and numerous followers after them throughout the centuries. Of the twelve disciples of Rāmānanda four others besides Kabīr have left some of their hymns behind—Dhannā, Pīpā, Sā'īn, and Raidās. The hymns of the first three are preserved in the *Ādigrantha* of the Sikhs, while Raidās's teachings have been collected and published separately.

Dhannā was a Jāt by caste and is said to have been born in 1415 A.D. He belonged to Rajputana, whence he went to Benares to become Rāmānanda's disciple. Nābhājī and Priyādāsa relate the legends of the supernatural occurrences of his life, which indicate that he was at first an idol worshipper. Later a change seems to have come over him, for he says:

> "When the *Guru* caused the wealth of divine knowledge to enter me, I meditated on God, and accepted in my heart that He was One.
>
> I have embraced the love and service of God and known comfort; I am satiated and satisfied, and have obtained salvation.
>
> He in whose heart God's light which filleth creation is contained, recognizeth God, who cannot be deceived."[1]

The *Bhaktmāla* and its commentary give an extended notice of Pīpā, the Raja of Gagaráungarh, and relate many stories of the marvellous events which happened in his life, and of the conversions which he effected. Macauliffe translates a hymn which is found in the *Granth,* and which shows the same tendency as is found in other contemporary saints, that is, God is the Primal Essence, the *Guru* is the means of attaining God, and that worship must be internal.

[1] Macauliffe: The Religion of Sikhs, Vol. VI, p. 110.

Sāī'n was a barber who lived at the court of the Prince of Bāndhavgarh, modern Rewa. He is said to have become the spiritual preceptor of this prince. Of him a story is told by Nābhājī which illustrates the saint's dependence on God and His readiness to help him.

Raidās was a worker in leather and thus belonged to a caste very low in social status. He was born at Benares, his father's name was Ragghū and that of his mother Ghurbiniya. He was devoted to religious men and saints and used to spend all the money that he could procure from his father in their service. His father became displeased and turned him out of the house. He then began to live with his wife in a dilapidated hut, engaged in devotion and earning his living by mending shoes. People were attracted to him by his life of simplicity and contentment, and it is said that a Rajput queen accepted him as her *guru*.

His hymns breathe a spirit of humility and self-surrender. He did not indulge in high philosophic speculation about the nature and essence of God and His relation with the world and man. His cardinal doctrines are not different from those of Kabīr, and like him he uses *Rekhta*, even the Persian language, and Sūfi terms, to show the identity of Hinduism and Islam. He believed in God as the Absolute Lord of all and identical with self. Says he:

> "*Govind* is immovable, formless, unborn, unique, of fearless gait, unlimited, beyond sight and reason, indivisible, unqualified, extreme joy."[2]
>
> And
>
> "*Hari* is in all and all is in *Hari*,"[3]
>
> "Thou art I, and the difference between me and thee is like water in a vessel of gold and in the wave."[4]

2 Raidās Kī Bāṇī, p. 25.

3 Ibid., p. 7.

4 Ibid., p. 15.

Thus although He is one He is yet many:

> "One is many and many is one *Hari,* how am I to say that there is a second," and "He is one, and only two by illusion."[5]

But, according to him, God is not identical with any of the incarnations; says he:

> "The *Rāma* in whom the people recognise Him, they are in error about it, O brother."[6]

Raidās looks upon the world as the play of God, and is inclined to the view that it is illusory, or, at any rate, not worth paying attention to:

> "He arranges it like a player (*Bāzīgar*), no one knows the secret of his play. The play is false, only the player is true, by knowing this the mind is satisfied."[7] Again, "the body is empty, the *māyā* (nature) is empty, emptily hast thou wasted life without *Hari.* The temple and luxurious living are empty and empty is the dependence on other gods."[8] Raidās has complete faith in His grace, for did He not come to the help of *Ajāmila,* the elephant, the prostitute, and if He broke their chains, undoubtedly He will do the same for him. Yet there is a pleasing conceit in his attitude; "Thou hast bound me by chains of illusion (*moha*), I have bound Thee with the ropes of love. I am making an effort to emancipate myself, but when I attain freedom then who will adore Thee?"[9]

The other attitude, of complete surrender and humility, is usual with him:

[5] Raidās Kī Bāṇī, pp. 25, 26.
[6] Ibid., p. 6.
[7] Ibid., p. 7.
[8] Ibid., p. 26.
[9] Ibid., p. 22.

"*O Rāma,* Thou alone art wise, thou art eternity without guise, Thou art King (*sultān*) of kings. I am thy ignorant broken (*shikasta*) servant (*bandā*). I have no manners, no fortune. I am senseless, foolish and given to evil. I am a sinner, an alien (*gharib*), heedless, cowardly and black-hearted. Thou art powerful (*qādir*) and capable of taking me across the ocean. I am greedy and cunning. This body of mine is shattered and broken, and my mind is full of many apprehensions. Raidās the slave, begs his Lord (*Sāhib*) vouchsafe to me a sight (*didār*) of Thee,"[10]

and therefore he calls upon Him out of the deepth of his heart:

"Save me, save me, O holy Lord of three worlds."[11]

It is necessary then to give up all external rites, the pilgrimages, fasts, shaving of head, singing and dancing in temples, offering of leaves to idols, and to betake to the devotion of One only, by losing the self in Him, as the river loses itself in the sea. Although

"My caste is low, my actions are low, and even my profession is low,

Says Raidās, yet the Lord has raised me high."[12]

Kabīr had many disciples who spread his message throughout Northern India and the Deccan. They founded twelve branches of the *Panth,* each one recognising some immediate disciple as its head. Some of the branches were merely nominal and took no root where they were planted; others produced important sects. Of his immediate disciples Srut Gopāl Dās succeeded him at Benares and was recognised at Maghar, Jagannāth and Dwārkā; Bhaggū (Bhagwān) Dās is known as the

10 Ibid., p. 16.

11 Ibid., p. 39.

12 Ibid., p. 20.

compiler of the *Bījak*; Dharamdās was the author of many poems in which Kabīr appears as answering his questions; Jīvandās was probably the founder of the famous Satnāmī sect; and Kamāl who is remembered in the *Ādigrantha* by the disparaging line, "the family of Kabīr foundered when Kamāl the son was born," apparently had a following in Western India. Others hardly need mention.

Of those in the generation following one of the most important was Dādū Dayāl. According to *Dabistan*, Dādū was a cotton cleaner, who came from Nārāinā, a village in Mārwār, and lived in the time of Akbar. Wilson follows *Dabistan* concerning Dādū's caste, but adds that he was born in Ahmedabad, from where he removed to Nārāinā in his thirty-seventh year, and where he lived till the end of his life. Farquhar and Traill, however, state that he was born of Brahmin parents at Ahmedabad in 1544 A.D. But Sudhạkar Dwivedī differs from them and is of opinion that he was a tanner or currier (*mochī*) and his family profession was that of making leather bags (*moth*) for drawing water from well. His first name was Mahābalī, he retired from worldly pursuits after the death of his first wife and became a disciple of Kamāl. The last authority produces the following couplet in proof of his opinions:

> "I found the true and mighty *guru*, who taught me the reality, Dādū is the leather bag (*moth*), Mahābalī is the vessel who churned and ate the butter."[13]

Dādū spent most of his life in Rajputana and he visited Ajmer, Delhi, Amber and other places. He is reported to have had an interview with Akbar. He died at Nārāinā in 1603. His poetic utterances consist of 5,000 verses which are divided into chapters, each dealing with a leading religious question. Their language is a mixture of the dialects *Braja Bhāṣā* and

[13] Sudhākar Dwivedi : Dādū Dayāl Kī Bāṇī. Introduction.

Rājasthānī; some of the verses are in *Panjābī* and a number in *Rekhta* and corrupt Persian. Of the last, one or two instances may be reproduced here:

Be mihr gumrāh ghāfil gosht khurdanī,
Be dil badkār 'ālam hayāt murdanī.[14]

which may be rendered thus:

Men are merciless, strayed from the path, heedless, meat-eaters, heartless, evil-doing, and living yet lifeless.

And,

Kul 'ālam yake dīdam arwāh akhlās
Bad 'aml badkār dui pāk yārān pās.[15]

which means;

He saw the whole universe as one, and the pure souls cleaned of evil actions, evil deeds and of the sin of duality in the company of the Friend.

And again, there is an entire poem beginning with the lines,—

Maujūd khabar ma'būd khabar arwāh khabar wajūd
Maqām chi chiz ast dālanī sujūd.[16]

This may be translated as follows:

The existent is known, the adored is known, the souls are known, what is the station of the being to whom it is necessary to bow?

The station of beiny, according to Dadu, is this:

When the lower self (*nafs*) is dominant, and pride is in possession and anger, egotism, duality, falsehood, greed, obstinacy are present, then there is not the name of righteousness.

The station of souls (*arwāh*) is this:

When love, worship, obedience, unty, purity, mercy, affection right, and goodness are present then there is the name of righteousness near.

14 Chandrikā Prasāda Tripāthī. Dādū Dayāl Kī Bāṇī, p. 186.
15 Dwivedī: Op. cit., p. 327.
16 Ibid., p. 80.

The station of the adored (ma'būd) is this:

There is one, the beautiful sight of the Beauty is amazing. To drink the cup of inebriation is a wonderful thing.

The animal stage is when men are away from the path and heedless; the first step is to be bound by law (sharī'at) to obtain from a wise person the knowledge of good and bad, and of lawful and unlawful. Then having completed this, it is necessary to abandon the world, and to engage in remembering epery day and every moment the Highest God, to love the Lover, and to feel the pain and to complain and cry.

Then the station of gnosis (*ma'rifat*) is to know that water, fire, heavens (*'arsh*), the chair were all forms of the *Subhān* who had taken the quality of fire (sharar). Says he:

"The Truth is found, I have seen the Light, the object is held which is the sight of the Friend, the spirits of Adam are the being of the being.

"I have told plainly what kind of goal I had attained, the *Pīrs* (Preceptors) have informed the soul of the *Murīds* (disciples) about the path to the Adored."

Dādū's description of the true Musalman shows how he rose above prejudices of creed and emphasized the true inwardness of religion. He says,

"Dādū the tank of His presence is in the heart and there I take my complete ablution; after performing the ablution in front of *Allah* I say the prayers there.

"Dādū makes his body His mosque, he finds the five members of the assembly (*Jamāat*) in the mind as well as the leader of the prayers (*Mullā'imām*); the indescribable God is Himself in front of him and there he makes his bows and greetings.

"Dādū regards the whole body as the rosary on which the name of the Generous one (*Karīm*) is repeated; there is one fast and there is no second, and the word (*kalima*) is He himself.

"Thus Dādū rises before Allah with concentrated attention

and goes himself above the heavens (*'arsh*) to the place where the *Rahmān* (Merciful) lives.

"Dādū the worshipper continues thus every day till his death, and then he stands before the gates of the Master and neither leaves Him nor goes."[17]

Dādū manifests perhaps even greater knowledge of Sufism than his predecessors, perhaps because he was the disciple of Kamāl who probably had greater leanings towards Islamic ways of thinking than others, perhaps because the Sūfīs of Western India—Ahmedabad and Ajmer—wielded greater influence upon the minds of seekers after God, Hindus or Muslims, than those of the East. At any rate, the effect of their teachings was to make him a staunch supporter of Hindu-Muslim unity. He repeats again and again the sentiment that,

"In all vessels whether Hindu or Muslim there is one soul,"[18]

and

"*O Allah Rāma,* my illusion has passed away, there is no difference at all between Hindu and Musalman."[19]

and

"The one invisible *Ilāhī* art Thou, Thou art *Rāma* and *Rahīm,* Thou are the beautiful Master (*Mālik*), Thy names are *Keśava* and *Karīm,*"[20]

and he asks,

"What is the *Panth* (sect) of *Brahmā, Viṣṇu and Maheś* which is the *dīn* (faith) of Muhammad and what is the way of Gabriel; the one *Allah* is their *Pīr* and *Murshid* (preceptor and director). Dādū knows in his heart to whom they were

17 Dwivedī : Op. cit., p. 95.

18 C. P. Tripāthī : Op. cit., p. 323.

19 Ibid., p. 383.

20 Ibid., p. 455

devoted, the Invisible *Ilāhī* is the *Guru* of the world and there is no other besides him,"[21]

and lastly says Dādū:

"The two brothers are hand and feet, the two are the two ears, the two brothers are the two eyes—Hindus and Musalmans."[22]

With regard to ritual and form, priests, caste, idol worship, incarnations, pilgrimages, ceremonial ablutions and so forth, he held the same opinion as his master Kabīr; to him also God alone is essential and He is sufficient:

"I am not a *Pandit,* I do not know the good of studying and I have not thought over knowledge.

I am not a prophet, I do not know the light, and I do not possess the ornaments of the face.

I am no ascetic, I have no control over my senses, and I have not performed pilgrimages.

I am not a worshipper in temples, and I do not put my trust in meditation.

I am not an adept in *Yoga* and I do not know the methods of worship.

I do not know anything else, and what after all is the need of other things.

Dādū has placed his whole soul under the protection of one Beautiful *Govind.*"[23]

His ideas of God, of the world and of man do not differ from those of his predecessors. He insists upon the unity of God and he regards Him in His twofold aspect of transcendence and immanence. To him He is one, unchangeable, immortal, incomprehensible Being; He is brightness, effulgence, light, illumination, perfection; He is within the heart of all beings. "I stay within me, I am the house for me, I am in the heavens

[21] C. P. Tripāthī: Op. cit., p. 201.

[22] Ibid., p. 323.

[23] S. Dwivedī: Op. cit., p. 76.

(*'arsh*), I am my own support, I depend on myself, so says the Merciful One, the Creator"[24]; and "the whole of nature is His own form, for He is inside all."[25] Withal He is Creator and Lord, who "by one word created all,"[26] and who wills it and the creation comes out of nothing or relapses into nothing.

Man, as long as he is separated from Him, is a sinful creature; his salvation consists in rending this veil; in realising that all otherness and duality, the world of sense, pleasure and pain is a sport and illusion, they are like the mirage in the desert after which the thirsty man runs in vain. The one road to salvation is to know and love Him alone, the one discipline is to die to self in order to live in Him. The man who journeys along this path must be prepared to lay down his life, for he will meet with terrible obstacles, he will feel weary and sick and maddened by pain, so that he will cry out, "my soul is sorely afflicted, because I have forgotten thee, O God, I cannot endure the pain, deliver me."[27] But if he perseveres the clouds will roll away and the sun will shine and the Light will illumine his soul, and filled with wonder he will exclaim "*O Rāma,* my God, I am amazed, no one can find Thy end. *Brahmā, Sanaka* and *Nārad* all failed to see Thee; I who am insignificant and low and little minded, Thou vouchsafest Thy vision to me."[28]

Dādū held that man passed through the whole cycle of births and deaths in one life-time. He says:

"The nature of the eighty-four lakhs of lives is within you, there are many births in a single day but few understand them,"[29] and

24 Ibid., p. 59.

25 Ibid., p. 81.

26 C. P. Tripāthī : Op. cit., p. 276.

27 Ibid., p. 511.

28 S. Dwivedī : Op. cit., p. 109.

29 Ibid., p. 159.

"There are as many incarnations (rebirths) as the changes which come over the soul. This is the transmigration which the Almighty Creator removes away."[30]

"The soul does not know of its births, they take place moment after moment, it undergoes the eighty-four lakhs but does not apprehend."[31]

And again,

"The swine, dogs, jackals, tigers and serpents reside in the heart, also the elephants and the insects, but the *Pandit* knows them not."[32]

It is only by destroying this chain of psychic modifications or spiritual births and deaths that one can become absorbed in God.

Dādū teaches that the *Guru* is the devotee's protector (guāl), and the whip which keeps the horse of the mind in control. The *Guru* is greater than books—*Vedas* and *Qorān*—for through Him realisation takes place and the abode of Light is attained. But it is difficult to obtain the right type of *Guru*, in which case Dādū recommends that one should make birds, beasts and the lord of the forest his *Guru*, for God is in all.

Dādū did not believe in complete actionlessness, for he says,

"Effort (*udyam*) does not produce evil effects, for him who knows it; in effort there is joy, but it should be directed towards the Lord only."[33]

The sect which Dādū established, has its chief seat at Nārāinā where he died. There they hold an annual festival which gives an opportunity to the *Dādūpanthīs* to assemble together in memory of the great man who tried to sink all differences of creed and caste in one religion of love.

[30] S. Dwivedī : Op. cit., p. 160.

[31] Ibid., p. 160.

[32] Ibid., p. 160.

[33] C. P. Tripāthī : Op. cit., p. 33.

The sect of the *Khākīs* arose from among a group of the followers of Dādū. The reputed name of the founder is Kilh who is mentioned by Nābhājī among the disciples of Paihārī Śrīkriśṇadāsa. But nothing more is known about him.

Malūk Dās is made out by Wilson as a disciple of Kilh, but the editor of the *Sant-bāṇī Pustak Mālā*, regards him as the disciple of Viṭṭhaldās, the Dravida saint. Who this Viṭṭhaldās was it is difficult to ascertain. Nābhājī mentions one Viṭṭhaldās who belonged to the sect of Raidās and was a member of Rāmānuja's *Śri Sampradāya*, and Rice speaks of Viṭṭhaldās as a *Vaiśṇava* singer among the Kanarese poets of the sixteenth century. Malūkdās was born in 1574 in the reign of Akbar and after a long life of one hundred and eight years died in 1682 A.D. Kara in the district of Allahabad is his birth-place. He married and had a daughter, and founded a sect which consists wholly of laymen without any ascetics. His order is said to have monasteries at Kara, Jaipur, Isfahābād (Gujarat), Multan, Patna, Katak, Sītā Kayal (Deccan), Kolhapur, Nepal, and Kabul.

Malūkdās taught the same religious doctrines which by his time had become prevalent all over India. He condemns the externalia of religion—pilgrimage, idol worship, good works, and others. He teaches that the true religion is an inward faith, that *Māyā* is the enemy of man, and God's name is the only protection against it, that the world is transitory and the worldly relations of no avail, that man is born of dust and will return to dust, that those who are not devoted to spiritual life are the dogs of the world, that salvation is obtained by knowing the self, killing pride and egotism, controlling passions, trusting the *Guru*, and loving God. This is his definition of the true ascetic (*darwīsh*):

"He who lives apart from the five elements, is the beloved of God, who gives water to the thirsty; his worship is considered great by Muhammad.

"He who feeds the hungry, soon finds the Lord. He who abandons passion and dies while alive, to him 'Izra'īl bows.

"He who considers all men's pain as his own, Malūkdās regards him as the true ascetic."[34]

He too taught oneness of religions and the unity of the Hindu and the Muslim; says he,

"Where is the string of beads (*mālā*) and the rosary (*tasbīh*), now awake and rely not on them.

Who is infidel (*kafir*) and who is barbarian (*malechchha*) look upon *sandhya* (Hindu worship) and the prayer (*namāz*) as one.

Where does *Yama* live and where is Gabriel? He himself is the judge (*Qāzī*), who else keeps accounts?

He calculates the good and the evil deeds, and renders account and sends one where he deserves to go.

Malūkdās, why art thou in error, *Rāma* and *Rahīm* are the names of One."[35]

Sundardās was a disciple of Dādū. He was born in 1596 A.D. at Deosā near Jaipur in Rajputana, in the family of a Bania. It is related that when Sundardās was six years of age Dādū came to Deosā. He saw the child and was struck with his handsome face. Since then the child became known as *Sundar* (handsome), and lived with Dādū his preceptor at Nārāinā. He soon became known for his precocious genius as a saint and poet. But on the death of Dādū in 1603 A.D. he left Nārāinā and returned home. After spending some time at Deosā he went to Benares where he remained engaged in his studies till the age of thirty, and then came back to Rajputana and worked with his co-disciples, Prāgdās and Rajjab, to spread the religion of *Bhakti* as taught by Dādū. He settled down at Fatehpur Shekhāvatī and became friendly with Nawāb Alif Khān and his sons Daulat Khān and Ta'bīr Khān. The Nawāb was himself a Hindi poet, and he highly appreciated the talents of Sundardās. In later years he took to travelling and visited numerous places in Rajputana and Panjab. He died in 1689.

34 Malūk Dās Kī Bāṇī, p. 22.
35 Ibid., p. 27.

Sundardās was a Sanskrit scholar; he had studied Persian and the languages of the North-Western Provinces of India also. His work *Sundarvilāsa* is divided into twenty-four chapters. Some of the chapters deal with the six philosophic systems of the Hindus, and the paths of action and knowledge, and show their inadequacy for the salvation of man. In the constructive parts he dwells upon the teaching of Dādū, but draws most of his arguments and illustrations from purely Hindu sources. Sundardās was a man of culture and a fine poet unlike many of the other religious leaders, but his outlook was not so broad and his spiritual experience not as rich as theirs. In the following poem he describes the self-forgetfulness of man:

> "As the fish swallows the flesh overpowered by greed, and distinguishes not the iron hook from the worm;
>
> As the monkey puts his hand into the jar and keeps his fist firmly closed, and does not open it forced by the temptation of taste;
>
> As the parrot fixes his beak into the coconut and remains hanging on it, and puts himself into trouble on account of his avidity,
>
> So man united with the body, falls into the power of senses, and urged by his desires for pleasure forgets that He is himself."[36]

[36] Malūk Dās Kī Bāṇī, p. 94.

A CONTEMPORARY of Dādū was Bīrbhān, who founded the famous sect of the *Sādhs* or *Satnāmīs*. He was born in 1543 A.D. at Bijesar near Nārnaul in the South-eastern Punjab. He was affiliated through Udhodās to Raidās. He was a strict monotheist, he called God by the name of *Satnām*—the Truth.

He looked upon his *Guru* as the inspirer of his teachings, and spoke about himself as *Udho Kā dās*, the servant of Udho whom he describes as the *Mâlik Kā Hukm*, i.e., the order of the Lord, the personified word of God. The teachings of the sect are in Hindī *Bhāśā*, and their collection is known as the *Pothī* (the book), which is reverenced like the *Granth* of the Sikhs. The book is read in a *Jumlāghar* (house of assembly) or a *Chaukī* (station), and the evening service is attended by men, women and children.

The *Sādhs* do not observe distinctions of caste and rank, they eat and drink together, and marry inside their sect. They permit divorce for offences in which the penalty is expulsion from the sect. They adore one God under the name of *Satnām*, do not keep any material representation of Him, and they do not bow before idol or man. Their worship consists of meditation and the practice of virtue and their ultimate aim is absorption in God. They abstain from intoxicants and animal food, maintain a strict standard of morals and do not allow the oppression of one by the other. They believe in earning one's living by lawful means only, they discourage inequalities of wealth and give their charities in secret.

Their chief seats are at Delhi, Rohtak in the Punjab, Agra, Farrukhabad and Mirzapur in the United Provinces and Jaipur in Rajputana. They became very prominent in the reign of Aurangzeb, when they broke out into rebellion. In 1672 A.D. Khāfi Khān in his notice of the rebellion gave them a very good character, but Īśwardās Nāgar calls them filthy and wicked; the head and front of their offending was that they made no distinction between Hindus and Musalmans.

Their twelve *Hukms* or commandments which are given in the *Ādi Updesh* (first precepts) are deserving of full reproduction. They are given below:—

1. Acknowledge but one God who made and can destroy you, to whom there is none superior, and to whom alone therefore is worship due; not to earth, nor stone, nor metal, nor wood, nor trees, nor any created thing. There is but one Lord, and the word of the Lord. He who medicates on falsehoods, practises falsehoods and commits sin, and he who commits sin falls into hell.
2. Be modest and humble, set not your affections on the world, adhere faithfully to your creed, and avoid intercourse with all not of the same faith, eat not of a stranger's bread.
3. Never lie nor speak ill at any time to, or of anything, of earth or water, of trees, of animals. Let the tongue be employed in the praise of God. Never steal, nor wealth, nor land, nor beasts, nor pasture. Distinguish your own from another's property, and be content with what you possess. Never imagine evil. Let not your eyes rest on improper objects, nor men, nor women, nor dances, nor shows.
4. Listen not to evil discourse, nor to anything but the praise of the Creator, nor to tales, nor gossip, nor calumny, nor music, nor singing except hymns; but then the only musical accompaniment must be in the mind.
5. Never covet anything, either of body or wealth; take not of another. God is the giver of all things, as your trust is in Him so shall you receive.

6. When asked what you are, declare yourself a *Sādh*, speak not of caste, engage not in controversy, hold firm your faith, put not your hope in men.
7. Wear white garments, use no pigments, nor collyrium, nor dentifrice, nor *mehndī* (henna), nor mark your person, nor your forehead, with sectional distinctions, nor wear chaplets, or rosaries or jewels.
8. Never eat nor drink intoxicating substances, nor chew *pān*, nor smell perfumes, nor smoke tobacco, nor chew nor smell opium; hold not up your hands, bow not down your head in the presence of idols or of men.
9. Take no life away, nor offer personal violence, nor give damnatory evidence, nor seize anything by force.
10. Let a man wed one wife, and a woman one husband, let not a man eat of a woman's leavings, but a woman may of a man's, as may be the custom. Let the woman be obedient to the man.
11. Assume not the garb of a mendicant, nor solicit alms, nor accept gifts. Have no dread of necromancy, neither have recourse to it. Know before you confide. The meetings of the pious (*Sādhus*) are the only places of pilgrimage, but understand who are the pious (*Sādhus*) before you so salute them.
12. Let not a *Sādh* be superstitious as to days, or to lunations, or to months, or the cries or appearance of birds or animals; let him seek only the will of the Lord.[1]

Commentary on these commandments is superfluous; their sturdy commonsense is as evident as their puritanism which

[1] Wilson : The Sects of the Hindus, Vol. I.

borrows from Islam and goes beyond it. The voice of Bīrbhān must have sounded like a clarion blast gathering together all those who were fighting for light and reason against superstition and darkness. It must, indeed, have been a wonderful age which could produce Kabīr and Nānak, Dādū and Bīrbhān together and which could render it possible for them to spread their purifying gospel broadcast. The account of the *Sādhs* may be closed with one of their hymns, which illustrates the deeply devotional aspect of their faith:—

"My frame aches without thee! I am wailing at thy door!
Now appear and let me see thee.
O my Lord! I pray thee make no delay!
I have become restless through weeping and wailing.
I cannot live without the sight of thee.
Flames rise within me and consume my frame. Who can endure my pain?
I am full of faults and sins; do thou have mercy upon me.
Take not my faults and faisings into thy regard!
O! thou that freest the soul from sin, maintain my honour!
Forget me not even for a moment, and have mercy upon me
Show me thy form and forget my sins of the present!
Cast thine eyes full upon me, and sever not thy love from me."[2]

Lāldās and Bābā Lāl flourished about the middle of the seventeenth century. The founder of the *Lāldāsī* sect belonged to Alwar and came from a predatory tribe known as the Meos. His teachings ran on the same lines as those of Kabīr. The teachers of the sect are married men, and the singing of hymns accompanied with music plays an important part in their worship.

Bābā Lāl who was a Kshatriya was born in Malwa about the reign of Jahāngīr. His preceptor was one Chaitana, whom he followed to Lahore. He settled down at Dehanpur near Sirhind where he built a temple and a monastery. The

2 Russel: The Castes and Tribes of Central India, Vol. IV, p. 250.

unfortunate Dārā Shikoh, who was one of his pupils, had many interviews with the saint in which he obtained instruction on religious questions. The conversations at these interviews were embodied in a book entitled *Nādir-un-Nukāt* written in Persian. The teaching is in the form of a dialogue between Dārā Shikoh and Bābā Lāl.

What was the creed of Bābā Lāl? He answers the question in these words:

"The creed of the lover differs from other creeds. God is the faith and creed of those who love Him, but to do good is best for the follower of every faith." And he quotes the verse of Hāfiz approvingly:—

"The object of all religions is alike,
All men seek their beloved—
What is the difference between prudent and wild?
All the world is love's dwelling,
Why talk of a mosque or a church?"[3]

Bābā Lāl and Lāldās were not by any means the only representatives of the religious synthesis which attempted to reconcile Hinduism with Islam in the seventeenth century. There were numerous saints and teachers who advocated the same ideas; but unfortunately the names and writings of most of them have disappeared; *Dabistan* has, however, recorded the names of some with whom the author came into contact or of whom he learnt by reputation. Writing of Pīrānā Kohāly he mentions the *Vāirāgīs* and their beliefs: "This sect do no harm to any living being.... They do not admit the *Avatāras* (incarnations), and say that God is exempt from transmigration and union; and according to those who profess the belief in the unity and solitariness of the Supreme Being, He is not susceptible of intimate friendship."[4] And again of the *Nārāyanīs*, a sect founded by Haridās, who died in 1055

[3] Wilson : Op. cit., Vol. I, p. 349.
[4] Op. cit., pp. 195-96.

A.H. (1644 A.D.), he says: "This sect knows nothing of idols, nor of temples, nor of the *Ka'bah*, nor of any sort of worship; they do nothing towards obtaining the knowledge of, or union with, God; they confine themselves to the veneration of *Nārāyaṇ* or the Supreme Being, from which they derive the name of *Nārāyaṇiān*. They do not occupy themselves with the affairs of the world; abnegation and solitude is their law."[5] He gives the following account of Gosā'in Jānī and his disciples:—

"They call their master Jahān, and his followers, composed of Hindus and Musalmans, adopted the creed of *Viśnavī*. This is as follows: They hurt no living beings; they avoid fellowship with men of another creed among the Hindus and Musalmans; they pray five times a day, with their face towards the east; they have the names of God, of the divinities, of the Prophet upon their lips, such as Allah, Mīkā'īl, 'Izra'īl, Jibra'il, Muhammad, and others; they bury their dead; they confer benefits upon others to the extent of their power, a number of their *dervishes* pretend to be afflicted with maladies and beg alms, and whatever they so collect they distribute to the blind and lame, and to people of that description."[6]

He goes on to speak of many others who were equally independent in their ideas, among them were Śivarīnā, Shidāyī, Harirām Purī, Sathrā, Jādū, Partāpmal Chadah, Bināvalī son of Hīrāman Kāyastha, Āzádah Brahman, and Meharchand Sunār.

To the latter half of the seventeenth century belonged Dharnīdās and Pran Nath whose lives extended on to the beginning of the eighteenth century. Dharnīdās was born in 1656, and lived at the village of Manjhī in the district of Chapra. He was a Srīvastava Kāyastha by caste, and a disciple of Chandradās. His teachings are contained in his

[5] Ibid., p. 232.

[6] Ibid., p. 233.

two works *Satya Prakāś* and *Prem Prakāś*. The followers of his sect are to be found all over India even to-day. The following poems illustrate his thought:—

"The lamp is within the house (body), it has neither wick, nor oil nor flame,
Dharnī one should attach himself to Him in thought, word and deed;
There (in the abode of God) one walks without feet and cheers without hands,
Without eyes one sees the sight, and without ears hears the voice,
Dharnī climbed up only half the height, when he saw the form of light arise,
And he beheld the fascinating image of exceedingly incomparable form,
Dharnī the throne is in the body, and the Lord (*Sultān*) is seated on it,
There he accepts in audience (*Mujrā*) all life and world (*Jahān*) to its uttermost limits."[7]

And

"He created you from water, hear, O! my foolish mind,
Such is the husband who is known as *Khudā*.
You burnt for ten months (within the Mother's womb),
And when you became helpless you moved.
You then promised with your own tongue, and vainly had the letters (of fate) written.
And then you promised, O! my foolish mind, that you would obey Him this time, if you were released from pain."[8]

Prān Nāth, founder of the sect of *Dharnīs,* was a Kshatriya who lived in the latter part of the seventeenth century in the reign of the Emperor Aurangzeb. He acquired great influence over Chhatrasāl Raja of Pannā by the discovery of a

[7] Santa Bāṇī Sangrah : Vol. I, p. 115.
[8] Ibid., Vol. II, p. 125.

diamond mine, it is said. He was well acquainted with the sacred books of Islam, and he attempted to propagate a faith which should combine the two religions. In his *Kulzum Sarūp*, a work in the Gujrati language, he brings together texts from the *Qorān* and the *Vedas* and shows that they are not incompatible. His creed proclaims the abolition of the worship of idols, of caste restrictions and the supremacy of the Brahmins. As a test of a disciple's assent to the real identity of the Hindu and Musalman creeds, the ceremony of initiation consists in eating in the society of both religions. He wrote fourteen treatises all in verse; some extracts from his *Qiyāmat-nāma* are given below:—

"Go to the followers (*ummat*) and tell them, rise the faithful ones, for the day of resurrection has come.
I tell you in accordance with what the *Qorān* says, and I relate before you the story.
He who is a special leader of the following should stand careful.
I will only give this warning, that in the eleventh century (of the *Hejira*) you will become fearless...........
All of you, whether Hindus or Muslims, will have a common faith."

He describes the history of the last eleven centuries, how Jesus Christ came first and then Muhammad and after him the *Imāms*; and then continues to give the story of Adam's fall, and Satan's (*'Azāzīl's*) determination to destroy the race of man; and then goes on to discuss the various prophecies Judaic, Muslim and Hindu which foretell the coming of the last prophet, with this mission:—

"There was strife in the two worlds, and the path of action (*Karma Kāṇḍa*) and of law (*Sharī'at*) prevailed, He made known to all the path of reality (*haqīqat*) and gnosis (*ma'rifat*). He cleared away the clouds from the sky, illumined the universe with the sun of light, and united the peoples of the world. The whole creation calls upon *Khudā*, makes its statement to Him, and accepts His command. All worship the word (*Sūrat*) of the Lord, or the *Kalām* (word) of *Allah*."[9]

The active careers of Jagjīvan, Bullā Sāhib, Keśava, Charandās, his two lady disciples Sahjo and Dayābaī, Gharībdās, Shivanārāyaṇ and Rām Sanehī, lay in the eighteenth century.

Jagjīvandās was born at Sārdaha in the Bārābankī district of the United Provinces in 1682 A.D. He was a Chandel Thākur and belonged to the school of Kabīr. He spent most of his life at Kotwa between Bārābankī and Lucknow. His teachings are contained in his three principal works—*Jñān Prakāś*, *Mahāpralaya* and *Pratham Granth*. His disciples were drawn from all classes of people—Brahmin, Thākur, Chamār and Muslim. "He succeeded in establishing some community of thought between himself and Islam. Two at least of his disciples were Musalmans."[10]

He either re-organised the older Satnāmī sect which had suffered defeat from Aurangzeb's armies, or set up a new one with the same name.

He taught the doctrine of the unity of God, whom he regarded as beyond all qualities (*nirguṇa*). He laid great stress upon self-surrender and indifference towards the world. He held that the goal of human endeavours was absorption in God through the help of a spiritual guide (*guru*). Truth, gentleness, and harmlessness were the main virtues in his moral code.

In the following hymn he preaches the inwardness of religion:—

"Oh what avail is the wearing of a rosary, or putting on the mark on the forehead;
Of what avail is the abandonment of food and fasting, or feeding on milk alone.

[9] Growse: Mathura, Aajawat Namah.

[10] Grierson: Satnāmīs, E. R. E., Vol. XI.

What is the use of mortification before five fires, of wearing skins,
Of standing with face turned upwards or sitting in smoke or giving up the use of salt.
What is the value of sitting and standing or of keeping silence and repeating the names;
Of being a learned man or a lecturer or of acquiring much knowledge.
Why abandon wife and retire into forest, and practise asceticism;
The world forgets that without love all is fruitless.
Stay at home, do not run away in all directions, meditate on the One who is beyond thought and beyond support; in the expanse of the mind's sky His image is seen. He is different from all.
He whose belief attains to Him, has ensured his destiny; O Jagjīvan, place your head on the feet of the *guru* and then you will escape from the net of errors."[11]

How to meditate on God is told here:—

"Give up all thinking (*fikr*), and become absorbed in meditation (*zikr*).
Make the parrot of attention (*śruti*) sit in the sky, and repeat the name of *Hari* and thus teach him.
The Lord (*Sā'īn*) is one, know Him as one,
Never allow your mind to have any doubts
Says Jagjīvandās, see there the word (*śruti*),
Fold the two hands together and adore the Lord."[12]

And all human beings are recognized as essentially equal:—

"O *Sādhu*, the one Light shines in all,
Think it over in your mind, there is no second.

[11] Jagjīvan Sāhib Kī Śabdāvalī, p. 38.

[12] Ibid., p. 49.

The blood and the body are the same, there is no Brahman or *Sādhu*;
Some are called men and some women, the Invisible (*ghaibī*) *Puruś* (male) is in all."[13]

Bullā Sāhib, whose real name was Bulāqī Rām, was a Kunbī by caste, he was employed for ploughing the fields of Gulāl Sāhib; but the latter, struck by his piety and devotion, became his disciple. Bullā was a disciple of Yārī Sāhib, and set up as a teacher in Bhurkuda, a village in the Ghāzīpur district of the United Provinces. His utterances are full of references to Yogic exercises, and he seems to have regarded the control of breath as an important part of worship. Apart from this, however, he is a *Bhakta* of the usual type. Here is an illustration of his teachings:—

"One who is mad (*divānā*) after the Beloved (*Mahbūb*) drinks the cup, in the obode (*khānā*) of the unconditioned (*nirguṇ*).
The unconditioned is the abode, the *Trikutī* is the goal, and the association of the devotees the means of knowledge.
Every moment one should go to the unconditioned abode, and should remain drunk during the eight parts of the day. Speak to the people of the unconditioned form, O Bullā, and you have found the secret of the heavens."[14]

And this is how he expresses his dependence on God from day to day:—

"O Lord, take my roll-call (*hāzirī*), and enter it into the register (*daftar*). I am a poor neglected soldier, give me something day by day."[15]

[13] Jagjīvan Sāhib Kī Śabdāvalī, p. 108.

[14] Bullā Sāhib Kā Śabda Sār, p. 13.

[15] Ibid., p. 29.

Keśavadās was a Bania by caste, and belonged to the order of Yārī Sāhib, a Muslim saint (1668–1723), who lived and taught at Delhi. His warning (*chetāvanī*) is given below:—

"He maintains wealth (*daulat*), standards (*nishān*), display, egotism (*khudī*) and pride.

He shows no mercy to any soul in the world.

He knows well that all this magnificence is transitory, and that Death goes about with its net to kill in an instant.

All this encampment of tents and elephants and horses, all these furnishings are illusory.

Except the name of *Hari* none of them will be of any use at the time of departure.

I warn you over and over again, give up pride and the love of *māyā* (world), why, O *Keśava,* are you agitated with the delusions of desire."[16]

Charandās was born in 1703 A.D. at Dehrā in Mewāt, Rajputana. He was a Dhūsar Bania by caste, and he founded his order at Delhi about 1730. He lived the life of a householder and accepted both men and women disciples. Of the later Sahjo and Dayābāī have acquired fame by their utterances (*bānī*). His teaching is similar to that of Kabīr. It emphasizes the unity of God, the value of reliance upon His name, the need of devotion and the necessity of having a *guru* who is to be regarded as divine. He died in 1780.

Charandās denounced idolatry. He says:—

"Keep your eyes on the Husband, what have you got to do with any other man?

Leave all the gods alone, and repeat the name of *Hari*."[17]

16 Sant Bāṇī Sangrah, Vol. II, p. 176.

17 Ibid., Vol. I, p. 147

He had unlimited reverence for the preceptor; says he:

"*Guru* is like *Śiva* who awakens you.

Guru is *Brahmā*, *guru* is *Viṣṇu*, he fills up your emptiness.

Guru is like the Ganges which washes away all sins.

Guru is like the Sun which draws away all darkness."[18]

Here is an illustration of his devotion:—

"O benefactor of the poor (*gharīb-nivāz*), protect my honour, who will put my affairs straight, for everything is wrong with me?

O *Hari*, you are called the lover of *Bhaktas*, the saviour of the fallen, fulfil the aspirations of thy people, look at them with eyes which will cool their burning.

You are a ship, I am your crew, I cannot leave you and go elsewhere.

O *Hari*, if you will punish me and throw me overboard, I shall never find a place of rest.

O Lord, the whole world knows that Charandās has thrown himself on Your protection.

If he is then laughed at, it will bring slight on You, please think of it."[19]

Sahjo and Dayābāī were two sisters belonging to the same caste as Charandās who was their *guru*. Their hymns are full of tenderness and love.

Gharībdās lived from 1717 to 1778 A.D. in the village of Chhudanī, Rohtak district, the Panjab. He was a Jāt by caste and a householder in life. He belonged to the school of

18 Sant Bāṇī Sangrah, Vol. II, p. 79.

19 Ibid., Vol. II, p. 185.

Kabīr, and consequently his verses abound with Persian terms and Sūfī allusions, for instance:—

"O *Sāhib* (Lord), hear the sound of my prayer in Your highest heaven (*'arsh*).

You are my father (*pidar*) and mother (*mādar*) and you are bestower of favour (*karīm*), it is becoming the Father to protect the honour of the son.

I pray to You with folded hands, O Creator,

My body and mind and wealth are an offering to You, vouchsafe to me your sight (*dīdār*)."[20]

And again—

"Good conduct, patience, discrimination, understanding, mercy, and continuous *dharma*, and maintain also, intelligence (*'aql*), certitude (*yaqīn*), and faith (*īmān*), and you will obtain the object which is their reality."[21]

Rāmcharan, the founder of the *Rām Sanehī* order, was born in 1718, at Surasena, in Jaipur territory. He was at first a *Rāmāwat,* but later became a staunch opponent of idol worship, and was therefore persecuted by Brahmins. The headquarters of his sect are at Shāhpur, but they are represented in several other places. The order consists of *Sādhūs* only, and there are no lay members. They "do not worship images. Their religious services are to some extent similar to those of the Muhammadans. Five services are held every day in their shrines."[22] The order admits men of any caste, their religious and moral discipline is strict, and they have regular officers to enforce it.

The *Shivanārāyaṇī* order was established about the middle of the eighteenth century (1734 A.D.). The founder, Swāmī

20 Sant Bāṇī Sangrah, Vol. I, p. 193.

21 Ibid.

22 Bhattāchārya : Hindu Castes and Sects, p. 447.

Nārāyaṇa Singh, belonged to the Naraunī Rajput tribe and was an inhabitant of Chandrāvar near Rasrā in the Ballia district. The order has three monasteries in the Ballia district and one in Ghāzīpur. The *Shivanārāyanīs* adore the Absolute (*Pāra Brahma*) alone, and hold their *Granth* (book) in reverence. Persons of all denominations are admitted without any distinction of caste or class. When a member of the sect dies his body is disposed of according to his instructions by burial, cremation or throwing in a river. Muhammad Shāh the Mughal Emperor was a disciple of the founder, which is borne out by the following couplet:—

> "He taught the word to Muhammad Shāh,
> And obtaining his seal propagated the sect."[23]

The adhesion of the emperor gave a prestige to the order, which obtained popularity for it. The seal is still kept in the headquarters.

In the latter part of the eighteenth century and the beginning of the nineteenth, flourished Sahajānand, Dūlandās, Gulāl, Bhīkā, and Paltoodās. They were amonp the backwashes of the great wave which had arisen with Kabīr in the fifteenth century, and which spread with great force and rapidity all over India in the succeeding three centuries, and which as the eighteenth century wore towards its close gradually ebbed away, creating a cultural hollow into which European currents began to pour down. All of them were devotees inspired by the same ideas, they were reiterators and popularisers, they hardly added anything new to the religiousness or anything of great value to the rich treasures of devotional poetry. The social impulse was exhausted, the empire was crumbling to pieces and society was torn by conflict and disorder. In such circumstances men's minds were benumbed and their activities were clogged. India ceased to create.

23 Grierson: Shivanārāyaṇīs, J.R.A.S., 1918, p. 114.

Sahajānanda, the founder of the *Swāmī Nārāyaṇī* sect, was born near Ajodhia in 1780 A.D. He taught the worship of one God whom he called *Krisna* or *Nārāyaṇa*, and whose incarnation he was himself. He prohibited killing and the use of animal food or liquor or drugs, he insisted upon strict sexual relations, and denounced theft, robbery, false accusations, suicide and other evils. He observed no distinction of caste, and he rejected the worship of images. His priests were celibate. His ideas spread among Kolīs, Bhīls and Kāthīs of Western India. He was persecuted by the Maratha Peshwas, but he taught the doctrine of suffering injury without retaliation, and consequently many of his followers were beaten to death.

Dūlandās was a disciple of Jagjīvandās who reorganised the *Satnāmī* order. He was a Sombansī Kshatriya, and lived in the district of Rāi Bareilī. He speaks of Mansūr, Shamsi Tabrīz, Nizāmuddīn, Hāfiz, in his poems, one of which is given below:

"Now the sorrow of the heart has vanished, the Beloved has come into sight.

Living in the company of saints, I have bowed my head before the true leader (*hādī*).........

Every moment I have His face in my imagination (*tasavvar*), and His image shines in my heart, Bu 'Alī Qalandar, Farīd and Tabrīz have all sung of this same faith.

With sincerity and patience, he has shown me Allah who is beyond space (*la makān*) and beyond sight.

See, O peoples, Dūlan, whose *guru* (preceptor) is Jagjīvan, has taken the Beloved to his heart.

And the unique Husband, the Invisible Presence (*Ghaibī hudhūr*) has entered into my heart."[24]

24 Sant Bāṇī Sangrah, Vol. II, pp. 166-67.

Gulāl, who was born in the last quarter of the eighteenth century, hailed from Bashārī, Ghāzīpur district. He belonged to the Kshatriya caste, and was a disciple of Bullā Sāhib. The following lines give an idea of his poetic skill and religious beliefs:

"The bee of the mind plays *Vasanta*,
The unstruck music sounds in infinite space.
The lotus opens and the bees make a noise,
The Light expands its illumination.
The heart is filled with joy to see it again and again;
When the mind becomes entangled, then it is enmeshed in the net.
The current of Light flows in wave after wave.
My heart is placed at the lotus feet.
It does not come (take birth), nor does it go, the soul dies not,
Gladly it drinks the immortal nectar again and again.
The Lord is beyond reach, beyond perception, beyond sight,
I have found the Lord by seeing him with my eyes.
Says Gulāl my desire is fulfilled,
I have triumphed over *Yama* and obtained an abode in Light."[25]

Bhīkā was a disciple of Gulāl. He taught in the district of Ghāzīpur, after the death of his *guru*, as his successor. His pantheistic outlook is expressed in the following poem:

"He himself (*Khud*) is the earth, from which a multitude of vessels are made, by the potter, whose creation has a wonderful variety.
The name is like gold, it becomes ornament and appears as other,
But whether it is pure or impure, the basis is gold itself.

25 Sant Bāṇī Sangrah, Vol. II, p. 205.

The foam, the bubble, currents and waves are many,
Know that the water is the same, whether it is sweet or salt.
The soul has one caste, *Bhīkā* holds this opinion,
The robbers belong to His government (*Sarkār*) as well as the travellers."[26]

Paltoo Dās was a resident of village Nāgpur Jalālpur in the district of Faizabad. He belonged to the *Kandu Bania* community and was of the school of Bhīkā. The following lines describe his career:

"He took birth in Nanga Jalālpur, and dwelt in Oudh says Paltooprasād, his birth created a stir in the world.
He destroyed the four castes and laid the root of *Bhakti*, and in the garden of Guru Govinda, Paltoo the flower, blossomed.
He became a monk in Jalālpur city, and in Oudh broke the belt.
God carries on transactions in the heart, Paltoo says, he is the unconditioned trader."[27]

He showed the same familiarity with Sūfī ideas as Kabīr, and attempted the same kind of reconciliation of the two faiths as his great predecessor had done. He says,

"I have known *Nāsūt, Malkūt,* and *Jabrūt,*
and I have tasted the delights of *Lāhūt.*
The mature devotee is one whose heart is illumined,
And who takes his seat in the spaceless abode (*lāmakān*).
The secret of heaven has been opened,
And the soul cries in the heart, *Haq* (the truth), *Haq*.

26 Sant Bāṇī Sangrah, Vol. II, p. 213.

27 Paltoo Sāhib Kī Bāṇī, Vol. I, Life, p. I.

F. 14

Paltoo Dās says, he sees every minute and on all sides, Mecca."[28]

And with regard to Hindus and Muslims:

"They say *Rāma* in the east, and *Khudā* in the west,
Who then lives in the north and the south?
Where is the Lord, and where is He not?
Why do the Hindus and Muslims raise a storm?
The Hindu and Muslim have engaged in struggle,
And the two faiths run into two opposing camps.
Paltoo the slave says, the Lord is in all.
He is not divided at all, this is the truth."[29]

Here the account of the radical reformers of Hinduism must close. It was noticed before that there were two classes of religious leaders in India; in the first class were Kabīr, Nānak and others whose careers have been traced above, and to the second class belonged those whose thought was of a more conservative type. Among the latter were some who adored *Rāma* and others who worshipped *Kriśna* or *Kriśna* and *Rādhā*. In all human societies there are groups of men of different spiritual needs; for instance, it is impossible for one group of men to conceive of God except in absolute terms, and their intellectual bias excludes from that conception every human quality; then there is another group which supremely feels the want of a God who has something in common with themselves, who is not a mere abstract impersonal entity, an abstract and impersonal consciousness, command, or love, but something that is personal, a teacher, a ruler, a father, a lover; still others need an even more concrete personality on whom they can depend, a person who can stand before them as an ideal, or a person in whose history they can take a living interest, in short, an incarnation of God who dwells amidst men and shares with men his sorrows, griefs and burdens.

28 Paltoo Sāhib Kī Bāṇī, Vol. II, p. 44 (I).
29 Ibid., Vol. II, p. 5.

The Hindus call the first group the worshippers of the absolute (*Nirguṇa upāsaka*), whether their path be that of action or knowledge or devotion; and the second group the worshippers of the qualified *Brahman* (*Saguṇa*); among them some believe in incarnations and the others do not. The Absolute may again be transcendent or immanent or both. The radical reformers were, generally speaking, worshippers of the Absolute who was both transcendent and immanent; and as the Muslim Sūfis had the same conception of God, the two came together and saw that there was no essential difference in their religions.

The second group among the Hindus was that of worshippers of *Śiva* and *Viśṇu*, the latter in his two manifestations as *Rāma* or *Kriśṇa*. They had their counterparts among orthodox Muslims who regarded God as the Lord and the Ruler; but it was impossible for these two to make any approach towards an understanding, because both were entrenched behind fixed systems of revealed books, inspired and irrevocable commands, and divinely sanctioned rites and institutions. To this group mainly belonged the conservatives, the learned on both sides, and the priests whose interests were vested in the maintenance of a particular social and economic order. But the presence of Islam in India could hardly fail to impress even them, and they too showed in certain aspects its influence. In an earlier chapter it has been shown how Hinduism in the south reacted towards Islam, how contact with Islam accentuated its monotheism, tended to remove disqualifications of caste, strengthened the movement of devotion, introduced new elements in its doctrines about the teacher, relaxed the rigours of the cult without entirely abolishing it, and encouraged the use of the popular languages.

In the north the same features appeared. It is hardly necessary to enter into a detailed analysis of the literature of the two schools, the one regarding *Rāma* as the supreme deity to be adored, and the other, *Kriśṇa*. Rāmānanda and Vallabha were the founders of the two schools in the north, but the best exponents of their ideas in the Hindi language were Tulasīdās and Sūrdās. Both have wielded an enormous influence upon the Hindu mind. But as the object of this thesis is not to describe all the sects which were developed in Hinduism, but only those which show the distinct influence of Islam, they fall outside its ambit. It may, however, be remarked that the language of both Tulasīdās and Sūrdās shows evident traces of this influence, for both use quite a number of words which had been made current by the Muslims.

REFORMERS OF BENGAL AND MAHARAŚTRA

Outside the vast region in which Hindī or some dialect of Hindī is spoken, among the peoples whose language is Marāthī or Bengālī, movements similar to that already discussed, arose. In Bengal the Musalmans appeared in the twelfth century and in Mahārāśtra a hundred years later. Their presence in both regions created upheavals—social, political and religious.

In Bengal at the time of the arrival of the Muslims, Buddhism was undergoing a complete transformation. The old faith was being replaced by either *Paurāṇic* Hinduism or a strange mixture of many cults, Buddhist, *Śaiva* and *Tāntrim*. The arrival of Hinduism which took place under Pāla and Sen Kings and which was not unaccompanied with persecution, led to the establishment of Brahman supremacy, caste differences and image worship. Sanskrit was the medium of its expression, and it naturally discouraged the language of the common people. But side by side with *Paurānic* Hinduism the old cults continued to exist, although in veiled forms. When, therefore, the Muslim conquest took place, it gave a definite check to Brahmanism, but encouraged the half-suppressed ancient cults, stimulated the movement of reform, and encouraged the growth of Bengālī literature.

Dinesh Chandra Sen in his monumental history of Bengālī language and literature handsomely acknowledge the debt which the language owes to the patronage of the Muslim rulers. He says:

"This elevation of Bengālī to a literary status was brought about by several influences, of which the Muhammadan conquest was undoubtedly one of the foremost. If the Hindu kings had continued to enjoy independence Bengālī would scarcely have got an opportunity to find its way to the court of Kings."[1] The Muslim rulers of Bengal appointed scholars to translate the Rāmāyaṇa and the Mahābhārata from Sanskrit into Bengālī which they spoke and understood. The translation of the Mahābhārata was undertaken by order of Nāsir Shāh who ruled at Gaur till 1325 A.D. Vidyāpati, the celebrated Maithilī poet, dedicated his song to Nāsir Shāh and spoke with admiration of Sultān Ghiyas-ud-dīn. Raja Kans whose successor became a convert to Islam, patronised Krittivasa, the translator of the Rāmāyaṇa; "his court was stamped with Moslem influence."[2] The Bhāgwata was translated under the patronage of the Emperor Husain Shāh; the translator Mālādhar Vasu received from him the title of Guṇrāja Khān. Husain Shāh's general, Parangal Khān, had another translation of the Mahābhārata made by Kavīndra Parameśwar. Parangal Khān's son Chhutī Khān, governor of Chittagong, employed Śrīkarana Nandī for translating the *Aśvamedha Parva* of the Mahābhārata. 'Alaol, a Musalman, translated Malik Muhammad Ja'isi's Hindi *Padmāvata* into Bengāli, as well as, some Persian work. "Instances of like nature, where Muhammadan emperors and chiefs initiated and patronised translations of Sanskrit and Persian works into Bengālī, are numerous, and we are led to believe, that when the powerful Moslem sovereigns of Bengal granted this recognition to the vernacular language in their courts, Hindu rajas naturally followed suit. Thus the appointment of Bengālī poets to the courts of Hindu Rajas, grew to be a fashion after the example of the Moslem chiefs."[3]

[1] Dinesh Chandra Sen: History of Bengālī Language and Literature, p. 10.

[2] Ibid., p. 12.

[3] Ibid., pp. 13-14.

The results of Muslim intercourse with the Hindu population appeared early in the history of Hindu sects in Bengal. The representatives of the older faiths were highly gratified with the suppression of Brahmanism and even with Muslim vandalism. The followers of the *Dharma* cult, a modified form of *Mahāyānism*, could hardly contain themselves with glee at the chastisement which their erstwhile oppressors suffered. In their sacred book entitled *Śūnya Purāna* and written in the eleventh century by Ramai Pandit, there is a chapter headed "the anger of Niranjan" (*Niranjaner Rukhm*), and evidently interpolated in the fourteenth century, which refers to a free fight between the Muhammadans and the Brahmanas at Jājpur. It is thus rendered by Dinesh Chandra Sen: "In Jājpur and Māldah sixteen hundred families of Vedic Brahmins mustered strong. Being assembled in groups of ten or twelve they killed the *Sat-Dharmīs* (Buddhists) who would not pay them religious fees, by uttering incantations and curses. They recited *mantras* from the *Vedas* and fire came out of their mouths, as they did so. The followers of *Sat-Dharma* trembled with fear at the sight thereof, and prayed to *Dharma*; for who else could give them succour in that crisis? The Brahmins began to destroy the creation in the above manner, and acts of great violence were perpetrated on the earth. *Dharma* who resided in *Baikuntha* was grieved to see all this. He came to the world as a Muhammadan. On his head he wore a black cap, and in his hand he held a cross-bow. He mounted a horse and was called *Khodā*. *Niranjana* incarnated himself in *Bhest* (heaven). All the gods being of one mind, wore trousers. Brahma incarnated himself as Mohammad, *Viṣṇu* as *Paigambar* and *Śiva* became *Adamfa* (*Adam*). *Ganeśa* came as a *Gāzī*, *Kārtika* as a *Kāzī*, *Nārada* became a *Sekhq* and *Indra* a Moulāna. The *Risis* of heaven became *Fakīrs*. The sun, the moon, and the other gods came in the capacity of foot-soldiers, and began to beat drums. The goddess *Chandī* incarnated herself as *Hayā Bībī* and Padmāvatī became *Bībī Nūr*. The gods being all of one mind entered Jājpur. They broke the temples and *maṭhas* and cried 'seize', 'seize'. Falling at the feet of *Dharma*, Ramai Pandit sings, "O what a great confusion!"[4]

The *Dharma Gājan* and *Bada Janānī* songs bristle with spite and jealousy against the Brahmans, and are interspersed with Muslim ideas. There is a *Dehāra Bhanga* (breaking of a temple) song entitled *Dharma Pūjā Paddhati* (the method of worshipping *Dharma*):

> "Then of Deharā Bhanga,
>
> The Khonkara is worshipping with his face towards the west.
>
> Some worship *Alla,* some *'Alī,* and others Mamud Sai (Lord).
>
> The *miān* kills no living things nor eats dead ones.
>
> He is cooking his food over a slow fire.
>
> The caste distinction will slowly be broken—for, behold, there's a Mohammedan in a Hindu family;
>
> *Khodā's Rahmān* has called a meeting.
>
> The crow is asking and *Dharma* is deciding where *Khodā* was first born......
>
> Thou art, *O Khodā,* I know, superior to all others.
>
> How I wish to hear the *Qorān* form thy lips!
>
> Niranjana transformed to *Alla* will confer blessings.
>
> May the enemies of *Amin* fall under the wrath of *Qutub.*"

The *Bada Janānī* (proclamation) ends thus:

> "May *Pīr Paygambara* shower his blessings on our heads and may our formidable enemies fall and die under the wrath of *Qutub.*

[4] Dinesh Chandra Sen : Op. cit., pp. 36–37.

Thus has Ramai Pandit sung only the Proclamation, (and he hopes that) the Lord will confer boons on the leader."[5]

The worship of *Śiva* was at one time a leading factor in the religion of Bengal as early as the times of Hiuen Tsiang. Śaśānka, a *Śaiva* ruler of Bengal, persecuted the Buddhists, destroyed their temples and set up images of *Śiva* in place of those of Buddha. Since his times the worship had grown in great favour. But with the changes produced by the Muslim conquest *Śiva* worship declined, and new beliefs grew up. In the words of Dinesh Chandra Sen, "the Muhammadans with their vigorous living faith, had by this time come to Bengal. Their *Qorān* which they believed to be inspired, lays it down that the God of Islam helps believers and destroys unbelievers. The strong belief of Islam in a personal God had to be counteracted in this country by forms of religion in which the personal element of divinity predominated. So the *Śākta* and the *Vaiśnava* religions flourished and the *Śaiva* religion with its impersonal ideal and mysticism in which man rose to the level of his God in the *Advaitvāda*, was gradually thrown into the background as the masses did not comprehend its speculative features."[6]

As a result of this interaction of Hinduism and Islam curious syncretic cults and practices arose. The Hindus offered sweets at Muslim shrines, consulted the *Qorān* as an oracle, kept its copies to ward off evil influences, and celebrated Muslim feasts, and the Musalmans responded with similar acts.

Out of this close comradeship grew the worship of a common God, adored by Hindus and Musalmans alike, namely, *Satya Pīr*. The Emperor Husain Shāh of Gauḍa is supposed to be the originator of the cult, and if that is so, he my be regarded as a precursor of the illustrious Akbar.

[5] Benoy Kumār Sarkār: Folk Element in Hindu Culture, pp. 226—29.

[6] D. C. Sen: Op. cit., pp. 234—35.

But of far greater importance was the effect of this interaction on the movement inaugurated by Chaitanya. The conditions of religious life before the birth of Chaitanya are thus summarised in the History of Bengālī language and literature: "The power of the Brahmans had become oppressive. The rules of caste became more and more stringent as *Kulīnism* was stereotyped. While better ideals in religion were upheld by the Brahmins, the gap between man and man was widened by caste restrictions. The lower strata of society groaned under the autocracy of the higher, who shut the portals of learning against the inferior classes. They were also debarred from having any access to higher life, and the religion of the new school (*Paurānik*) became the monopoly of the Brahmins as if it were the commodity of the market-place."[7]

The simple faith and the democratic ideals of Islam impinged upon this society and produced a ferment which was focussed by Chaitanya.[8] He was born of Brahman parents at Nadia, in 1485 A.D. His father died when he was quite a child, his mother sent him to school, where he became proficient in grammar and logic. He was married at the age of eighteen, and he set up as a teacher when he was twenty. But later the spirit which has called so many earnest Hindus away from the world came upon him; he left home and wandered over the whole country. In his travels he came into touch with *Sādhūs* and *Faqīrs*. In his biography written by Kriśnadās, a meeting with *Pathāns* near Brindāban is thus described: "One of the Muslims, a grave man clad in black and called a *Pīr*, was melted at heart on seeing the master (Chaitanya). He propounded monotheism and one common God, on the basis of his holy book," but of course the master refuted him. "There are various incidents in the life of Chaitanya which prove con-

[7] D. C. Sen: Op. cit., pp. 413–14.

[8] Jadunāth Sarkār: Chaitanya, p. 226.

clusively that he dearly loved the *Yavana*."[9] But whether he loved the *Yavana* or not, it is undoubted that his teaching was affected by the *Yavana's* ideas. He died in 1533 A.D.

The essence of Chaitanyaism is given in two sentences by Kriśnadās: "if a creature adores *Kriśna* and serves his *Guru*, he is released from the meshes of illusion and attains to *Kriśna's* feet,"[10] and, "leaving these (i.e., temptations) and the religious systems based on caste, (the true *Vaiśṇava*) helplessly takes refuge with *Kriśna*."[11] Chaitanya thus condemned the whole ritualistic system of the Brahmans, and preached faith in *Hari*. According to him worship consisted in love and devotion, and song and dance, producing a state of ecstasy in which His presence was realised. All men were competent to perform this worship, irrespective of caste and creed. Chaitanya had disciples from the lowest strata of Hindu society and among Musalmans too. Three of his principal disciples were Rūp, Sanātan and Haridāsa.

From the school of Chaitanya branched out the sect of Kartābhajas. The founder of the sect was a Sadgop, named Rām Samran Pāl, known as Kartā Babā. He was born about the end of the seventeenth century near Chakdahā in Nadia. His birth was foretold by a Muslim *Faqīr*, who also brought him up. Kartā lived for eighty-four years and died in a village near the place of his birth. He left behind twentytwo disciples (*Bāīs Faqïr*), one of whom named, Rām Dulāl, succeeded as the head of the sect; in him the spirit of the Muslim *Faqīr* was incarnated. He organized the sect and laid down its precepts in a series of songs. The doctrines of the Kartābhajas are:

(1) There is only one God, who is incarnate in Kartā.

(2) The *Mahāśaya* or spiritual guide must be all in all to his *Baratï* or disciple.

9 Jadu Bhathāchārya: Hindu Castes and Sects, p. 464.

10 Jadunāth Sarkār: Op. cit., p. 278.

11 Ibid., p. 281.

(3) The Mantra or religious formula of the sect to be repeated five times a day, was a means of salvation and of obtaining material prosperity.

(4) Meat and wine must be abstained from.

(5) Friday must be held sacred and should be spent in religious meditation and discussion.

(6) There is no distinction in the cult between high caste and low, or between Hindus, Musalmans and Christians. [A Musalman has more than once risen to the rank of a teacher. The members of the sect eat together, at least once or twice in the year].

(7) No outward sign of adherence to the sect is required. A Hindu may retain his sacred thread, and a Musalman need not shave on becoming a member of the sect.

(8) Fervid love or *Bhaktī* is the only religious exercise necessary.

About the end of the thirteenth century the Muslims began the conquest of the Deccan. By the middle of the fourteenth century they had not only completely subjugated it, but they had also established an independent Muslim kingdom there. The Bahmanī rulers of the Deccan like their contemporaries in Bengal, fostered the growth of the literature and art of the people whom they governed. The Marāthī language was used in the offices of the 'Ādil Shāhī and Qutb Shāhī kingdoms, and Marāthās were employed as revenue officers and even as commandants. Qutb Shāh was a patron of culture and himself a poet of considerable power, and wrote extensively in the *Dakhnī* language which was a mixture of Hindī and Persian. The intercourse of Hindus and Musalmans produced the same cultural phenomena in Mahārāśtra as it had done in Hindustan and Bengal.[12] The Marāthī saints and hymn-singers effected the

[12] Census of India (1901, Vol. VI, Bengal).

same kind of synthesis of the two faiths as was done by Kabīr and Nānak in the north. Rānāde describes the beginning of the movement thus: "The severity of the monotheistic creed of the Muhammadans was distinctly impressed upon the minds of these prophets (Kabīr, Nānak and others). The worshippers of Dattātraya or the incarnation of the Hindu Trinity, often clothed their God in the garb of a Muhammad *Faqīr*. This same influence was at work with greater effect on the popular mind in Mahārāśtra, where preachers, both Brahmans and non-Brahmans, were calling the people to identify *Rāmā* with *Rahīm*, and ensure their freedom from the bonds of formal ritualism and caste distinctions, and unite in common love of man and faith in God."[13]

The history of religious upheaval in Mahārāśtra goes back to the time of Jñāneśvar who completed his Marāthī commentary of the Bhagavad Gītā in 1290 A.D. Jñāneśvar had a tremendous influence on the language and thought of Mahārāśtra, but the first of the saintly array of men who changed the faith of this region and turned the minds of men from the priest-ridden ceremonial of a narrow creed to freedom and love was Nāmdev. He is remembered by every saint of Mahārāśtra, Hindustan, Rajputana and the Punjab as the grst historic name in the long list of *Bhaktas*. The date of his birth according to tradition is 1270 A.D., but Bhandārkar, for very good reasons, assign him to the fourteenth century.

Bhakti in Mahārāśtra centred round the shrine of Vithobā at Pandharpur on the banks of the Bhīmā. But although thus associated with a particular temple and a particular image, it was really not idolatrous in its character. Vithobā was a symbol and a convention but not an idol. Thus the characteristics of the *Kriśnaite* religion of devotion in Mahārāśtra were hardly distinguishable from those of the radical reformers of the north. Its results as summarised by Rānāde, were the develoment of the vernacular literature, the modification of caste exclusiveness, the

[13] Rānāde: Rise of the Maratha Power, pp. 50–51.

sanctification of family life, the elevation of the status of women, the spread of humaneness and toleration, the partial reconciliation with Islam, the subordination of rites and ceremonies, pilgrimages and fasts, the learning and contemplation, the worship of love and faith, the limitation of the excesses of polytheism, and the uplift of the nation to a higher level of capacity both of thought and action.[14]

Nāmdev was a disciple of Khechar who was definitely hostile to idol worship; he received the following instructions from his *Guru*:—

> "A stone-god never speaks. What possibility then of his removing the disease of mundane existence? A stone image is regarded as God, but the true God is wholly different. If a stone-god fulfils desires, how is it he breaks when struck? Those who adore a god made of stone lose everything through their folly. Those who say and hear that a god of stone speaks to his devotees, are both of them fools. Those who extol the greatness of such a god and call themselves his devotees, should be regarded as worthless persons, and their words should not be heard by the ear. If, by chiselling a stone, a god is made of it and is worshipped with care for many years, will he be of use at any time? Do reflect on this well in your mind. Whether a holy place is small or large, there is no God but stone or water. In the village of Dvādasī (Barsī) instruction was given that there is no place which is devoid of God. That God was shown to Nāma in his heart, and thus Khechar conferred a blessing on him."[15]

[14] Rānāde: Op. cit., pp. 50–51.

[15] Bhandārkar: Vaiśnavism and Śaivism, p. 90.

This is how Nāmdev exposes the inefficiency of the external acts of religion:—

> "Vows, fasts, and austerities are not all necessary; nor is it necessary for you to go on a pilgrimage. Be you watchful in your hearts and always sing the name of *Hari*. It is not necessary to give up eating food or drinking water; fix your mind on the feet of *Hari*. *Yoga* or sacrificial ceremonies or giving up objects of desire is not wanted. Realise a fondness for the feet of *Hari*."[16]

The following hymn describes the goal which Nāma desired to attain:—

Now all my days with joy I'll fill
Full to the brim,
With all my heart to *Viṭṭhal* cling
And only Him.

He will sweep utterly away
All dole and care;
And all in sunder shall I rend
Illusion's snare.

O! altogether dear is He
And He alone,
For all by burden He will take
To be His own.

Lo! all the sorrow of the world
Will straightway cease,
And all unending now shall be
The reign of peace.

For all the bondage He will break
Of worldly care,
And all in sunder will He rend
Illusion's snare.

[16] Bhandārkar: Vaiśnavism and Śaivism, p. 90.

From all my foolish fancies now
Let me be free.
In *Viṭṭhal* only is
Tranquillity.[17]

Nāmdev was the leader of a goodly host, which carried forward the traditions which he handed over to them. Among these saints a few were women, a few were Muslim converts to Hinduism, nearly half of them were Brahmins, while the remaining ones were drawn from all the other castes—"Marāthā, Kunbī, tailors, gardeners, potters, goldsmiths, repentant prostitutes, and slave girls, even the outcaste Mahārs."[18]

Nāmdev's spirit breathed in their teachings. This is how Chokhamela, a Mahār, replied to the remonstrances of a Brahman priest on entering the temple of Pandharpur. He said: "What availeth birth in high caste, what availeth rites or learning, if there is no devotion or faith? Though a man be of low caste, yet if he is faithful in heart, and loves God, and regards all creatures as though they were like himself, and makes no distinction between his own and other people's children, and speaks the truth, his caste is pure, and God is pleased with him. Never ask a man's caste when he has in his heart faith in God, and love of men. God wants in his children love and devotion, and he does not care for his caste."[19]

Bahirām Bhaṭ twice changed his religion in order to find the truth that would satisfy the cravings of his heart. Both Hindus and Muslims found fault with him for these changes of faith, but he disclaimed being either Hindu or Muslim.

The followers of Shaikh Muhammad who became *Bhaktas* observe both the *Ramazān* and the *Ekādaśī* fast, and make pilgrimages both to Mecca and to Pandharpur.

[17] Macnicoll: Hymns of the Marāthā Saints, p. 47.

[18] Rānāde: Op. cit., p. 146.

[19] Ibid., p. 154.

Tukārām who after Nāmdev was the greatest of Mārathā saints, and who wields the widest influence in Mahārāśtra, was equally eclectic. He was a contemporary of Śivajī, and one of the inspirers of the spirit which welded the Marāthās into a people united in common aims and aspirations) He was born at Dehu, near Poona, about 1608 A.D. He belonged to the Marāthā caste, and came from a family which had been for several generations devoted to the worship of *Vithobā*. His father was a petty trader, who entrusted his business to him when he was only a boy of thirteen. On the death of his father four years later the business fell into confusion, out of which it was rescued for a time through the help of one of his wives. But this prosperity did not last long, he gave away his money to a needy person who was threatened with imprisonment and himself became bankrupt. A famine followed, and one of his wives was starved to death. Tukārām became intensely disgusted with worldly life, gave up all business and devoted himself completely to contemplation and devotion. His life of piety and service made him popular with the people all round. But the Brahmans became jealous of his fame and subjected him to persecution. Śivajī whose star was just rising, however, became his admirer and tried to offer him wealth, comfort and ease, which of course were refused.

Tukārām's teachings are embodied in his numerous *Abhangas* which number between five and eight thousand. They deal with all aspects and every problem of religion as it presented itself to the peoples of India in that period, namely, the nature of God, His relation with the world and man, His grace, the destiny of man, the method of realization, the standard of virtue, the path of devotion, the obstacles, sufferings, and triumphs of the devotee, the emotions accompanying various stages of religious life, the snares of the world and of sense, the character of saints, the need of the preceptor, the uselessness of externalia, the iniquity of social distinctions and so on.

Tukārām's conception of God was almost identical with that of Kabīr, He says:—

> "He has neither form nor name, nor place of abode; He is present wherever we go, *Vitthal* our mother and sister. He knows neither form nor change of form. He pervades the moving and immovable world. He is neither with nor without attributes; who, indeed, can know Him? He will turn to none, says Tukā, who has not faith in Him."[20]

The immanence of God and the sanctity of life and the offering of all actions to Him, are taught in the following hymn:—

> "We see Thy footprints everywhere; form, name and shape belong all to the cloud-coloured one. If we roll on the ground it is nothing but a place for God's images to stand on; because our mind is fully fed on Thy love, every moment of time is auspicious to us. Thou art all to us, O God; our life, our hope and our vocation. When we finish our meal and eat fruit of betel nut, it is all an offering in Thy honour. When we walk we are walking round Thy image; in sleep we are prostrate before Thee, like a rod on the earth. When we meet people to talk with them, we see Thy image in every one. Lakes, rivers and wells to us are holy places, full of the water of the Ganges. Palaces, storeyed mansions and huts of grass are all temples of God. Every sound that we hear is *Hari's* name, whatever words are or have been uttered. Tukā says, we servants of *Viśṇu* are fully fed on His love."[21]

God's grace is spoken of thus:—

> "They need not ask God for anything; He comes running to serve them,"[22] and

[20] Fraser and Marathe: Hymns of Tukārām, Vol. II, p. 154.
[21] Ibid., Vol. II, pp. 169–170.
[22] Fraser and Marathe: Op. cit., Vol. II, p. 186.

"At a call Thou art drawn to Thy worshippers. So sure is Thy mercy, says Tukā, that with Thee there can be no delay."[23]

In a number of *Abhangas*[24] he indicates the nature of true worship, and rejects ceremonies, offering Vedic sacrifices, visiting holy places, worshipping stones, putting on saints' guise, fasts, and austerities. And this is how he describes the goal of human life:—

"Calm is life's crown; all other joy beside
Is only pain.
Hold Thou it fast. Thou shalt, whate'er betide,
The further shore attain.
When persons rage and we are wrung with woe
And sore distress,
Comes calm, and then—yea, Tukā knows it—lo!
The fever vanishes."[25]

Tukārām's attempt at reconciling Hindu and Muslim faiths is evidenced in the hymns translated below:—

"What *Allah* wishes that is accomplished, O! my friend (*Bābā*), the Maker is the sovereign of all.

Cattle and friends, gardens and goods all depart.

My mind dewells, O! friend, on my Lord (*Sāhib*) who is the Maker.

I ride there on the back of the horse (mind) and the self becomes the horseman.

O! friend, meditate (*zikr*) on *Allah*, who is in the guise of all,

23 Ibid., Vol. II, p. 190.

24 Ibid., Vol. II, pp. 411, 415.

25 Macnicoll: Op. cit., p. 80.

Says Tukā, the man who understands this becomes a
Darwīsh."[26]

And

"First among the great names is *Allah*, never forget to
repeat it.

Allah is verily one, the prophet (*nabi*) is verily one.

There Thou art one, there Thou art one, there Thou
art one, O! friend.

There is neither I nor thou."[27]

[26] Tukārām: Abhanga (Godbole's edition), p. 86.

[27] Ibid., 85.

INDIAN ARCHITECTURE

RELIGION and art are expressions of culture in two different media. The evolution of culture may, therefore, be traced equally well in either of them, for the consciousness of a race changes organically and in all parts together. Perhaps art is a more sensitive indication of change than even religion, which in its nature is more subjective, while art lives in objective form alone. In estimating then the influence of Islam upon Hindu art, it is essential to understand the formative influences which mould civilizations and shape their aesthetic needs and values.

Civilization is the organization of experience, which man gains by working both in harmony and in conflict with nature. Common pursuit with and struggle against nature are the warp and woof from which is woven the stuff of civilization. The character of a particular civilization depends upon the disposition and temperament of man as well as the nature of his environment, and on their mutual and dynamic interaction. Men are fundamentally alike everywhere; they all possess similar psychological endowments, they are all moved by the same set of instincts, impulses and feelings, and they all function intellectually in a similar manner. But, although essentially alike, men have enormous differences in the strength and temper of their emotional, intellectual and volitional powers. Living together in similar surroundings for long periods tends to develop in different groups, different types of character and mentality, which distinguish one community from another.

Thus it happens that, in spite of the unity of human nature, diversities of culture are produced. Although the instincts remain the same they are differently stimulated, the flow of emotional energy occupies different channels, sentiments are organized from different groups of emotions, intellect is exercised on different elements of perception and thought, and the mutual relationship of the conative and affective aspects of the mind so varies as to produce from similar elements entirely different attitudes and behaviours. The different groups organize differently the psychological facts of their experience and entertain dissimilar outlooks upon life, and although no two individuals are alike in a community, each community as an organism differs from the others in its institutions and ideals.

Each distinct community so organized has a history. It develops from an inner impulse of its life and its course is directed, stimulated or retarded, by its environment which itself is changing. Then the communities interact upon one another, for they do not live in isolation. They coalesce, absorb or conquer. New material is always pouring into the old casts, and either breaking them up or taking their mould. Thus the world process continues, and out of the conflict of races and the clash of civilizations new communities and new civilizations grow.

Every civilization which is thus formed passes through a cycle of change. It starts with definite, although unconscious, tendencies which it seeks to realize in its career. It attains the period of its highest expansion, when its capacities are matured and their expression is most adequately achieved. Then follows a downward movement; the original impulse is exhausted and either the civilization decays and dies out or its life is renewed by the appearance of a new impulse. The impulse whether sociological or intellectual may come from within or without. The character of the new civilization will be determined by the power of the new impulse, which may be so violent as to revolutionize the old civilization or it may only modify it.

The history of the Balkan Peninsula affords the aptest illustration of the principles enunciated here. The Ægean peoples who were originally settled there took nearly two thousand years to pass through the many stages of their culture, and then they developed a highly characteristic civilization whose magnificent monuments are to be seen at Mykenæ, Tiryns and Crete. When they had apparently attained the climax of their achievement, the Greek races broke through the Balkan passes and put an end to their development. Then the Greeks started on the path of civilization, and out of the alchemy of the mixing of races grew Athens and Sparta and the city states of Greece. It took several hundred years to accomplish the process of assimilation and then a new culture arose which, in the case of Athens, mounted the crest of the wave in the Periclean age. Then followed the stasis of Hellenism, of that culture which was as different from the Mykenian as from any other that the world has ever known. Although Hellenism spread beyond the bounds of Hellas and became a world culture, the civilization of Greece became moribund. Later in the same land, another civilization, the Byzantine, passed through its cycles of growth and decay; and the future may yet see in the same theatre the enactment of the drama of the rise and fall of the new Greek race. The Ægean, Hellenic, Hellenistic, Byzantine and modern Greek civilizations succeeded one another and yet each differs fundamentally from the others.

Greece is the epitome of world history. For humanity is like a sea in which billows arise under the urge of wind and moon and cosmic forces, and they gather volume and speed, and they travel. For a while on their crest appears the play of light and spray and of wondrous scenes, and then they gradually begin to fall and become slow, until they settle down and disappear in the deep calm of the sea from which they rose. And so the process of human life goes on.

What part has India taken in this world process, and how has its civilization been shaped under the age-long effort of humanity to explore the most varied avenues and to sound the most profound depths of human experience? How has the Indian mind sought to grasp reality and what insight and vision have helped to illumine its art and culture?

To understand the Hindu mind it is essential to know its environment. Warde Fowler noticed the wide difference in the development of the Indo-Germanic races in Asia and Europe, and sought its cause in the nature of the terrain on which the Aryan tribes entered. The Greeks and Italians settled down in small river valleys separated by mountains and seas, and the Persians and Indians in vast plains unending and unlimited. The first crystallized into small city states where life became intense and the bonds of community close, while the second spread out into loosely joined, free and easy tribal organizations ruled by autocratic sovereigns. Rabindranath Tagore, searching for the secret of European culture, the fierce antagonisms of its nationalities, the almost complete anarchy of its domestic and personal life, the wonderful order and discipline of its social and political organizations, the peculiar character of its analytic intellect most victoriously working itself out in science and industry, finds it in tde walls and moats which surrounded the cities of Europe, and which were at once the symbols of defiance and strife, protection and order.

Such being the influence of man's surroundings, it is necessary to understand the Hindu's environment. Vast, flat, unending plains watered by broad slow-moving rivers, the horizon limited in the far distance by lofty mountain chains covered with white eternal snows, or thick, impenetrable forests, or inhospitable barren hills—such is the outward aspect of the land. Nature plays upon it in fierce but well-regulated moods. Summer, rains and winter follow one another in unfailing succession. The intense heat of the tropical sun dries up all vegetation and leaves the open plains naked, bare and lifeless; and when man and earth are panting with thirst come the rains with storm and thunder suddenly, swiftly and widely but on almost the appointed day, and in the twinkling of an eye the whole aspect of the land is changed, life is re-born with an abundance and luxuriance which are utterly bewildering. Then follows the mild, exhilarating winter with its sowings, swift ripening and joyful harvesting when the heaps of corn lie thick upon the ground and overflow the granary. The sky of India is always bright, and its nights wonderfully, unspeakably, beautiful; for when the sun sets swiftly ushering in the night, the silent procession of a myriad stars gradually comes out filling in the dark mysterious firmament, and it whispers unutterable mysteries to those who lie listening under the vault of heaven gazing into the immeasurable immensities above. Day follows night, one season another, the exuberance of rains, the drought of summer, and the wheel of life moves on its regular, uninterrupted rhythm.

What wonder then if the clear and strident notes of a nature so distinct and unique playing on the human instrument, age after age, should have evoked in him a music attuned to its own peculiar assonances. It would be surprising, indeed, if the Hindu mind had not evolved a culture, a view of life and a system of society peculiar and individual. The very conditions of living were peculiar. The hamlets and villages in which dwelt India's teeming millions, or the hermitages where abode her seers, poets and prophets, were cradled in the thick copses of plants and trees, or deep glens of crowded forests. The impress that nature made on their souls in the morning freshness of their lives they bore in the ripeness of their age. The stamp of the forest became affixed upon the Hindu mind.

Indian consciousness developed a sense of time and space, and a conception of reality peculiarly its own. To the Hindu reality functioned in a time which was full and continuous and cyclical in its measure, and in a space which abhorred emptiness and which was sinuously curved like the soft tendrils of the lotus; and both his time and space had many orders. His universe ran riot in inexhaustible form and throbbed with the intensity of life, it was a universe of infinite subtle distinctions, of innumerable interweaving shapes, beginningless and endless, and yet a cosmos and a whole.

Another feature of this consciousness, noticeable in the triumphs as well as the defeats of Indian civilization, was its mystical intuitionalism. The dominant fact in the consciousness of Europe is the will to act, in that of India the will to know; and the peculiar emphasis of each has profoundly influenced the growth of their civilizations. Religion, philosophy, art, custom and institutions all bear the same mark, and all reiterate in their different languages that fundamental concept of reality which forms the stuff of Hindu consciousness.

Religion and philosophy have been dealt with elsewhere; it is now necessary to turn to art—architecture, sculpture and painting. But religion and art are inseparably linked together, they are but two aspects of the same vision of reality. The one gives significance to life, the other to form. All changes in the religious consciousness affect the expression of art, and whenever art forms change they imply a corresponding modification in faith. Human mind is a unity and an organism and it acts and reacts as a whole. How then did the Hindu religion inspire Hindu art?

The Hindu is a spiritual anarchist. His faith is intensely personal and individualistic. His worship consists in ardent self-communion, it implies an abstraction from all outward phenomena and realization in mystic ecstasy of the identity of the self with God; and when this vision of inner unity is gained he returns to the world and reduces the multiplicity into oneness again. He is a pantheist who sees God as *Hiraṇyagarbha*, the golden germ of creation and the *Virāṭ* or the total aggregate of all. His pantheis is, moreover, an intellectual translation of his primeval sense of the forest. Every twig and branch, every little flower and leaf that is born is a form in which the forest manifests itself; every twig and branch, flower and leaf changes rapidly and constantly, while the forest as such goes on for ever transcendent and eternal. And like the flower in a forest is the life of man in the universe. He, too, must live and die and be born again until he has exhausted all possibilities of action either through a whole series of lives or by intense and deliberate self-realization at once, in either case his final goal being unification with that Universal reality which is his primal source. And when this consummation is reached the cycle of life is ended to be followed by another one, perhaps similar, perhaps different.

Hindu architecture is the objectification of this consciousness in solid mass. It is a twofold symbol of the mystery and splendour of the deity. The shrine inside is a small dark cell, with overhanging roof and heavy columns and overladen with sculptural forms. In the bosom of the cell furthest removed from the entrance, without a ray of light falling directly upon it, is the image standing, seated or reclining. Scarcely more than a man may enter into the dim, silent mysterious arcana of the temple. In the shrine of the heart the soul of man must stand alone face to face with the mystery. Outside, the temple luxuriates in form: plinth stands upon plinth, base upon base, mouldings and friezes and bands in unending succession, the walls broken into numerous vertical steps, not an inch of empty space anywhere; and above the shrine rises the pyramidal dome, or tower, tier upon tier, and each tier studded with niche and figure, and the tower decorated with miniature towers on every face. The treatment of the walls is reproduced in the pillars, and each pillar is a model of the temple itself; on the bases are shrines of the guardians of the quarters, the shaft is divided by bands and friezes representing religious scenes, one capital is topped by another, and between the lower brackets and the achitraves the space is spanned by caryatid figures. The doors and windows are encased in jambs of numerous members on which are designed floral, geometrical, and other conventional patterns. The slanting eaves projecting from the walls and the mouldings cut deeply into the building give the happy play of light and shade on the surface. The vertical lines of the aspiring *śikhara* and the horizontal lines marking the roof of the *mandapa,* emphasize the feelings of sublimity and stability, the low columnar porches or storeys of pillared halls, and the unbounded opulence of detail and ornament all serve to manifest the Reality which is the transcendent totality of all forms. Altogether, the temple has a strong virile exterior, which inspires the sentiments of dignity, grandeur and majesty.

This general æsthetic feeling of the Hindu found its expression in the many styles of architecture which flourished in the period just before the conquest of India by the Musalmans, from about the beginning of the eighth century to the end of the thirteenth. These Hindu styles, which were derived from earlier styles of the Buddhist period, may be classified according to the region in which the monuments were erected, into three main divisions: (1) North-Indian, (2) Deccanese or Chālukyan, and (3) Southern or Dravidian. Then there are subordinate styles under the main divisions and transitional ones between them. The distinctions of the styles are mainly due to the difference in the form of the roof or spire. In the North-Indian temples the spire is a lofty tower with curvilinear sides narrowing towards the top and crowned with a large, fluted, bulbous block called the *amalasila*, over which rises the finial in the shape of a vase or *kalaśa*. The whole is richly ornamented with carving in horizontal courses and on bold vertical bands or ribs and the corners. Examples of this style are the Orissan temples of *Bhuvaneśwar*, the Central Indian temples at Khajurāho and Gwalior, and the temples of Rajputana and Gujarat. Sometimes the lines of the *śikhara* are straight as at Gayā, and in most *śikharas* one of the ornaments consists of the reduplication of the form on the faces.

In the Dravidian style the pyramidal roof rises in several stages and is crowned by a small dome either circular or polygonal. The *vimāna* of a Dravidian temple could have any number of storeys up to fifteen. In the earlier times each storey had a number of residential cells, but later the cells became merely ornamental, and thus the *gopuram* was evolved from the pyramidal tower. The later temples of the south are distinguished by having many enclosures with *gopurams* over the gates, and cornices having a double curve. The earliest examples of this style are the monolithic *rathas* at Māmallāpuram and the *Kailāś* temple at Ellorā, the *Virupakśa* temple at Pattadakal, the *Rājrājeśwara* temple at Tanjore and others; while of the later style the examples are the temples of Madura, Śrīrangam, and others.

The Chālukyan style is transitional between the northern and southern styles. The *śikhara* has lost the distinctively Dravidian storeyed form and become stepped without acquiring the continuous line of the northern style, and forming pyramids of different heights. The sanctuary usually has a star-shaped plan and is raised upon a broad terrace; the deeply stratified lower parts of the walls are covered with the most lavish sculpture, and perforated stone screens are set between the columns. The temples of this style extend over the Deccan including Mysore, the Kanarese districts and the territories of the Nizām, as far as Nagpur. The most magnificent examples are the temples at Halebid in Mysore.

An analysis of the Hindu buildings of this period will reveal the character of their architectural achievement. The usual plan on which the temple is arranged consists of a square cell (*garbha griha*) which contains the image and forms the basis of the tower, and a porch (*manḍapa*), and between them an intermediate chamber (*antarāla*); in larger temples the porch may be a hall and then it will have a second porch in front of it and a roofed verandah may surround the shrine. The walls are divided into plinth, basement and face up to the entablature, and stepped by deep projections. They are built in two shells, the outer with the mouldings and the inner dressed smooth, and they have unequal thickness in different parts, being thick at the back and sides and thin at corners. The proportion between the space occupied by the walls and that by the enclosed rooms is fixed by rule, in Orissan temples the ratio being four-tenths and six-tenths. The result of this proportion is that the walls are extremely solid and stable.

The openings of the Hindu temples are rectangular, columns and lintels being employed for spanning the spaces. In the doors the usual proportions of the height to the width is two to one. The jambs are carved into antepagments or vertical mouldings some of which are projecting and others recessed. The door-frames may have three or five or nine fasciæ. Their decoration consists of creepers and leaves, lozenge-shape ornaments or squares and circles, animals, dancing human figures, and other devices. In the ancient Buddhist, Jain and Hindu caves the facade of the entrance is elaborately treated; over the rectangular gate they have pierced arches whose intrados are divided by purlins and the meeting point of the curves is elongated to give it a *pipal* leaf shape. The use of pillar, bracket and lintel, however, is universal and strongly marks the trabeate character of the Hindu architecture.

In order to cover larger spaces and rooms two methods of roofing are employed. The simplest form of the first method is to erect four pillars and place stone beams on them and then cover the opening by a slab; but this is only possible when the space is small, and, therefore, the next step is to reduce the extent of the central space by cutting off its corners by triangular stones placed in each angle of the square; this process can be carried on by heaping tier upon tier till the area is diminished to the required size. The second method is to arrange the columns at the corners of an octagon to support the lintels, and to raise a dome upon them in successive diminishing horizontal courses, laid flat upon one another and corbelling inwards. When necessary the octagon is reduced to a polygon of sixteen sides. The interior of the dome is always richly decorated with carved mouldings running in horizontal circles and marking the joints of the masonry, and pendants hang from the centure of the dome. The exterior of the dome is treated symbolically. The shrine of *Viśṇu* has a standing (*sthānīka*) image and therefore an elevated spire with vertical ribs (*śikhara*), that of *Śiva* a seated (*āsana*) image, and a domical roof or a terraced roof and dome with horizontal mouldings, and that of *Nārāyaṇa* a recumbent (*śayana*) one, and consequently a roof like a waggon vault or an upturned board or a parallelpiped, with pointed arch gables at the ends.

Vaulting by means of radiating voussoirs is not found, although it was probably known. The dread of the lateral thrust exerted by that kind of construction forced the use of the principle of building in which only vertical loadings were encountered: the substantial walls sufficiently supported it and the weight of the coping *amalaka* and *kalaśa* served to lock the sides of the *śikhara* together. The dome and the spire are never kept plain, the whole surface being covered with most elaborate carvings and profuse sculpture. In the ancient Stupas and the Dagabas of the *Chaitya* halls, however, the bulbous profile was maintained.

The columns and pillars of Hindu architecture exhibit an infinite richness and variety. They may be square, pentagonal, hexagonal, eight or sixteen-sided, or circular. Their orders are rigidly fixed as well as the proportions between the diameter and the height and the intercolumniation. The various parts, pedestal, base, shaft, capital and entablature and the innumerable mouldings, square, semi-circular, convex, concave, are all made according to rules. In general, the parts of the pillar correspond to the members of the walls. The pillars may have double capitals, capitals of different shapes of animals and bells and fruits, and they carry brackets which support lintels upon which rests the roof. Their corbels may be used as rests for the lower tenons of bracket figures, usually *Gāndharvas*, and to support the wreath-arches (*toranas*). Their decoration is extremely rich and varied—niches of *Lokapālas*, gods and goddesses or in the case of Jainas, their *Tīrthānkaras* and saints, friezes of scenes of worship, bands with animals, lotus leaf members and so on.

The cornices are boldly projecting eaves or dripstones resting upon brackets, and usually slanting from the walls at an angle of 45°. They may be corrugated or shaped especially in the south) into a double curve. They protect the walls from weather and serve to throw off rain. The panels between the brackets under the cornice are usually ornamented, and the brackets are carved beautifully.

The variety of mouldings and the richness of ornament are extraordinary; no other school of architecture in the world can rival the opulence of the Hindu. In the ornament, organic forms, vegetable and animal dominate, and the human figure is freely employed. In fact, the whole building is so entirely covered with decoration that its only purpose appears to be to set off the exuberant form in which life manifests itself. In spite, however, of this abandon, ornament is never allowed to hide the essential features of the structure or to depreciate the value of the unified mass as a whole. This is achieved by the observance of those laws of predominance and subordination of masses, of the relation and grouping of parts, of the proportion and symmetry of members, which make the harmony and unity of an architectural monument, and which evoke the feelings which inspire the master-builder, and give expression to the æsthetic purposes to which he attaches value.

The character of Muslim consciousness is as different from that of the Hindu as possible. It has been remarked that Islam is the religion of the heat belt, perhaps it will be more accurrate to say that Islam flourishes in the region of scanty rainfall. The vast stretch of territory which includes the whole of Africa north of the line of latitude twelve degrees above the equator, Arabia, South-Eastern Persia, the Aralo-Caspian region, the Gobi and Takla makan deserts, has a rainfall of less than ten inches in the year; while Asia Minor, Mesopotamia, Northern Persia, Afghanistan, Southern Siberia and Eastern Turkestan, have a rainfall of between ten and twenty inches. This arid expanse of land bordering on the Atlantic in the west and the Chinese wall on the east, is the home of Muslim people. Here Musalman inhabitants are either in total possession or in overwhelming majority; outside these regions they are found in great numbers but mixed with followers of other faiths, and numerically in a minority. But Malaya and Indonesia are exceptions. Here from the dawn of their history, they have lived and erected the great fabrics of their cultures, here are situatd all the great cities which contributed to the building of these cultures—Samarqand and Bokhārā, Ghaznī and Herāt, Isfahān. Tabrïz and Shīrāz, Baghdād and Damascus, Mecca and Medina, Cairo, Tunis and Cordova.

What is the character of these lands and how has it impressed itself upon the mentality of the peoples inhabiting them? The Muslim lands are not all absolutely alike. Central Asia is a basin of some ancient depression, Persia a plateau, Asia Minor a mountainous tract with deep river valleys, Syria and Hedjaz desert and sea coast, Iraq and Misr river valleys. But there is one thing common to all; the lands of fertility are oases large or small, surrounded by howling wastes of sand. The contrast between the patch of land which is productive and the barren, stony or sandy desert which enclosed it, is tremendous. The vast extent of the infinite stretch of arid expanse all round, the immensity of the cloudless sky overhead, the day with its dazzling slpendour and the night filled with innumerable brightly glowing stars, the regular succession of seasons, the cruelty and economy of a stern nature, the tremendous effort to keep vegetation alive and to save the intricate system of irrigational canals and hard-won pieces of garden and pleasance from destruction, the nomadic life fostered by the scanty pasturage and desert and the sedentary occupations intensely pursued in the city and the fertile spot, all leave deep marks upon the mind of men living in these regions. The transcendence and masterfulness of the Reality, the insignificance of man and his works, the stretches of emptiness between instants of time and points of space, the sense of directness moral and intellectual, the preiodicity of passionate energy and pathetic lethargy, the abstractness of thinking logical and geometrical, the absence of plastic feeling, the devotion to pure ideas and abhorrence of iconism and anthropomorphism, clarity and definiteness in seeing outlines, infinite elaboration of detail, a mystic faith in the immutable order of nature, a quiet resignation and a calm dignified submission to divine will, are the leading characteristics of the Muslim mentality in its original phase. The Byzantine, Christian, Mongol, Indian or Hispano-Roman influences might colour it and diversify it, but cannot completely transform it. This consciousness finds expression in religion, literature and art.

A fierce monotheism, an intolerance of other religions, a clear demarcation between the faithful and the infidels, a unique eschatology—one birth, one death—a resurrection followed by eternal reward or punishment, an absence of hierarchy, religious or social, such is its religious aspect; and in literature the *Ghazal* with its infinite variations upon the same theme, with its amazing cleverness in the selection of polished word and appropriate rhyme, with its subtle inter-relation of verse and verse by means of sound like the interlaced pattern of Muslim geometrical ornament, is the poetical expression of the same consciousness.

Muslim art, like Indian or any other art, is conditioned by certain practical needs of religion and worship. The Muslim worshipper must have a house of worship embodying his vision of reality. It must be a symbol of transcendent majesty of vast spaciousness, of sublimity and purity, and it must be a shelter for the combined prayers of an assembled congregation. Its forms must suggest to him one-pointed devotion, and the all-enveloping nature of the Reality.

These feelings are realized in the mosque, whose pointed arch, aspiring dome, tall minaret, lofty portals, pillared naves and aisles, clear-cut outlines, bereft of all sculpture and possessing a minimum of mouldings, but adorned with surface decoration of conventional arabesques, interlaced geometrical patterns, and beautiul calligraphic inscriptions, whose well-proportioned and symmetrical exterior often covered with enamelled tiles or faierce, and cool, shaded and spacious interior, fulfil all the aspirations and longings of a devout Muslim's soul. The impression of these elements on the existing local schools of architecture, resulted in the growth of different styles of Muslim art in *Maghrib*, Egypt, Syria, Persia and Turkey.

On the soil of India the clash of the two divergent mentalities and their cultures resulted in the creation of a new culture whose religious aspect has already been considered. In art a similar development took place. Hindu and Muslim elements coalesced to form a new type of architecture. The buildings erected by the Musalmans for religious, civil or military purposes were not purely Muslim-Syro-Egyptian, Persian or Central Asian, nor were the Hindu buildings, temples or palaces or cenotaphs purely Hindu. The simple severity of the Muslim architecture was toned down, and the plastic exuberance of the Hindu was restrained. The craftsmanship, ornamental richness and general design remained largely Hindu, the arcuated form, plain domes, smooth-faced walls, and spacious interiors were Muslim superimpositions. The artistic quality of the buidings erected since the thirteenth century whether by Hindus or by Muslims is the same, although differences are introduced by considerations of purpose and use, and styles are varied according to differences of local tradition and regional peculiarities.

"In all the Indian–Muhammadan styles of Fergusson's academic classification—at Delhi, Ajmer, Agra, Gaur, Malwa, Gujarat, Jaunpur and Bijapur—whether the local rulers were Arab, Pathan, Turk, Persian, Mongol, or Indian, the form and construction of the domes of mosques and tombs and palaces, as well as the Hindu symbols which crown them; the *mihrābs* made to stimulate Hindu shrines; the arches Hinduised often in construction, in form nearly always; the symbolism which underlies the decorative and structural designs—all these tell us plainly that to the Indian builders the sect of the Prophet of Mecca was only one of the many which made up the synthesis of Hinduism; they could be good Muhammadans but yet remain Hindus."[1] Havell has so brilliantly sustained this

[1] Havell: Indian Architecture, p. 101.

thesis in his works on Indian art that it is hardly necessary to expatiate upon it.

It must, however, be remembered that although some of the elements of Muslim architecture—the pointed arch and the bulbous dome—were probably derived from Hindu origins—and Fergusson[2] has described the process by which the Jaina temple was developed into a Muslim mosque—the Muslim æsthetis feeling is decidedly different from the Hindu; and whatever importance may be attached to origins of elements, it cannot be gainsaid that in the mediæval art of India the effect of Muslim impact was to transform the ancient Hindu æsthetic values.

The earliest Muslim constructions were the two great mosques at Delhi and Ajmer built by Qutb-ud-Dīn Aibak about the end of the twelfth century, and from this time onwards every city which the Muslim armies occupied was adorned with mosques, palaces, tombs and other buildings belonging to the new Hindu-Muslim style of architecture. The overthrow of most of the northern Hindu kingdoms and the constant pressure on those that successfully withstood the early onrush of the Muslim armies were not conditions favourable to indulgence in expensive architectural display. Consequently for the two centuries which followed the building of the last great monument of Hindu architecture, the temple of *Vastupāla* and *Tejahpāla* at Girnār (1230 A.D.), no building of great importance was erected in Northern India. About the middle of the fourteenth century a kind of political equilibrium was reached. The high tide of conquest had receded, and the Tughlaq empire, after Muhammad's brilliant but unfortunate experiments, was breaking up into provincial kingdoms; the Hindu princes of Rajputana and Bundelkhand, who had never been subdued, took advantage of the opportnuity and acquired surrounding territories and obtained command of large re-

[2] Fergusson: Eastern Architecture, Vol. II, p. 69.

sources in men and revenue. Their political importance was soon established; they treated the Muslim rulers of Gujarat, Malwa and Jaunpur on equal terms; they harassed their frontiers, fought with them, made alliances with them and were no longer menaced with extinction by the power of the empire at Delhi. With the restoration of self-confidence and prosperity, they were again able to devote their energies to the patronage of art, and at the commencement of the fifteenth century they began to erect monuments which set the example to their co-religionists throughout India in the succeeding generations.

For the selection of style they had the alternative of either reviving the ancient Hindu style, whose examples were still standing around them both in Rajputana and in Bundelkhand, or adopting the new Hindu-Muslim style which the Muslim patrons and Hindu artists had combined to create. They wisely, or perhaps inevitably, chose the latter course. Probably the earliest example of a Hindu structure in which this departure from ancient traditions makes its appearance, is the temple at Rampur,[3] near Sadar in the Godwar district of the Jodhpur State. The temple was built by a Jain named Dharanaka in 1439 A.D. during the region of Kumbha, Rānā of Mewar.

The temple which belongs to a group situated in a lonely but picturesque valley of the Aravalli mountains is overlooked by the fort of Kumhalner, the favourite residence of Rānā Kumbha. It is nearly square in plan and is raised on a lofty basement which with the exception of a few horizontolly continuous string courses, is without any other decoration, and thus exhibits the newly-acquired feeling for plain surfaces which was taking possession of the Hindu mind. The temple encloses four courts and five shrines, the great one in the centre and the others at the four corners. The shrines are covered with

3 Burgess: Archacological Survey, Vol. VII. The Muhammadan Architecture of Ahmedabad, p. 32.

domes, the central one being carried on a third storey. A range of cells for images each with a pyramidal roof of its own, surrounds the whole. The pillars of the shrine which support the domes are almost identical in design with those of the Jāmi mosque of Ahmad Shāh, and the exterior of the domes is left plain and undecorated like those of the Muslims. In spite of the want of ornament on the exterior faces, Fergusson admits, "I know of no other building in India, of the same class, that leaves so pleasing an impression."[4]

The ruins of Rānā Kumbha's palace at Chitore show amidst Hindu balconies and crested walls scattered over the terrace, kiosks covered with plain and segmented domes resting on lintels and columns. [5]

To the same period, that is, the pre-Mughal, belong the fort and palaces built by Rānā Mān Singh of Gwalior, who ruled from 1486 to 1516, and the palace of his successor Vikramāditya Singh built in 1518. The *Bārādarī* in the fort was 45 feet square and had a stone roof supported on twelve pillars. "It was, besides, singularly interesting from the expedients to which the Hindu architect was forced to resort to imitate the vaults of the Muslims."[7]

The Mān Mandir, in spite of its ruined state, makes a magnificent pile with projecting towers, open pillared balconies, and arrow-headed cresting. It is 360 feet long and 160 broad, and rises 100 feet above the ground. The chief entrance, called the *Hathiyā Paur* (elephant gate), is made of four handsome pillars on which rests a fine dome. Flanking the gate are two

[4] Fergusson: Op. cit., Vol. II, p. 47.

[5] Rousselet: Less Indes des Rajahs, p. 232.

[6] Griffin: The Monuments of Central India. Cole: Preservation of National Monuments, India, plate 2. Cunningham: Archaeological Survey, Vol. I. Gwalior State Gazetteer, Vol. I, Part IV, by Luard and Dwarkanath Sheopuri.

[7] Griffin: Op. cit., p. 46.

projecting towers surmounted by domes resting on fine clustered pillars. The handsomely carved balconies and the windows enclosed between graceful pilasters with wreath-arches between them, greatly enhance the picturesqueness of the exterior. "Its ornament. . . .reveals the same eclectic spirit that characterized the buildings of Akbar."[8]

Inside the palace are two artistic courts. The first court, which is a square of 33 by 33 feet, has rooms opening on it. One of the large rooms has a curious pitch roof which rests on a paling of perforated screen work, and is supported by a colonnade of sixteen pillars with fan capitals. Over the colonnade runs a balcony with sloping balustrade. The western room has an entrance of three handsome arches resting on stout piers beautifully carved. The southern room is roofed with a flat topped arch, and the room at the south-west corner has a roof composed of Saracenic arches.

The second court is slightly larger, having a side of 37 feet. The small room in the eastern face is often on all sides, the openings being arcuated. The roof is a vault composed of four semi-circles.

Both the courts are richly decorated, every part of the structure is carefully treated—corbels, brackets, caves, balconies, arches and walls—and both trabeate and arched forms are freely employed.

When Bābur visited Gwalior in 1526, he greatly admired the palace and noted that it was, "a building with five domes, and round about them smaller domes, the small domes are on each side of the greater according to the custom of Hindustan."[9] The domes were covered with gilt copper and the walls were inlaid with green painted tiles, while the front was covered with white stucco. The palace of Mān Singh furnished points of imitation to Bābur's successors as well as to Hindu builders.

[8] *Ibid.*, 48.

[9] Erskine: Babur's Memoirs, p. 384.

Under Akbar's enlightened rule a great impetus was given to the reconciliation of the Hindu and Muslim cultures. The buildings of Fatehpur Sīkrī are the expression of the same spirit as inspired the *Dīn-i-Ilahī*. The Panch Mahal was the translation into stone of the *Allah Upaniśad*. By his encouragement a number of temples were built, which show that the Hindu builders had at last overcome the hesitance and incomplete mastery of Muslim constructional methods which they had exhibited at Gwalior. Of these temples three at Brindāban[10] and one at Govardhan[11] were built in the reign of Akbar and one at Brindāban in that of Jahangir.

The temple of Govind Deva at Brindāban was built by Raja Mān Singh Kachwāhā, the celebrated general and governor of Akbar, in the year 1590. The plan of the building is cruciform, the length of the nave and the breadth across the transcept are nearly equal, measuring 117 feet and 105 feet and its porch is covered by a vault with radiating arches—a truly Muslim feature. Although the spire has fallen down, the external appearance of the building is remarkable. The accentuated corners, the boldly projecting balconies, the combination of vertical and horizontal lines, the use of both lintel and arch, the unsculptured plain surfaces—all impart to it a unique strength and grandeur.

The temple of Madan Mohan is in ruins. The vaulted roof has disappeared, as well as the choir tower. The gate of the *mandap* is a rectangle set inside an arch whose soffit is ornamented. The walls of the facade are plain, but two balconies project on either side of the arch; the spandrils have no decoration except for a lotus in the middle. The tower over the sacrarium is a lofty octagon of curvilinear outline tapering towards the summit and is quite plain. The chapel tower is similar in form but enriched with carved pannels, in which are placed medallions and diamonds, but no human figures.

[10] & [11] Feuhrer: Archaeological Survey, Vol. XII. Growse: Mathura. Le Bon: Les civilisations de l'Inde, Impey: Delhi, Agra and Rajputana.

The temple of Gopīnāth was built by Rā'isil of the *Shaikhāvati* clan, an officer in Akbar's service. The history of the clan is interesting. Mokal Rānā was long childless. He became a father through the blessings of Shaikh Burhān and called his son *Shaikhjī* and he became the patriarch of the *Shaikhāvati* race. "At the birth of every male infant a goat is sacrificed, and while the *kalima* is recited the child is sprinkled with blood. He is invested with the *Baddhiya*, or cross strings, usually worn by little Muhammadans; and when he laid them aside, he was bound to suspend them at the Saint's *Dargah* still existing six miles from Achrol. For two years he wears a blue tunic and cap, and for life abstains from hog's flesh and all meat in which blood remains."[12] The temple is now in ruins.

The temple of *Harideva* at Govardhan was built by Raja Bhagwān Dās. The nave of 60 feet by 20 feet has five arches on either side with clerestory windows above, and was covered with an arched vault.

The temple of Jugal Kishore at Brindāban was erected in 1627. Its plain walls, unornamented conical tower, arched niches, and absence of sculpture, clearly point to Muslim æsthetic inspiration.

The Jaina temples of Sonāgarh[13] in Bundelkhand date from the sixteenth and seventeenth centuries. There is a great variety of styles among them, but the immense influence of Muslim architecture is distinctly visible. The body of the edifice usually stands on a terrace and is surmounted by one or more spires, which are encircled by a row of gables, *chhatris* and bell-towers. The ancient *śikhara* overloaded with ornament is rare, and has been replaced either by a modern plain spire conical in shape and strongly marked with horizontal mouldings, or domes of various shapes. One temple (Griffin's monu-

12 Growse: Op. cit., p. 131.

13 Griffin: Op. cit.

ments of India, Plate LXXI) which is reached by a high flight of stairs, has a facade in which there is an arched gateway planted by two smaller arches, and the wings are decorated with blind arcades. All the arches are cusped. The facade is surmounted by a waggon-shaped vault in the middle and small domes on either side. The ribbed dome over the sanctum rises behind them. Not a single sculptured figure adorns the temple. The other temples show similar features.

The temples of Muktāgirī[14] near Gāwilgaḍh, in Berar, are like the Sonāgaḍh temples of the domed style copied from Muslim art.

Further south in the Madras State the influence of Islamic styles appears in the civil buildings of the Hindu rulers, in the palaces and pavilions of Vijayanagar and Chandragirī, Madura and Tanjore. The temples and other sacred buildings continued to be built on traditional lines although in the north even their style was modified in accordance with the new tastes.

In spite of the fact that the Vijayanagar Kingdom was continually at war with the neighbouring Muslim kingdoms, there appears to have been much religious tolerance and great appreciation of each other's cultures. The 'Ādilshāhī Sultans of Bījāpur, like their more illustrious successors the Moghul emperors, were notorious for their leanings towards Hinduism; and both the 'Ādilshāhīs and Nizām-Shāhīs of Ahmadnagar freely patronized Marāthā chiefs and employed Hindu officers for their administration and Hindu troops for their armies. The latter gave a great impetus to the Marāthī language by making it the language of their official transactions. The Hindu rulers of Vijayanagar reciprocated these feelings, they took Muslim troops in their employ, encouraged Muslim traders and built mosques for their worship. In their civil architecture they

[14] Fergusson: Op. cit., Vol. II, p. 45.

borrowed the arch from their neighbours. A photograph of one of the pavilions built before the downfall of Vijayanagar in 1565 A.D. is given by Fergusson (Vol. I, p. 417), who remarks: "It is a fair specimen of that picturesque mixed style which arose from the mixture of the Saracenic and Hindu styles."[15] Its repeated cusped arches, slanting dripstones and unornamented walls, are an eloquent proof of the justness of the remark.

The successors of the fallen Vijayanagar dynasty settled at Chandragirī[16] in the North Arcot district. There they built their palaces, the principal one of which presents a well-balanced facade of three storeys surmounted by turrets of pleasing form. Each floor consists mainly of a pillared hall, the piers are arched across both ways, corbelled at the angles and closed with flat domes. The walls pierced with arches are built of brick, but the vaults are worked in stone.

Tīrumalai Nāyak's palace at Madura[17] which belongs to the seventeenth century, is one of the most magnificent pillars erected in the Hindu-Muslim style. The principal apartments are situated round a courtyard measuring 160 feet east and west by 100 feet north and south, and surrounded on all sides by arcades of very great beauty. The pillars which support the arches are of stone, 40 feet in height, and are joined by foliated brick arcades of great elegance of design, carrying a cornice an an entablature. The celestial pavilion (*Swarga Vilâsam*) stands on the west side of the court and measures 235 feet by 105 feet. It is arranged on the plan of a great mosque with three domes, "in fact the whole structure, if not first erected as a splendid mosque is marvellously like one."[18] The central

15 Fergusson: Op. cit., Vol. I, p. 416.

16 Ibid., p. 417.

17 Ibid., p. 411 ff.

18 Ibid., p. 413.

dome is supported on twelve columns linked together by massive Saracenic arches. Four similar arches are thrown across the corners and above these rests the octagonal drum which is pierced by clerestory windows. The drum is carried up and then changed from an octagon into a circle over which the dome is built. A second hall 125 feet by 69 feet is placed at the northwest corner of the main building, and the two together correspond to the *Dīwān-i-Khās* and *Dīwān-i-Ām* of Muslim palaces.

The palace at Tanjore[19] was commenced by the Marāthā chief who established his dynasty in the last quarter of the seventeenth century. It follows the arrangements of the Madura palace and belongs to the same style.

In the north the seventeenth century saw the erection of a number of noble edifices in the states of the Hindu princes of Rajputana and Bundelkhand, at Amber, Udaipur, Būndī, Datia, and Orchha. Apparently the new style had now become universal and architecturally it was henceforward impossible to distinguish a building erected by the Hindus and the Muslims. Another effect of this cultural synthesis was the construction of tombs among the Hindus. It is impossible to fix the date of the earliest structures of this type, but the *mahāsatis* and *chhatrīs* (cenotaphs), to commemorate the dead, begin to make their appearance about this period. As burial has never been a Hindu custom, the new departure can only be ascribed to the influence of the Musalmans.

The palace at Amber[20] was commenced by Raja Mān Singh who ascended the throne in 1592 A.D., and was completed by Jai Singh (1625—1666). It ranks after the great Gwalior palace as the finest piece of architecture among the Rajputs. The palace stands in a valley which slightly mars the effect of impressiveness, otherwise it contrasts favourably with the contemporary work of the same kind at Fatehpur Sikrī. Its elephant

[19] *Ibid.*, p. 415.

[20] Rousselet: Op. cit., p. 277 ff. (English Edn., p. 278, Impey: Op. cit., Plate 42.

capitals, figure sculpture and use of colour and mirrors, make it very picturesque.

Udaipur became the capital of Mewār after the sack of Chitor by Akbar in 1568. Mahārānā Udai Singh began the building of the new capital; the great palace called the *Barī Mahal*[21] was erected by Amar Singh I, in 1597. It is a five-storeyed stone edifice. The superstructure is made of marble, which is fancifully wrought into corbelled windows and trellis screens, resting on a marble string course, and decorated with elephants carved in low relief. The later Mahārānās added pavilions and kiosks. The palace stands on the verge of the Pichola lake which is surrounded by charming hills. In the lake there are two other palaces situated on an island. The palace of *Jag Niwās* was built by Rānā Jagat Singh in white and black marble, and the principal chambers, according to Rousselet, were decorated with historical frescoes of great value. The use of the Bengālī bent cornice, cusped arches, domes, kiosks, balconies and open terraces, gives to it a unique charm. The other palace *Jag Mandir* was built by Rānā Karan, son of Rānā Amar Singh, for Shāh Jahan who was in rebellion against his father and had sought refuge with the Rānā. The whole island is "a fairy's mirage with its lines of domes and of palms reflecting in the water."[22]

The palace at Būndī[23] of about the same age as that at Udaipur, almost equals it in architectural effect. Its situation is very similar to that of the *Baṛī Mahal* on the side of a lake which has an islet on which stand temples. The distinguishing feature of the palace is its bold and richly decorated balconies, and the principal halls have double rows of columns of serpentine.

The palace at Datia[24] in Bundelkhand was built at the beginning of the seventeenth century by Bīr Singh Deo, the

21 Cole: Op. cit., Plate I. Rousselet: Op. cit., p. 195.
22 Rousselet: Op. cit., p. 187.
23 Ibid., p. 188.
24 Griffin: Monuments of Central India.

Bundela chief of Orchhā. It is a square structure built of granite. The base is a vaulted terrace on which rises the seven-storeyed pile. The first four storeys consist of immense halls with arched roofs supported by numerous pillars, in the middle of which rises a square tower crowned by the central dome. Bīr Singh Deo built another palace at Orchhā similar in style but more varied in outline, and also the temple of Chaturbhuj.

The plan of the temple is a reversed Latin cross. A large flight of steps leads up to the porch, which forms a pavilion projecting from beyond the main front. Behind it is the main front which is divided into four storeys by large ogives and flanked by two square towers which are surmounted by steeples. Two similar towers are at the other end of the temple, and the flat roof of which they form the four corners, has in its centre a large round cupola with a small lantern at its summit. The granite terrace on which the temple stands is fifty feet high. There is no ornament on the exterior, but the magnitude and the proportions are admirable.

The mausoleum of Bīr Singh Deo at Orchhā[26] is a gigantic structure. It is a large square block flanked by two massive towers, and crowned by an enormous dome, of which a portion only was extant when Rousselet visited it. There is no sculpture or decoration upon the facade, which has three arches in the middle, and is pierced with rectangular recesses in which blind dentelled arches are carved. The mausoleum in its imposing grandeur resembles the Pathan edifices of the same kind.

To the next century belong the palaces of Raja Sawāī Jai Singh at Jaipur[27] and Raja Suraj Mal at Dīg. The last, according to Fergusson, wants "the massive character of the

25 Griffin: Op. cit.

26 Ibid.

27 Impey: Op. cit., Plate 46.

fortified palaces of other Rajput states, but for grandeur of conception and beauty of detail it surpasses them all."[28] The cenotaphs of Sangrām Singh at Udaipur,[29] of Sūraj Mal at Govardhan[30] between Mathura and Dīg, of Chhatrasāl and his queen Kamalāvatī, the Jaina temple at Delhi,[31] Ahalyābāī's temple at Ellorā,[32] and the temple at Kantanagar[33] near Dīnājpur in Bengal, all exhibit in their architecture the same elements of the Hindu-Muslim style which are found in that of their predecessors.

The temple in Bengal is probably the first Hindu building of the kind raised during Muslim rule which imitated the style of the mosques of Gauḍ and Mālda. It was built between 1704 and 1722 A.D. It is of considerable dimensions, and square in design; it has three storeys and above the third rises the central tower with its pyramidal spire. The first two storeys have four octagonal towers at the corners. The pointed arch prevails throughout. The whole surface is covered with terracotta, but no figure sculpture is seen anywhere. The curved lines, horizontal and vertical, and the arcuated forms, give a unity to the whole which is very pleasing.

The influence of the style spread in the eighteenth century to all arts of India. Even far off Neal did not escape the contagion. According to Le Bon's classification, the third category of Nepal temples consists of stone shrines from which Chinese influence has disappeared and on which Hindu influence has become sensible. Among these temples there are some in which traces of Muslim influence may be observed,

28 Fergusson: Op. cit., Vol. II, p. 178.

29 Rousselete: Op. cit., p. 210.

30 Impey: Op. cit., Plate, 39.

31 Fergusson: Op. cit., Vol. II, p. 66.

32 Burgess: Archaeological Survey, Vol. III, Western India, Plates LVI, LVII.

33 Fergusson: Op. cit., Vol. II, p. 159.

e.g., the dome. The temple at Khatmandu[34] furnishes an illustration.

The palaces, cenotaphs and temples of the nineteenth century, whether built in the west at Jāmnagar[35] or the east at Calcutta or in the Punjab by the Sikhs, or in Central India by the Jains, are all in the same style of the Hindu-Muslim architecture. The Viśweśwar temple at Benares,[36] the Golden Temple of the Sikhs at Amritsar,[37] the temple built by Sindhiā's mother at Gwalior,[38] the Pagoda at Calcutta,[39] the palaces of Mahārājā Ranjit Singh at Lahore,[40] of the Rāo of Jāmnagar in Kathiāwād, of the Raja of Chhatarpur[41] in Chhatarpur, of the Seths of Ajmer,[42] the mausoleums of Mahārājā Ranjit Singh,[43] Mahārāo Umed Singh at Kota,[44] Mahārājā Bakhtāwar Singh at Alwar,[45] Mahārānā Sangrām Singh at Udaipur,[46] of the Bharatpur Rajas Randhīr Singh and Baldeva Singh at Govardhan.[47] In fact, almost every building of architectural importance erected in modern times, except of course those of the Western styles, follows the Hindu-Muslim style. Even the Jain temple of Hutti Singh at Ahmedābad,[48] which may appear to be an

[34] Le Bon: Op. cit.

[35] Burgess: Op. cit., Vol. II, Western India.

[36] Le Bon: Op. cit., Fig. 291.

[37] Ibid., Fig. 294.

[38] Fergusson: Op. cit., Vol. II, 153.

[39] Le Bon: Op. cit., Fig. 297.

[40] Ibid., Fig. 276.

[41] Ibid., Fig. 298.

[42] Rousselet: Op. cit., p. 246.

[43] Le Bon: Op. cit., Fig. 275.

[44] Fergusson: Op. cit., Vol. II, p. 169.

[45] Impey: Op. cit., Plate 53.

[46] Rousselet: Op. cit., p. 210.

[47] Growse: Op. cit.

[48] Le Bon: Op. cit., Fig. 295.

exception, is not really one; its unsculptured spires, unornamented walls, and smooth-surfaced domes, are enough testimony to the failure of the attempt, if any was made, to revive an ancient taste, and to the compelling force of the new art values and æsthetic feelings. And not only did this Hindu-Muslim style become dominant in the monumental art of India, but it also acquired the same hold over all utilitarian architecture—houses, streets, landings and bathing places (*ghāṭs*).

INDIAN PAINTING

The history of Indian painting is but the history of Indian architecture. Pre-Muslim Indian paintings—Hindu, Jain or Buddhist—have a character of their own. The vision of reality which inspires them and gives significance to their form is their own. They are the æsthetic expression of a culture which grew out of the synthesis of the racial experience, a synthesis which implies a balance between opposing tendencies—joy and sorrow, pleasure and pain, success and failure, worldliness and other-worldliness, attachment to life and renunciation of life, domination by sense and control of sense, ambition, activity and passion, and satisfaction, passivity and calm serenity. It is not true that the Hindu culture is more religious or less materialistic than other cultures, but the quality and content of its religious consciousness is different, the point of equilibrium between the opposing forces of life is differently situated. The whole mentality is cast in a different mould and naturally all that issues from it has a different stamp. What the character of this consciousness was, has been delineated above, it remains to describe how it manifested itself in Indian painting.

The frescoes of Ajanta are almost the only surviving remains of the Indian art as it was practised in the ancient period, although the legendary accounts refer its origins to *Brahmā* as *Viśwakarmā* the architect of the gods. Scholars have discovered references to the art in the pre-Christian literature, for instance, in the *Vinaya Pitaka,* and in later Hindu poetry, *Mahābhārata, Rāmāyaṇa, Śakuntalā,* and so forth. There are actual fragments of paintings belonging to great antiquity existing in various caves, but the only adequate remains which truly reflected the character of the art which at one time was spread widely all over India and was extremely prolific in its output, are found at Ajanta. The paintings adorn the ceilings and walls of the temples excavated out of living rock. In all probability, all the twenty-nine cave temples were embellished with paintings but the ravages of nature and time and the vandalism of man have destroyed the greater part. They were executed during the first six centuries of the Christian era.

Who were the artists who painted these pictures and what was the motive of their work? It has been suggested that the artists were priests who were engaged in self-edification. If that is so they were absolutely unlike any other priests whom India at any rate has known. The Brahmins or the Hindu monks would never have dreamt of such pursuits, and it is not probable that their Buddhist or Jain *confrères* whose life was more or less modelled on theirs would have done so. The whole work is really much too professional to have been left to the amateurs of the monasteries. The *Chaitya* halls were excavated by a professional class of architects and masons, as they were constructed on the ground, and again a professional class of sculptors and painters must have decorated the edifices built or dug by their brother craftsmen. The wealth of kings and merchant princes, must have been poured out in order to create the works in which both ambition and piety were satisfied.

The conditions of production are reflected in the creation itself. The walls and ceilings were covered with scenes drawn equally from the life of the court and the world and the life of the devotee and the history of religion. The first class of pictures are inundated with joy in life; they throb with the aspiration and glory which are of the here and the now. They desight in the pomp and splendour of the royal state,[1] in the

[1] Griffiths: Ajanta Frescoes. Plates 5 and 74.

pride and triumph of war[2] and chase,[3] and are eagerly interested in the daily concerns of life, in the romance of love-making,[4] in the delights of feasting, singing and dancing,[5] in the busy hum of the market with its haggling over prices, purchase and sale.[6] They represent the noontide in the life of man and society when the sap of youth, ambition and power runs violently in the veins. But life is not all noon, for the sun must run its course and the shadows must lengthen as the evening advances. The synthesis of culture is incomplete without the wisdom of age and of detachment, and so there are the second class of pictures which depict the mild, unexciting, tranquil and serene life, which with its suggestion of the infinite and the beyond, gives healthy tone and proper perspective to the first world. They are pictures of Buddha's life,[7] of his struggles and eventual victory,[8] of the crowded career of beneficence and propagation of faith,[9] of the stories of previous lives,[10] and of allegories that stop the teachings.[11] But the two worlds do not lie apart, they weave and interweave with one another, for they are both part patterns of the same fabric.

The artistic treatment of the two is informed with the same æsthetic purpose. That consciousness of the intense pressure and throng of life which is observable in the Hindu architecture, is present in their paintings. The figures crowd upon one another; men, women and children in all postures and atti-

2 Herringham: Ajanta Plate 17.

3 Ibid., Plate 33.

4 Griffiths: Op. cit., Plate 83.

5 Ibid., Plate 12.

6 Ibid., Plates 30, 15.

7 Ibid., Plate 41.

8 Ibid., Plates 45, 54.

9 Ibid., Fig. 64.

10 Ibid., Plates 49, 80.

11 Ibid., Plate 85.

tudes, are put together in bewildering confusion, their numbers are beyond tale or count, as if the artist was oppressed with the illimitable, inexpressible fecundity of the reality that was life and was struggling to grasp, and render it.[12] Every form, animate or inanimate, rock or stream, bird or beast, flower or tree, man or superman, is equally interesting, equally sacred, for all form is the articulation of the One. This sanctity of all, expresses itself through the wonderful intimacy which the artist establishes between his human and non-human figures, between man and landscape, man and architecture, man and animals and plants, and between all of them together. The cows and bulls listen to the Buddha's teaching,[13] the geese tell their story to the prince,[14] the angels and gods hover round the teacher,[15] all the creatures of earth and heaven crowd round him with eager attention.[16] *Rākśasas* and birds and men are engaged together in strife,[17] the lion and the snake and human crowds are united in anger and terror;[18] processions of elephants, horses and soldiers with arms and banners pass in and out of city gates and the wall and gate and animals and men swing with the same rhythm of movement;[19] men and women stand amidst rocks and the overspreading branches of the trees darken the glen and a calm passivity rests upon them all;[20] the roots of plants are hidden in the crevices of rocks, their soft tendrils and slender

[12] Herringham: Op. cit., Plate 25.
Griffiths: Op. cit., Plates 6, 28, etc.

[13] Griffiths: Op. cit., Plates 19, 50.

[14] Herringham: Op. cit., Plate 25.

[15] Griffiths: Op. cit., Plates 37, 38, 51.

[16] Ibid., Fig. 64.

[17] Ibid., Plate 67.

[18] Ibid., Plate 57.

[19] Ibid., Plates 69, 71.

[20] Ibid., Plate 55.

stalks wind upwards almost clinging to them;[21] the river flows amidst crowded scenes, and the fishes and boats and swimming creatures animate its surface,[22] women peer through small oblong windows and look like medallions, decorating panels in the wall,[23] the bananas stand along with courtiers and ambassadors and officers in the halls of reception.[24] The same feeling works itself out in the grotesque bogeys, frightful looking figures, creatures—half man half horse, half man half bird, mermaids and celestial beings flying through air;[25] in the scenes of strife where bears hug men,[26] snakes attack elephants,[27] and bulls fight;[28] and in the attempt to render the features of all known races of men and of beings of the superior and inferior worlds.

The medium through which the intensity of this thronging and unified life is rendered is the line. It is one of the unexplained mysteries of civilization why Europe chose colour and Asia line as the language of its art. Whatever the reasons, the results have abundantly justified the choice. Each civilazation has attained its supreme success in its own medium. Thus what colour is to the West, line is to the East, for its schools are divided according to the character of their line. The line employed by the artists of Ajanta is unique for its firmness, breadth and sweep; it moves over vast spaces with an unhesitating assurance, unhalting swing, uniform and rhythmical. It is equally efficacious in rendering the calm, passionless rapture of an illumined Buddha, and the agitated, eager, trembling emotion of the devotee of song and dance. The artist employs it with the same

[21] Griffiths: Op. cit., Plate 63.

[22] Ibid., Plate 34.

[23] Ibid., Plate 76.

[24] Ibid., Plate 5.

[25] Ibid., Plate 60.

[26] Ibid., Fig. 28.

[27] Ibid., Fig. 31.

[28] Ibid., Plate 114.

knowledge and success whether he has to render the tenseness of flight through the air, the upward spring of plant and tree, the waving trunk of an elephant, or the wonderful gestures of the hands, and he is equally at home in creating with it types or individualities, forms of man or of nature, idealistic or realistic. In fact, it is impossible for the purpose—that of painting on large surfaces, on ceilings and walls—to suggest a line of character different from the one he has used. The line of the Indian painter, in the suppleness of its form, in the gentle sinuousness of its curve, shares indeed the plastic character of Indian sculpture and architecture.

The process of the Ajanta frescoes consisted in first preparing the ground by two layers of plasters; the layer below was made of a mixture of clay, cow-dung and pulverised trap rock, and occasionally of finely-chopped straw or rice husks. This was applied to the thickness of one-eighth to three-quarters of an inch to hide the rough-hewn surface of the walls. Over this ground was laid an extremely thin egg-shell layer of white plaster which was polished. The next step was to paint the surface thus prepared, and for this purpose a combination of fresco and tempera methods was used. The dry surface of plaster was thoroughly drenched with water the night before, and the next morning it was again wetted with lime water. On the damp surface the painting was made with the pigments which included metallic and vegetable colour.

The outline was first freely sketched out in red on the plaster, but was subsequently corrected in black or brown as occasion demanded. Then a semi-transparent green glaze was applied to the surface, over which the local colours were washed in flat. The colours used were white sulphate of lime, ferruginous red, green iron silicates, and blue ultramarine.

The treatment of the various *motifs* used in the paintings is worthy of attention. The human figure is slender and supple without muscularity or anatomical details. The eyes are long, almond like, hands full of meaning, attitudes graceful "of stylistic breeding," hair done in ringlets or tied in chignons at back or in loops at side and usually adorned with flowers. Side, back and half-averted views are not avoided The dresses vary from the diaphanous translucent drapery of the high placed to the coarse jackets and tight-fitting breeches of soldiers and servants, and the headgear is of many kinds. Jewellery is profusely used. Many animals are represented; the elephant is drawn with wonderful insight, the horses have rounded, full-bodied, high-crested and Roman-nosed heads, hogged manes, tails sometimes neatly clipped, legs adorned with bangles;[29] the deer have calf-like broad faces, the lions are crude, resembling distantly the Assyrian variety; the buffaloes, bulls, monkeys and others do not call for particular notice. Among the birds the geese and peacocks are noteworthy. In the landscape the rocks are made in masses of rectangular forms with ends brokes in fret-like pattern; the water is conventional like basket work or flowing wave scroll; fishes, tortoises and mermen are added as symbols; the clouds have folds and masses of rounded forms, edged with shapes like petals of rose, or scales of fish In plant life the banana, betelnut, palm, *aśoka*, banian, *pipal;* among fruits the mango, custard apple, pomegranate, gourd, and among flowers the lotus, are most frequent.

The art of Ajanta continued to exist after the last fresco was painted, but hardly any examples of it remain to show what developments it underwent. A few Jain and Buddhist palm-leaf manuscripts illuminated with religious paintings of unrecorded dates, a Nepālese or Behārī manuscript of *Asta-sahasrika Prajnaparamita,* dated 1090 A.D.,[30] the coloured panels of Mān Mandir at Gwalior from the end of the fifteenth cen-

[29] Griffiths: Op. cit., p. 12.

[30] Vredenburg: The Continuity of Pictorial Tradition in the Art of India; Rupam, January 1920.

tury,[31] Tārā Nāth's history, and indirectly the fragments of paintings from the sand-burried cities of Serindia—these show the continuity of the ancient tradition. In reality, however, the second period of Indian art of painting begins with the Chaghtā'ī rulers of India after an almost unfilled gap of nearly nine hundred years. The painting of this period belongs to a new style, a style created by the absorption of new elements from across the frontiers of India into the ancient traditions.

Before discussing this new school of Hindu-Muslim art it is necessary to enquire into the characteristics of painting in the Islamic schools of Samarqand, Herat, Ispahān, and Baghdad. It is not possible here to disentangle the ramifications by which Muslim art is affiliated to the antique and the Christian art of the West, and the arts of China, Khotan and Gandhāra in the East. But, when this art appears in its full-fledged form in the fourteenth century, it is so deeply coloured with eastern hues that it might almost be mistaken as a branch of the Chinese art. Under Tīmūr this Muslim—Mongol style becomes more individualized, more independent, and then by insensible gradations passes into the Safavid and Bokhāriot schools. The father of the Tīmuride school was one Gung entitled *Naqwat-ul-Muharrirīn,* whose pupil was Jahāngīr of Bokhārā, who was the master of Pīr Sayyid Ahmad. The last had for his disciple Bihzād, the greatest glory of the school. Bihzād was born in the middle of the fifteenth century and became the court painter of Mansūr ibn Baiqara, the Tīmuride ruler of Khorāsān. He migrated from Herat in 1506 and took service under Shāh Ismā'īl Safavī and continued in the service of the Safavid till he died about 1526 A.D., residing mostly at Tabrīz.

When Bābur conquered India the star of Bihzād was in its zenith, his style was the standard of perfection; naturally the connoisseurs of art, Bābur and his companions, and, afterwards on the return of Humāyūn from his enforced exile from Persia to India, the Chaghtā'ī nobles set Bihzād before Indian painters

[31] Griffiths: The Monuments of Central India.

as the master in whose footsteps they should follow and whose paintings they should copy. Bihzād and his school thus became the exemplars of Indian painters and the elements of the Tīmurid school were engrafted upon the traditions of Ajanta.

The character of this art is its intense individualism. This art is not interested in masses and crowds; it has hardly any direct interest in composition. It sees things limned in clear light and in definite outline, it looks at every detail of the individual figure and takes infinite pains with it, it feels the urge of life with tremendous force, and it communicates this passionate energy to what it delineates, but inter-relations of form and the infinite multiplicity of form it does not feel and does not care for. Its life has a different pulse and a different rhythm.

This art, born and cradled in the courts of Changīz and Tīmūr, the world-shakers of their age, could not conceivably be soft and sentimental. The scenes of battle[32] and siege and hunt, and of man and animas battes, are naturally frequent. But chivalry and romance,[33] the loves of Lailī and Majnūn, Shīrīn and Farhād, youths and maidens dallying in the garden by the side of a stream,[34] gorgeous receptions in princely courts,[35] feasts and merriment where the wine passes freely round and toothsome viands are spread in plenty,[36] are represented equally. And of piety and mysticism there is no lack, for in that curious age of self-abandonment the transformation from the intense pleasures of life to the rigorous discipline of sainthood was never difficult; the *Shāh* (king) and the *Gadā*

[32] Martin: The Miniature Painting of Persia, India and Turkey, Plates 60—61.

[33] Ibid., Plates 68, 79, 95, 96, 112.

[34] Ibid., Plate 105.

[35] Ibid., Plate 147.

[36] Ibid., Plate 71.

(beggar) were the two poles between which the individual constantly moved. The Sultan of to-day may be the *Darwīsh* of to-morrow, nay the king was always an ascetic at heart. Hence the frequency of the scenes where *Darwīsh* is depicted—the *Darwīsh* living in wild forests and lonely caves,[37] the *Darwīsh* as the miraculous master leading fierce animals like lambs,[38] and the Darwīsh dancing in the ecatasy of mystic joy.[39] Then like every age of romance, conquest and mystery, this age was greatly interested in the supernatural and the marvellous.[40] Genii, goblins, monsters and fairies moved amidst men as common, well-known, familiar figures. They were the stock-in-trade equally of the story-teller and the painter.

And in every scene the mark of individualism is unmistakable. There is system and order and arrangement sometimes fatal to composition, but each man has a fixed status and recognised position, and each one is engaged in his own pursuits energetically. It is the action of each which gives action to the whole and not the movement of the whole manifested through each. Here is the picture of siege[41]—one man is brandishing his huge axe and giving mighty blows to the closed gate, he is utterly oblivious of the missiles descending from the top, a pair of men is climbing up a ladder and never were men more self-confident and self-centred, the stars in heaven may stop in their revolutionary course, but nothing will deter them or daunt them, they know not how to stop; the horseman on his charger charges madly up the boards that have been thrown across the moat, and so on.

37 Martin: Op. cit., Plate 165.

38 Ibid., Plate 59.

39 Ibid.

40 Ibid., Plate 148.

41 Shāh Nāmah, Khuda Bakhsh Library, Bankipore, Folio 153-A.

Take the picture of a chase.[42] The riders form round a semi-circle, in the middle in the large broken space the royal huntsmen pierce the victims with their spears, each deer is separately rendered as well as each rider; there is no mêlée, no confusion. Again the builders[43] are busy erecting a mosque, one labourer mixes the mud plaster, two or three water carriers placed round in a circle pour water out of their skins, one man is carrying a tray of plaster, another of bricks, on the walls masons are dressing bricks or putting them in layers, the ladder occupies its individual position along the wall, there is activity all round but no hubbub. In the feasts[44] each man receives attention separately, even the dancers and the musicians do not get mixed up. Why let the warriors fight[45] and they will arrange themselves in a symmetrical pattern, with the horses rearing, the spears crossing and the curved swords dangling by the side. Even the leaves of the trees spread themselves out so that each may be separately counted.[46]

This interest in individuality grows to such an extent that painting becomes merely portraiture and portraiture of such amazing cleverness that it becomes itself a marvel.

As in the case of Ajanta so here, the line is the medium of expression. Yet what a vast difference between the character of the two lines! Here the line bends and breaks, thins and broadens, makes circles and angles, in short, does all that the requirements of a fastidious calligraphist demand. The geometrical and epigraphist bias of the Muslim surely would make calligraphy his own.

The elements which combine to make these paintings are very different from those found in the work of Ajanta. Of men, not only is the racial type different, but the proportions

[42] Martin: Op. cit., Plates 60-61.

[43] British Museum: Persian Paintings, C. 100.

[44] Martin: Op. cit., Plate 71.

[45] British Museum: Persian Paintings, C. 101.

[46] Martin: Op. cit., Plate 66.

of the body and the limbs and their rhythm, too, are different. The attitude is extremely graceful and the product of high culture. Its drapery in the simple flow of line is charming. In the rendering of animals the horse receives special attention: swiftness, lightness and slenderness are the ideals, as in depicting gazelles and antelopes; the lion is powerfully drawn. Slender flowering trees with overhanging boughs, blossoming creepers twined round them, and trees with knots and gnarls and almost always bent out of the straight line, and grounds strewn with flowers, are characteristic. The clouds are usually Chinese swirling lines like those of the sea shell, the rocks have rounded cactus-like shapes, the trees and bushes and shrubs grow on the surface, the grounds are rolling, narrow streamlets are lined with stones, and a single tree stands usually in the foreground. The architecture is Persian, highly decorated with faience and geometrical patterns, and with railings separating it from the garden behind and on the sides. Architecture plays an important part in the picture, it gives a setting to the scene, but it is not intimately related with the characters.

The meeting of these two art-consciousnesses under the fostering care of the Mughal emperors was productive of a new style. Upon the plasticity of Ajanta were imposed the new laws of symmetry, proportion and spacing from Samarqand and Heart. To the old pomp new splendours were added, and to the old free and easy naivete of life a new sense of courtly correctness and rigid etiquette. In the result a certain amount of the energy and dynamism of both the Hindu and the Muslim were sacrificed; and a stiff dignity was acquired, but along with it a marvellous richness of colour and subtlety of line.

The evolution of the new style was rapid. Probably Bābur introduced the models of the Tīmūrid school to the Hindu and Muslim artists of India at Agra. Under Humāyūn the copying was continued, so that when the *Dāstān* of Amīr Hamzah was produced in twelve volumes with illustrations for no less than one thousand and four hundred passages, there was a sufficient number of trained artists to commission for the work. Among them were Persians and Qalmāqs, certainly, but not exclusively. The work was of prodigious volume and was probably finished in the early years of Akbar's rule. It is interesting to find even in this early school—called the school of Humāyūn by Clarke—an unmistakable Indian feelng. The manner of the Tīmūrid style is dominant, in the delineation of landscape and architecture, in the rendering of clouds, rocks, water, trees, and animals; but in the selection of racial types, drapery, and attitudes there is greater freedom and in grouping still more.

The later artists of Akbar must have been trained in this school, probably under the four Muslim masters mentioned by Abul Fazl[47] namely, Farrukh Qalmāq, 'Abdus Samad of Shīrāz, Mīr Sayyid' Ali of Tabrīz and Miskīn. The pupils who were Hindus were in all likelihood painters who had acquired proficiency in traditional methods and were possessed of sufficient repute to be summoned to the Imperial court. They had only to transfer their talents to the services of their new masters and paint the pictures that pleased them. This explains why so early in Akbar's reign the new Hindu-Muslim school made its appearance fully developed. The names of Daswant, Basāwan, Keśo Lāl, Mukund, Mādho, Jagan Nāth, Maheś, Khem Karan, Tārā, Sānwalah, Haribans, and Rām, are recorded in the *Ā'in-i-Akbarī*. Many other Hindu names appear on the paintings of the period, for instance, in the *Tīmūr Nāmah*,[48] which is a history of Tīmūr and his successors till the twenty-second year of Akbar's reign. Among the illustrators of the manuscript, now preserved in the Khudā Baksh Library at Bānkīpore, occur the names of Tulsī, Surjan, Sūrdās, Īśar, Śankar, Rām Ās, Banwālī, Nand, Nanhā, Jagjīwan, Dharam-

[47] Blochmann and Jarrett: Ā'īn-iAkbarī, Vol. I, p. 108.

[48] Timūr Nāmah: Khudā Bakhsh Library, Bankipore, (Photographic reproductions).

dās, Nārāyan, Chatarman, Sūraj, Deojīva, Saran, Gangā Singh Pāras, Dhannā, Bhīm, etc. In some cases the place from which the artists came is denoted, and it is interesting to find only Gwalior, Gujarat and Kashmir mentioned. These three were pre-eminently centres of Hindu culture during the early mediæval period, and the fact that the painters of Akbar came from these places confirms the tradition that the Hindu art continued to flourish after Ajanta. It also clearly establishes the contention that the Mughal art was not altogether an offshoot of Central Asian and Persian styles, but a development of the ancient Indian art under new impulses.

Under Jahāngīr the Indian school completely freed itself of imitation, portrait painting acquired unusual fineness, and scenes of hunting became very popular. The reign of Shāh Jahān saw the culmination of the art, the rules of perspective and foreshortening, of modelling and shading were introduced, the finest brushes and the most costly colours were used. Again among the artists the Hindus were more numerous. The Hindus—Kalyān Dās *alias* Chatrman, Anūp Chatar, Rā'ī Anūp, Manohar, and the Musalmans—Muhammad Nādīr Samarqandī, Mīr Hāshim and Muhammad Faqīr Allah Khān, are selected by Smith[49] for special mention. In Muhammad Nādir Samarqandī portraiture attained its highest development. After Shāh Jahān taste gradually declined and decadence set in.

The artists of the court were usually engaged in painting either portraits or scenes. In portraiture the principal aim of the artists was the natural and truthful delineation of the features of the face and the character of the individual as revealed through them. Most of the portraits were drawn in profile, in some three-quarters of the face was shown; in all the position of the body was conventional with the exception of the hands which were always charmingly rendered. Of the portraits those of Akbar and Mahārājah Jaswant Singh by some un-

49 V. A. Smith: A History of Fine Arts of India and Ceylon, p. 482.

known artist and that of Āsaf Khān by Muhammad Nādir Samarqandī might be selected to show how different types of men of action were portrayed with such keen insight.

Among the scenes in the early period war and conquest received the greatest amount of attention, especially in illustrating works like *Dārāb Nāmah*,[50] *Tīmur Nāmah*,[51] *Razm Nāmah* (*Mahābhārata*)[52]; hunting and forest scenes also abounded; later a taste for durbār, mythological, genre, domestic and fanciful (*e.g.*, pictures of beauty) pictures developed. Through them all a mystic interest always remains in evidence; religious incidents, portraits of Darwīshes, scenes of princes learning divine wisdom from ascetics, of prayers in mosques, or of studying the holy book by candle light, or of assemblies of saints, are scattered through the albums and picture collections from Akbar's time onwards.

Of this Hindu-Muslim style, related on the one hand with the mural art of Ajanta, and with the true miniature painting of Samarqand and Heart on the other, there were many offshoots differing in their character as they approached the one or the other pole of this style. The Rajput and Pahādī styles of Jaipur, Kāngḍā and the Hindu states of the Himalayan hills, had a greater inclination towards the ancient Hindu; the *Qalams* of the Deccan, Lucknow, Kashmir, Patna gravitated more towards the Muslim; the Sikh *Qalam* was somewhere between them. They are all, however, sub-styles derived from the parent stock which is the style of the court at Delhi or Agra.

It would not have been necessary to stress the point, but for the fact that Coomāraswāmy has unduly emphasized the difference between the Rajput and Moghul schools. The differences of technique are negligible, the processes of painting whether Persian, Mughal or *Rājasthānī* are alike. The choice

50 Dārāb Nāmah: British Museum, Or. 4615.

51 Tīmūr Nāmah.

52 Razm Nāmah: Hendley's Jaipur Art.

of subjects was conditoned by the traditions of the prince. In the Hindu courts Hindu mythology afforded opportunities to the painter which in the Imperial courts were offered by the glories of conquest. Both arts are essentially courtly for in either case the patrons are princes. There is undoubtedly greater freedom and variety in the Rajput schools because their social manners differed from those of the Mughals, but the æsthetic quality of the two arts is much the same. The line of the Hindu retains more of Ajantan feeling in a certain class of pictures,[53] otherwise the beauty of life is envisaged in the same sharp, intense, well-defined, individualized manner as by the Mughal artist. The illustrations[54] of Rajput paintings given by Coomāraswāmy themselves testify to these facts. The setting of the three first and crudely though forcefully executed pictures is exactly like that of any of the Mughal school. The *Rāginīs*[56] and *Nāyakās* are Rajput ladies sitting like Persian maidens[57] under overhanging branches of blossoming trees. The clarity of outline, the emptiness of spaces, the devotion to details like the ornaments and drapery, the picturesque scenery, the graceful pose, are all Hindu versions of the Persian art. The subject matter may belong to Hindu society; the draughtsmanship, the setting, the colouring is Mughal or Hindu-Muslim. In fact, in painting the same synthesis took place as in architecture. If Akbar adorned the palaces of Fatehpur Sīkrī with paintings on the walls, the Mahārājās of Bīkāner and Udeypur followed his example, and not only were the edifices alike, but the adornments were also of the same character. The Muslim rulers set the example of

53 Coomaraswamy: Rajput Painting, Plate X, LI, LII.

54 Ibid., Plates I, II, III.

55 Coomaraswamy: Selected Examples of Indian Art Plates IV, CV, CXII.

56 Ibid., Plate CXLVIII.

57 Martin: Op. cit., Plates 101, 111.

patronage of art and literature, and the Hindu princes imitated them. Naturally it followed that the style created by the Hindu and Musalman artists of the Mughal court was copied with local variations by the court artists of Jaipur, Jammū, Chambā, Kāngda, Lahore, Amritsar, and distant Tanjore; and a common style prevailed throughout India.

BIBLIOGRAPHY

(a) RELIGION:—

(i) *General*

Barth, A. A. — The Religions of India.

Hopkins, E. W. — The Religions of India, Boston, 1895.

Macdonnel, A. A. — The History of Sanskrit Literature, London, 1900.

Frazer, R. W. — Indian Thought, London, 1915.

Elliot, Sir Henry — Hinduism and Brahmanism.

Oltramare, P. — L' Histoire des Idées théosophiques dans I'Inde.

Deussen, P. — Outline of Indian Philosophy.

Farquhar, J. N. — An outline of the religious literature of India, London, 1920.

Macnicoll, Nicol — Indian Theism.

Monier Williams, M. — Vedism, Brahmanism, Hinduism, London, 1889.

Weber, A — History of Sanskrit Literature.

Barnett, L. D. — Heart of Hinduism.

Barnett, L. D. — Indian Antiquities, London, 1913.

Wilson, H. H. — Works, London, 1871.

Colebrooke, H. T. — Miscellaneous Essays, London, 1873.

(ii) *Vedic*

Macdonnel, A. A. — Vedic Mythology.

Macdonnel, A. A., and Keith, A. B. — The Vedic Index, London, 1908.

Bloomfield, M. — The Religion of the Vedas.

Bergaigne, A. — The Rig Veda.

Wilson, H. H. — Translation of the Rig Veda.

Buhler, G. A. — Sacred Laws Part I, Apastamba and Gautam, S. B. E., Vol. 2., Oxford, 1879-82.

Buhler, G. A. — Sacred Laws Part II, Vasishta and Baudhyāyana, S. B. E., Vol. 14., Oxford, 1879-82.

Buhler, G. A. — The Laws of Manu, S. B. E., Vol. 25, Oxford, 1886.

Oldenburg, H. — Grihya Sutras, S. B. E., Vols. 29, 30, Oxford, 1921.

Hume, R. E. — Translation of Thirteen principal Upanishads, Edinburgh, 1901.

Deussen, P. — Philosophy of the Upanishads, translated by A. S. Geden. Edinburgh, 1908.

(iii) *Epic*

Hopkins, E. W.	The Great Epic, New York, 1901.
Williams, Monier	Indian Epic Poetry.
Fausboll, V.	Indian Mythology.
Buhler, G. and Kirste, J.	Indian Studies.
Vaidya, C. V.	Epic India.
Barth, A. A.	Quarante ans d' Indianisme.
Roy, P. C.	*Mahabharata* (English translation).
Dutt, M. M.	*Hari Vamśa* (English translation).

(iv) *Philosophical*

Max Muller, F.	Six Systems of Indian Philosophy.
Royce, J.	The World and the Individual. New York, 1859.
Keith, A. B.	Sāmkhya System.
Rāma Prasād	Yoga; S. B. H.
Chatterjee	Hindu Realism. Allahabad, 1910.
Garbe	*Karma Mīmānsā* E. R. E.
Thibaut	Vedānta Sūtras, S. B. E., Vols. 34, 38, 48.
Cowell, E. B.	*Sarvadarśana Sangraha.* London, 1894.

(v) *Early mysticism*

Bhagwān Dās	Translation of the Bhagawad Gita.
Barnett, L. D.	Translation of the Bhagawad Gita.
Grierson, G. A.	The Nārāyanīyā Section of the Śanti Parva of the Mahābhārata.
Seal, B. N.	Vaiśnavism.
Rām Prasād Chanda	Indo-Aryan Races. Rajshahi, 1916. n
Rām Prasāda Chanda	Memoirs of Archæological Survey; No. 5.
Shrader, F. O.	Introduction to Ahirbudhnya and Panchratra Samhitas.
Bhandārkar, R. G.	Vaiśnavism, Śaivism and other minor sects. Strassburg, 1913.
Sinhā, N.	Nārada Bhakti Sūtras, S. B. E. 1911.
Cowell, E. B.	Śāndilyā Bhakti Sūtras, Bib. Indica.
Grierson, G. A.	Monotheistic Religion.
Wilson, H. H.	The Viśṇu Purāna (Eng. translation). London, 1865.
Wilson, H. H.	The Purānas, (Eng. translation).
Dutt, M. N.	Agni Purāṇa, (English translation).

Pargiter, F. E. — *Mārkandeya Purāṇa* (Eng. translation).

Dutt, M. N. — *Bhāgawat Purāṇ.*

Pargiter, F. E. — The Purāṇa text of dynasties of the Kali age. Oxford, 1913.

(vi) *Buddhism and Jainism*

Kern — Manual of Indian Buddhism. Strassburg, 1896.

Rhys Davids — History of Indian Buddhism.

Oldenberg, H. — Buddha. London, 1882.

Poussin, Valle de la — The way to Nirvana.

Suzuki — Outlines of Mahāyān Buddhism.

Rhys Davids (Mrs.) — Buddhism.

Rhys Davids (Mrs.) — Psychology of Buddhism.

Jaini, J. B. — Outlines of Jainism. Cambridge, 1916.

Stevenson, S. — The heart of Jainism. London, 1915.

Jacobi, H. — Jainism; E. R. E.

(vii) *Reformed Hinduism*

Bhāshyāchārya, N. — Age of Śankara.

Krishnsvāmy Aiyar, C. N. — Śankara and his times.

Anandagirī — Śankara Vijaya.

Deussen, P. — Outline of Vedānta.

Thibaut, G. — The Vedānta Sūtras, S. B. E. 1890.

(viii) *Mysticism in the South*

Purnalingam Pillāi — Ten Tāmil saints.
Some milestones in the history of Tāmil literature.

Śrīnivāsa Aiyangar — Tāmil Studies.

Kingsbury and Phillips — The hymns of the Tāmil Śaivite saints. 1921.

Pope, G. U. — Manikka Vacagar.

Rājgopālāchariyar, T. — The Vaiśnava reformers of India.

Govindāchārya, H. — The divine wisdom of the Dravidian saints.

Śrīnivāsa Aiyangar, M. B. — Nityanusandhanam series.

Rangāchārya, M. — Life and teaching of Rāmānuja.

Aiyangar, K. S. — Rāmānuja.

Rājgopālāchariyar, T. — Rāmānuja.

Thibaut, G. — Vedanta Sutras; S. B. E. 1890.

Sukhtankar, V. A. — The teaching of Vedanta according to Rāmānuja.

Estlin Carpenter, J. — Theism in Medieval India. London, 1920.

Siddhānta Dīpaka

Gover, C. E. — Folk songs of Southern India. Madras, 1871.

(ix) *Islam*

The Encyclopedia of Islam

Hastings — Encyclopedia of Religion and Ethics.

Hughes — Dictionary of Islam. London, 1885.

Muhammad Alī — The Qorān (translation).

Rodwell — The Qorān (translation).

Houdas, et Marcais — Al-Bukhārī.

Mathews, A. N. — Mishkat ul Masābih.

Amīr 'Ali, S. — The Spirit of Islam. London, 1922.

Margoliouth, D. S. — Muhammadanism.

Margoliouth, D. S. — Early development of Muhammadanism.

Margoliouth, D. S. — Muhammad.

Sale, E. — Historical development of the Qorān.

Sale, E. — Essays on Islam.

Tisdall, St. Clair — Islam.

Hurgronje — Muhammadanism.

Stanton, A. U. W. — Teaching of Qorān.

Bosworth Smith — Muhammad and Muhammadanism.

Macdonald, A. B. — The development of Muslim Theology.

Goldziher, I. — Vorlesungen überden Islam, translated by Felix Arin. Heidelberg, 1910.

Khuda Bakhsh, S. — Contributions to the history of Islamic civilisation.

Boer, T. J. — History of Muslim philosophy, translation by E. R. Jones.

Iqbal, Dr. M. — Development of Metaphysics in Persia.

Schmolders — Essai sur les écoles philosophiques des Arabes.

Munk, S. — Mélanges de philosophic Juive et Arabe.

Dugat, G.	Histoire des philosophes et de théologiens Musulmans.
Carra de Vaux, B.	Ghazālī.
Carra de Vaux, B.	Avicenne.
Field, C.	Ghazālī, the Alchemy of Happiness.
Renan	Averroes et Averroisme.
Gautheir, L.	La philosophie Musulmane.
Mehren, A. F. M.	'Asharī.
Shiblī N'umānī	'Ilm-ul-Kalām.
Shiblī N'umānī	Sirat-un-Nabī.
Shiblī N'umānī	Al-Ghazālī.
Shiblī N'umānī	Rasā'il.
Seeley, K. C.	Moslem Schisms and sects.
Friedlander, I.	Heterodoxies of the Shiites from Ibn Hazm; I. A. O. S. Vols. 28 and 29.
Mustafā ibn Khāliqdād Hāshimi	Tandhīh-ul-Milal., Persian translation of Shahrastānī.
Nicholson, R. A.	Hujwirī's Kashful Mahjūb.
Nicholson, R. A.	Farīdud Dīn 'Attār's Tadhkirat-ul-Auliyā.
Nicholson, R. A	A historical enquiry concerning the origin and development of Sufism; J. R. A. S. 1906.
Nicholson, R. A.	Tarjuman ul Ashwāq of Ibn-ul-'Arabī.
Nicholson, R. A.	Studies in Islamic mysticism.
Nicholson, R. A.	Dīwāni Shams-i-Tabrīz.
Massignon, L.	Kitāb ul Tawāsīn.
Wilberforce Clarke, H.	Awāriful Ma'ārif of Suhrāwardī.
Palmer	Oriental mysticism.
Browne, E. G.	Literary history of Persia. London, 1902.
Whinfield, E. A.	Gulshan-i-Rāz of Shabistarī.
Whinfield, E. A.	Jalāl Uddin Rūmi's Masnavī m'anavī.
Farid-ud-Dīn 'Attār	Pand Nāmah.
Hāfiz	Dīwān.
Malcolm	History of Persia. London, 1815.
Brown, J. P.	The Derwishes. London, 1868.
Jāmī, 'Abdur Rahmān	Lawā'ih.
Muir, Sir W.	The Caliphate, its rise, decline and fall. Edinburg, 1915.

	A narrative of a year's journey through Central and Eastern Arabia.
Berlein, H.	Abul 'Alā'al Ma'arī, diwan.
Lane, E. W.	Arabian Society in the middle ages.
Lane-Poole, S.	Egypt.
Gibb	History of Ottoman poetry; Vol. I.
Sedillot, A.	Histoire des Arabes.
Huart, C.	Histoire des Ārabes.

(b) INDIAN CULTURE IN THE MIDDLE AGES:—

Beal	Buddhist records of the Western World.
Beal	Life of Hicen Tsiang.
Takakasu, M. J.	A record of Buddhist religion.
Watters	On Yuan Chwang's travels in India. London, 1904-03.
Rhys Davids	Buddhist India.
Reinaud, J. J.	Memoire géographique et historique, etc.
Reinaud, J. J.	Relation de voyages faits par les Arabes et Persans.
Reinaud, J. J.	Géographie d'Aboul Feda.
Ferrand, G.	Relations de voyages et textes géographiques Arabes, Persans et Turques, relatifs à I'extréme Orient.
Sachau	Alberunī's India, 2 Vols. Leipzig, 1925.
MacCrindle	India as described by Greek and Roman authors.
Elliot and Dowson	History of India.
Rowlandson	Tuhfatul Mujāhidīn.
Yule	The book of Ser Marco Polo.
Defremery and Sanguinetti	Ibn Batutah.
de meynard, B. and de Corteille, P.	Masudi, Les Prairies d'Or.
Major	India in the fifteenth century.
Day, F.	The land of the Perumāls.
Rice	Mysore and Coorg.
Sewell, R.	A sketch of the dynasties of South India.
Logan, W.	Malabar.
Innes, C. A.	Malabar and Anjengo, Madras District Gazetteer.

Moore, L.	Manual of Trichinopoly district.
Hemingway, F. R.	Trichinopoly, Madras Dist. Gazetteer.
Nelson, J. H.	Madura district manual.
Francis, W.	Madura, Madras Dist. Gazetteer.
Hemingway, F. R.	Tanjore Dist. Gazetteer.
Caldwell	Tinnevelly, Madras District Manual.
Pate, H. R.	Tinnevelly, Madras District Gazetteer.
Richards, F. J.	Salem, Madras District Gazetteer.
Sturrock, J.	South Canara, Madras District Manual, Madras, 1894-95.
Francis, W.	Anantapur, Madras Dist. Gazetteer.
Campbell, E. J.	Gazetteer of Gujarat, Bombay Gazetteer, Vol. IX, part II.
Thurston, E.	Castes and tribes of Southern India. Madras, 1909.
Aiyangar, S. I.	South India and her Muhammadan invaders.
Aiyangar, S. I.	The beginning of South Indian history.
Aiyangar, S. I.	Ancient India.
Subrahmanya Aiyer, K. V.	Historical sketches of ancient Dekhan.
Menon, S.	History of Travancore.
Arnold, T. W.	Preaching of Islam. Westminister, 1896.
Abdul Haq	Akhabār al Akhiyār.
Abdul Qādir Badāunī	Muntakhab-ut-Tawārīkh.
Abul Fazl	Ā'īn-i-Akbarī.
Muhammad Dārā Shukoh	Safīnat-ul-Auliyā.
Hāmid bin Fazl Allah Jamālī	Siyar-ul-Ārifīn.
Tod, J.	Rajasthān.
Forbes, K.	Rās Mālā.
Kern, H.	Varāhamihir, Verspreide Geschriften, 1913, 14.
de Tassy, G.	Histoire de la litérature Hindouie et Hindoustanie.
Muhammad Husain Āzād	Āb-i-Hayāt.
Mīr Ghulām 'Ali Āzād	Maasir ul-Kirām.
Shyām Vihārī Misra and others	Misra Vandhu Binod.
Sri Rām	Anthology of Urdu poets.
Dinesh Chandra Sen	Anthology of Bengālī language and Literature.

Rice	History of Kanarese literature., 1921.
Kaye, G. S.	Jaya Singh's astronomical observations. Calcutta, 1918.
Roy, P. C.	History of Hindu Chemistry.
Hoernle	Hindu Medicine.
Sedillot, A.	Récherches pour servir á I'histoire des sciences mathèmatiques shez les Orientaux.
Sedillot, A.	Memoire pour servir I'histoire comparée des sciences mathématiques.
Woepke	Récherches sur l'histoire des sciences mathématiques chez les Orientaux.
Cajori, F.	A history of Mathematics.
Sedillot, A.	Prolégomènes des Tables astronomiques d' Oloug Beg.
Carra de Vaux, B.	L'astrolabe linéare ou Baton d' at-Tousi.
Le Bon, G.	Le civilisation des Arabes.
Browne, E. G.	History of Arab medicine.
Mukharji, T. N.	Art manufactures of India. Calcutta, 1888.
Birdwood, G. C. M.	Industrial arts of India. London, 1880.
Grierson, G. A.	History of Medieval Vernacular literature of Hindustan.
	Lalla Didda.

(c) MEDIEVAL SECTS, SAINTS AND REFORMERS:—

Sitārām Saran Bhagwān Prasad	Nābhajī's Bhaktamāl, Nawal Kishor Press, Lucknow.
Kabīr	Bījak, with commentary, by Vishwanāth Singh of Rewah.
Kabīr	Bījak, with Trijya of Devīdāsa, Lucknow.
Kabīr	Siddhānta Dīpika collected by Ananta Dās, Rānchī.
Kabīr	Sākhī, collected by Yugalānanda, Lucknow.
Kabīr	Gyān Gudrī and Rekhtās, Belvėdere Press, Allahabad.
Kabīr	Ashtanga Yoga, edited by Yugalānanda, Lucknow.

Kabīr	Anurāga Sāgar, collected by Nand Kumār Lāl of Gole, Lucknow.
Kabīr	Bījak with commentary of Purandās.
Kabīr	Collection of hymns by K. M. Sen, Sāntiniketan.
Kabīr	Kabīr Manshūr, life and teachings of Kabīr, and the doctrines of the Kabīr Panth, by Parmānanda Dās.
Kabīr	Bījak, Ahmad Shāh, English translation, Hamīrpur.
Kabīr	Bījak, translated into English by Prem Chand, Calcutta.
Kabīr	100 poems, translated into English by Rabīndra Nāth Tagore. London, 1914-15.
Kabīr	Kabīr and Kabīr Panth, by H. G. Westcott.
Kabīr	Kabīr Bachanāvalī, by Ayodhyā Singh Upādhyāya, Allahabad.
Macauliffe	The Sikh Religion.
Khazān Singh	History and Philosophy of the Sikh religion (English).
Gurumukh Singh	Nānak Parkāsh (in Urdu). ..
Sant Bānī Sangrah	Belvedere Press, Allahabad.
Raidās Jī Kī Bāṇī	Belvedere Press, Allahabad.
Dādū Dayāl Kī Bāṇī	Edited by Sudhākar Dvivedī.
Dādū Dayāl Kī Bāṇī	Edited by Chandrika Prasād Tripāthi.
Malūkdās Kī Bāṇī	Belvedere Press, Allahabad.
Jagjīvan Sāhib Kī Śabdāvali	Belvedere Press, Allahabad.
Bullā Sāhib Kā Śabda Sar	Belvedere Press, Allahabad.
Paltoo Sāhib Kī Bāṇī (4 Vols.)	Belvedere Press, Allahabad.
Sundardās	Belvedere Press, Allahabad.
Charandās Kī Bāṇī	Belvedere Press, Allahabad.
Gharībdās Kī Bāṇī	Belvedere Press, Allahabad.
Dulandās Kī Bāṇī	Belvedere Press, Allahabad.
Dariyā Sāhib Kī Bāṇī	Belvedere Press, Allahabad.
Bhīkā Sāhib Kī Bāṇī	Belvedere Press, Allahabad.
Dharnīdās Kī Bāṇī	Belvedere Press, Allahabad.
Yārī Sāhib Kī Bāṇī	Belvedere Press, Allahabad.

Mīrā bā'ī Kī Bāṇī	Belvedere Press, Allahabad.
Sahjobā'ī Kī Bāṇī	Belvedere Press, Allahabad.
Dayābā'ī Kī Bāṇī	Belvedere Press, Allahabad.
Rajjabdās Kī Bāṇī	Belvedere Press, Allahabad.
Tulasīdās	Rām Charita Mānas. Paryaga, 1938.
Malik Muhammad Jāyasī	Akharāvat, Benares.
Raskhān	Sujan Raskhān, Benares.
Benoy Kumār Sarkār	Folk elements in Hindu culture. London, 1917.
Jadu Nāth Sarkār	Chaitanya, Calcutta, 1932.
Rānāde, M. G.	Rise of the Marāthā power.
Macnicoll, N.	Hymns of the Marāthā Saints.
Fraser and Marāthe	Hymns of Tukaram, 3 Vols.
Jogendra Nāth Bhattāchārya	Hindu castes and sects.
Rose, H. A.	A glossary of the tribes and castes of the Panjab.
Russel, R. V.	The tribes and castes of C. P. (Madhya Bharat), London, 1916.
Crooke, W.	The tribes and castes of N. W. P. and Oudh. Calcutta, 1896.
Risley, H. H.	The tribes and castes of Bengal. Calcutta, 1891.
Crowse, F. S.	Mathura.
Troyer and Shea	Dabistān-i-Mazāhib (English Translation)
Herklots	Qānūn-i-Islam, edited by W. Crookes.
De Tassy, G.	Memories sur les particularites de la religion Musulmane dans l'Inde.
Mīr Hasan 'Alī, Mrs.	Observations on the Indian Musalmans. London, 1832.
Oman, J. C.	The Brahmans, Theists and Muslims of India, London, 1907
Oman, J. C.	The mystics, ascetics and saints of India. London, 1903.

(d) ART :—

Fletcher, B.	A History of architecture. London, 1901.
Choisy, A.	Histoire de l'architecture.
Lethaby, W. R.	Architecture, mysticism and myth.
Robinson, J. B.	Architectural Composition. London, 1914.
Della Seta, A.	Religion and art.
Sturgis, R.	A dictionary of architecture and building. New York, 1901-02.

Gousset — Les cupoles d'orient et d'occident.
Spiers, R. P. — Architecture, east and west.
Dieulafoy, M. — L'art antique de la Perse. Paris, 1884-85.
Prise d' Avennes — L'art Arabe.
Rivoire, G. T. — Moslem architecture. London, 1918.
Saladin, H. — Manuel d'art Musulman.
Gayet, A. — L'art Persan. Paris, 1880.
Gayet, A. — L'art Arabe.
Simakoff — L'art dans l'Asie centrale.
Bourgoin, J. — Les arts Arabes. Paris, 1873.
Olufsen, O. — Old and new architecture in Khiva, Bukhara and Turkestan. Copenhagen, 1904.
Coste, P. — Architecture Arabe.
Coste, P. — Monuments modernes de la Perse.
Fergusson, J. — History of Indian and Eastern architecture. London, 1899.
Le Bon, G. — Les civilisation de l' Inde.
Maindron — L'art indien. Paris, 1898.
Rousselet, L. — Les Indes des Radjahs.
Ram Raz — Architecture of the Hindus. London, 1834.
Prasanna Kumar Acharya — A summary of Mansara.
Cole, H. H. — Illustrations of ancient buildings in Mathura and Agra. London, 1873.
Griffin, L. H. — Famous monuments of Central India.
Smith, V. A. — A history of fine art in India and Ceylon. Oxford 1911.
Havell, E. B. — Indian architecture.
Havell, E. B. — A study in Aryan civilisation.
Havell, E. B. — Benares. London, 1905.
Growse — Modern Indian architecture.
Golubev, V. — Ars Asiatica.
Cunningham, A. — Archæological Survey of India reports Vol. 1—23.
Burgess, J. — Survey of Belgam and Kaladgi Districts. London, 1874.
Burgess, J. — Survey of Belgam, Vol. II, and Kathiawar and Kuch. London, 1874.
Burgess, J. — Survey of Belgam, Vol. III, and Bidar and Aurangabad. London, 1878.

Burgess, J. and Cousens H.	Antiquarian remains of Bombay Presidency. Bombay, 1885.
Burgess, J.	Muhammadan architecture of Baroch, Cambay and Dholka. London, 1876.
Burgess, J.	Ahmadabad architecture.
Burgess, J. and Cousens, H.	North Gujarat architecture, London, 1903.
Cousens, H.	Bījāpur architecture. Bombay, 1916.
Fuhrer, A.	Sharqī architecture. Calcutta, 1880.
Fuhrer, A.	Monuments of N. W. P. and Oudh. Allahabad, 1891.
Smith, E. W.	Fatehpur Sīkrī. Allahabad, 1894–98.
Martin, F. R.	Miniature painting of Persia, India and Turkey.
Migeon, G.	Manuel d'art musulman.
Griffiths, J.	Ajanta cave paintings. London, 1896–97.
Herringham, C. J.	Ajanta frescoes. London, 1915.
Havel, E. B.	Indian sculpture and painting. London, 1908.
Havel, E. B.	The ideals of Indian art. London, 1911.
Brown, P.	Indian painting.
Anesaki, M.	Buddhist art.
Handley, T. H.	Memorials of Jeypore exhibition.
Handley, T. H.	Alwar and its art treasures.
Coomārswāmy, A. K.	Arts and crafts of India and Ceylon. London, 1913.
Coomārswāmy, A. K.	Indian drawings. London, 1910.
Coomārswāmy, A. K.	Selected examples of Indian art.
Coomārswāmy, A. K.	Rajput painting. London, 1918.
Okakura, K.	Ideals of the east.

Miniatures :

1. The Bodleian Library

    MSS. Ouseley Add 166, 167, 169, 170, 171, 172, 173, 174.
    MSS. Laud, OR 149.
    MS. Elliot, 254.
    MS. Pers. b. I.

2. The British Museum :—

OR, 4615, Shāh Nāmah (Dārab Namah).

Reproductions of Persian and Indian paintings.

3. The India Office Library :—

Johnson : Collection of 65 albums.

4. The Victoria and Albert Museum, South-Kensington, Indian section :

(a) Clarke MS. of Akbar Nāmah.

(b) Dāstān-i-Amīr Hamzah.

(c) Miscellaneous paintings on cotton and paper.

Photographic Reproductions of illustrations from the three Mss. Bādshāh-nāmah, Shāhnāmah, Tīmūrnāmah.

APPENDIX A

ARCHITECTURAL TERMS

Āmalaka, p. 239

Amalasila—the large-fluted bulbous block—the characteristic of N. Indian temples, p. 236

Antarāla--or intermediate chamber in a Hindu temple, p. 237

Brackets, *toraṇas*—in Hindu architecture and their use, p. 239

Columns of Hindu architecture, p. 239

Cornices—in Hindu architecture, pp. 239-40

Dome, the Hindu—and its construction, p. 238, the—never kept plain, p. 239

GARBHA GRIHA—the square cell which contains the image, forms the basis of the temple tower, p. 237

Gopuram—evolved from pyramidical tower—a characteristic of the Dravidian style of architecture, p. 237

Kalaśa—the finial in Hindu temples, p. 236, p. 239

Maṇḍapa—or porch, p. 237

Ornaments—in Hindu architecture p. 240

Rathas—monolithic—at Māmallāpuram, characteristic of the Dravidian style of architecture, p. 237

Śikhara—straight at Gaya—a characteristic of N. Indian style, p. 236, in the Chālukyan style, p. 237, p. 238, p. 239, in the temples at Sonāgarh in Bundelkhand, p. 249

Stūpās, p. 86, and the Dagabas, p. 239

Vimāna, chief feature of the Dravidian style temple—could have any number of storeys, p. 237

APPENDIX B

HINDU THEISTIC AND BHAKTI TERMS

APPENDIX C

SUFI TERMS

A

Ahadiya, p. 75
Al-haqq, p. 75
Al-khalq, p. 75
Allah—p. 154, p. 165, Dādū Dayal, p. 184, p. 185, Gosā'in Jānī, p. 197, Prān Nāth, p. 200, *Lāmakan,* p. 207, Ramai Pandit, p. 216. Tukarām, p. 227, and p. 228
'Ama—cecity, p. 75
'Aql, p. 52, the M'uitazalites make—the chief source of knowledge, p. 55, equivalent to human soul, its constituents, p. 73, p. 78, Gharībdās, p. 205
A'rsha—Dādū, p. 184, and p. 185, Gharībdās, p. 205
'Āshiq—p. 152
Azal—pre-eternal existence of God, p. 70

B

Baqā—Kharraz the first to explain its meaning, p. 69, p. 79

D

D̲hāt—essence, p. 76
D̲hikr—repetition of God's name, the tendency in Islam accentuated by the Christian contact, p. 65, the discipline of the seeker, of two kinds, *K̲hafī* and *Jalī,* p. 82, p. 158
Dīvāna—Bulla Sahib, p. 202
Dīdār, p. 181, Gharībdās, p. 205

F

Faiz, p. 79
Fanā, p. 67, Kharraz the first to explain its meaning, p. 69, the destination of individual soul, a state of absolute annihilation, p. 73, p. 79
Fikr—Jagjīvandas, p. 201
Fuqr—indifference towards suffering or sickness, etc., the tendency in Islam borrowed from Christianity, p. 65, p. 80, or faqīr, p. 174

G

G̲haibat—absence, p. 161
G̲haibī—unknown, p. 150, p. 169, Jagjīvandas, p. 202,—*huzur,* Dūlandās, p. 207
Gharīb-Nivāz—Charandās, p. 204

H

Habīb, p. 152
Hādī—Dūlandās, p. 207
Hāhūt, p. 162, explained by Kabir, p. 162
Hairat, p. 161
Haj—Shī'ah interpretation of—, p. 52, p. 78
Hākim—Nanak conceived God as—, p. 169
Hāl or states—7 according to Sufis, p. 80, experienced by Kabīr, p. 161
Haq (Truth), p. 162, Paltoo Dās, p. 209
Haqīqat—*Union* with Divinity, p. 79, al-haqāiq, according to Jīlī the idea of ideas, p. 156, Prān Nāth, p. 199
Hayūlā, substance, p. 76
Hubāb—Kabīr both the—and sea, p. 152
Huzūr—p. 161
Hulūl—incarnation, the doctrine held by extreme *Sufis,* p. 69
Huwiya, p. 75

I

J

K

L

M

N

INDEX

B

D

E

I

J

N

S

T

U

V

PLATE No. I

Buddha answering questions (Ajanta)

PLATE No. II

Buddha answering questions (Ajanta)

PLATE No. III

Departure of Bodhisatva as a deer (Ajanta)

PLATE No. IV

The agony of Prince Sibi (Ajanta)

PLATE No. V

The king of Banaras and the golden geese (Ajanta)

PLATE No. VI

Raja going out to attend the Sermon of the Hermit (Ajanta)

PLATE No. VII

Temptation of Buddha by Mara (Ajanta)

PLATE No. VIII

A Court Scene–The Game of Dice (Ajanta)

PLATE No. IX

A Palace Scene–Dancing Girls (Ajanta)

PLATE No. X

Husband and wife in a forest (Ajanta)

PLATE No. XI

Vijay's conquest of Ceylon (Ajanta)

PLATE No. XII

A Procession of Vidhura-Pandita Jataka (Ajanta)

PLATE No. XIII

A Royal Procession–Raja riding on an Elephant (Ajanta)

PLATE No. XIV

A Procession—(Ajanta)

PLATE No. XV

Farud slays Zarasp on Mount Sapad (Persian, about 1440)

PLATE No. XVI

A disputation of Doctors (Mir Ali Shir Nawai, 1485)

PLATE No. XVII

Scene in a Public Bath (Bihzad 1495)

PLATE No. XVIII

Zahir-ud-din Md. Babar Padishah in his youth, at the time of his campaign against Kandahar and India, (1505)

PLATE No. XIX

Battle between the armies of Alexander the Great and those of Darius, King of Persia (Mir Ali Shir Nawai, 1526)

PLATE No. XX

Pastoral Scene (Mir Sayyid Ali, 1539–43)

PLATE No. XXI

A Picnic (Persian, 1569)

PLATE No. XXII

Baz Bahadur and Rupmati (Rajput School)

PLATE No. XXIII

Shikar by night (Bichitar, Rajput School)

PLATE No. XXIV

Agata–Patika (Rajputana)

PLATE No. XXV

Ragini Sarangi (Jaipur School)

Dance of Shiva (Kangra School)

PLATE No. XXVII

Birth of Krishna (Kangra School)

PLATE No. XXVIII

Gai-Charan Lila (Kangra School)

PLATE No. XXIX

Hori Lila (Kangra School)

PLATE No. XXX

Rape of Yadava Women (Chaiter Tehri-Garhwal School)

PLATE No. XXXI

Hour of Cow-Dust (Chamba School)

PLATE No. XXXII

Siege of Lanka (Jammu School)

PLATE No. XXXIII

Siege of Lanka (Jammu School)

PLATE No. XXXIV

Maharaja Shatrujit on horseback Bundela School (1762–1801)

PLATE No. XXXV

Temple of Visvanath at Khajuraho (Northern Style)

PLATE No. XXXVI

Temple of Nuggehalli, Mysore (Deccan Style)

PLATE No. XXXVII

Temple of Subrahmanya, Tanjore (Dravidian Style)

PLATE No. XXXVIII

Hoysalesvara Temple, Halebid (Sculpture on Eastern Side)

PLATE No. XXXIX

Jerusalem—Exterior of the Qubbat As-Sakhrah, Dome of the Rock

PLATE No. XL

Exterior from the East

PLATE No. XLI

Cairo, Madrasah of Qayt Bey

PLATE No. XLII

The mosque of Sultan Barquq

PLATE No. XLIII

Mosque at Tabriz

Mosque at Isphan

PLATE No. XLIV

Tomb of Uljaitoo

PLATE No. XLV

Mosque in Mirzapur Quarter at Ahmedabad

PLATE No. XLVI

Central portion of Facade of Jami Masjid at Ahmedabad

PLATE No. XLVII

Atala Devis Mosque, Jaunpore

PLATE No. XLVIII

Lower Group of Jain Temples at Sonnaghur

PLATE No. XLIX

Chaumukha Temple, Rampur

PLATE No. L

The Man Mandir Palace–S.-W. Corner

PLATE No. LI

The Man Mandir Palace–Interior West Room

PLATE No. LII

The Man Mandir Palace–General View

PLATE No. LIII

Mausoleum of Birsing Deo at Oorcha–Rear View

PLATE No. LIV

Cenotaph of Maharaja Chatarpur

PLATE No. LV

Chhattri of Maharaja Baladeva Singh, Gobardhan

PLATE No. LVI

The pavilion of Jain Mandir, in the Palace of Amber

PLATE No. LVII

Kantanagar Temple

PLATE No. LVIII

Temple of Gobind Deva, Brindaban

PLATE No. LIX

Temple of Jugal Kishor, Brindaban

PLATE No. LX

Court in Palace, Tanjore

PLATE No. LXI

Qadam-ul-Rusul Mosque, Gaur